AS

ENGLISH LANGUAGE

for AQA B

Ron Norman
Consultant: Tim Shortis

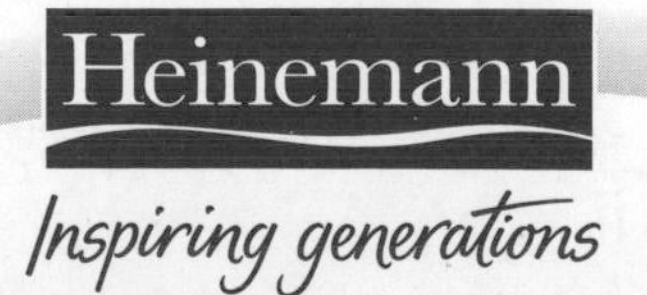

Heinemann Educational Publishers
Halley Court, Jordan Hill, Oxford OX2 8EJ
Part of Harcourt Education

Heinemann is a registered trademark of Harcourt Education Limited

First edition published 2000
Second edition published 2003
Revised edition published 2006

10 09 08 07 06
10 9 8 7 6 5 4 3 2

British Library Cataloguing in Publication Data is available
from the British Library on request.

10-digit ISBN: 0 435 11536 7
13-digit ISBN: 978 0 435115 36 4

Typeset by Tech Type, Abingdon, Oxon
Original illustrations © Harcourt Education Limited, 2006
Printed in China by CTPS
Photographs: Seicento; Corbis; Alamy

Tel: 01865 888058

Contents

Introduction

We hope that this book will support you as you discover how fascinating and challenging the study of language at Advanced Level can be. Its three-module structure follows the AQA English Language B specification.

You may be taught and then tested on the three modules consecutively, or you may cover elements of each throughout the year and take all three unit tests together. Either way, it is probably best to start with Module 1, as it introduces many ideas and terms that arise in the other two modules. Where you see one of these symbols in the margin, there is a link to one of the other modules.

Note on the third edition

The specification continues to evolve. This revised edition reflects the experiences of teaching, learning and preparing for each of the modules. Much of the most successful material from the first edition has been retained, but Module 2, Language and Social Contexts, has completely new sections on 'Language and occupational groups' and 'Language and technology'.

Using this book

We hope that this book will provide a sound basis for your course, but it cannot contain everything that you need. Therefore, at various points in the text there are suggestions for additional reading, indicated by a symbol in the margin.

The book uses several different types of text:

- *teaching text* that introduces ideas and explains and comments on linguistic material; study these sections before tackling the activities
- *data and extracts* composed of excerpts and examples of language in use; these form the raw material of your study, so read and respond to them carefully
- *instructions or suggestions for activities*, which are usually data gathering or research, group discussion or individual work
- *commentaries* and answers to the activities; try to do the activities before you read these, and remember that the commentary is not the only 'correct' response or analysis.

Linguistic terminology

As you work through this book you will encounter a number of specialist terms. The first time one of these appears, it is printed in **bold** text. They are listed in the **Glossary** at the end of the book.

Assessment Objectives

The course has been designed to enable students following any specification to meet the same set of **Assessment Objectives**. These define the skills and knowledge that you must demonstrate in your assessments.

At the start of each module you will see how marks are attached to each Assessment Objective; it is important to know which objectives you must meet.

The specification says you have to . . .	In other words. . .
AO1 – communicate clearly the knowledge, understanding and insight appropriate to the study of language, using appropriate terminology and accurate and coherent written expression	you should write clearly, with accurate spelling and grammar, using specialist technical terms where they help you to define ideas and features of language
AO2 – demonstrate expertise and accuracy in writing for a variety of specific purposes, drawing on knowledge of linguistic features to explain and comment on choices made	you should show that you can write in different styles to suit different purposes and audiences, and must be able to explain how and why you have done this
AO3 – know and use key features of frameworks for the systematic study of spoken and written English	when analysing texts, you must use the knowledge you have acquired during the course – this demands more than just a 'common sense' approach
AO4 – understand, discuss and explore concepts and issues relating to language in use	you must show that you understand some important ideas about language and the factors that influence how it is used
AO5 – distinguish, describe and interpret variation in the meanings and forms of spoken and written language according to context	you must show that you understand how language is influenced by the situation in which it is produced

Key Skills

The activities in the book offer opportunities to produce evidence of attainment of most of the Key Skills: data gathering may tie in with Application of Number as well as ICT, group work gives scope for 'Working with others', and as you progress you may generate evidence for 'Improving own learning and performance'. However, we confine ourselves to flagging up opportunities for Communication-related activities at Level 3; these are indicated with the Key Skills symbol, e.g. **C3.1a**.

Key Skills Communication: level 3	
C3.1a	Contribute to a group discussion about a complex subject
C3.1b	Make a presentation about a complex subject, using at least one image to illustrate complex points
C3.2	Read and synthesise information from two extended documents about a complex subject. One of these documents should include at least one image
C3.3	Write two different types of documents about complex subjects. One piece of writing should be an extended document and include at least one image

Topic and Skills Map: English Language AS and A2

This map indicates which topics or skills either receive coverage or are applied in each module. Units ENB 1–3 are covered in English Language AS; Units ENB 4–6 are covered in English Language A2.

	ENB1: Introduction to the study of language	ENB2: Language and social contexts	ENB3: Original writing and commentary	ENB4: Investigating language	ENB5: Editorial writing and commentary	ENB6: Language development
Classifying and describing language	✓	✓	✓ Commentary	✓	✓ Commentary	✓
Studying variation in audience, register and purposes	✓	✓	✓	✓	✓	✓
Writing for different purposes and audiences	✓		✓	✓	✓	
Writing a commentary on your own work	✓		✓		✓	
Using levels of linguistic description, or **frameworks**, to analyse data and texts	✓	✓	✓ Commentary	✓	✓ Commentary	✓
Phonology: the sounds of English	✓	✓		✓		✓
Orthography: the spelling of English	✓			✓		✓
Morphology: the structure of words	✓			✓		✓
Etymology: the study of the origins and development of words and meanings				✓ (possibly)		✓
Lexis: looking at word classes	✓		✓ Commentary	✓		✓
Semantics: the study of meaning	✓	✓	✓	✓		✓
Syntax: the grammar of sentences and word order	✓	✓	✓ Commentary	✓	✓ Commentary	✓
Discourse: the structure of different kinds of spoken and written texts	✓		✓ Commentary	✓	✓ Commentary	✓
(includes the study of cohesion and coherence)	✓	✓	✓	✓	✓	✓
Pragmatics: the study of the meanings of language in specific social contexts	✓	✓		✓		✓
Comparing spoken and written language	✓			✓		✓
Analysis of conversation	✓	✓		✓		✓
Language and gender		✓		✓ (possibly)		✓
Language and power		✓		✓ (possibly)		
Language and occupational groups		✓				
Language and technology		✓				
Accents and dialects of the British Isles		✓		✓ (possibly)		✓
Social class and language		✓		✓ (possibly)		
Language and thought		✓		✓ (possibly)		
Historical change in language				✓ (possibly)		✓
Contemporary language change				✓ (possibly)		✓
Child language acquisition				✓ (possibly)		✓
Learning to read and write				✓ (possibly)		✓
Carrying out independent research and investigation of data	✓	✓	✓	✓		✓

MODULE 1 Introduction to the Study of Language

This unit counts for **35%** of the AS qualification, or **17½%** of the total A Level marks.

ASSESSMENT OBJECTIVES

The skills and knowledge you develop in this module, which will be tested in the examination you take at the end of it, are defined by the examination board's Assessment Objectives. These require that you:

- **AO1:** communicate clearly the knowledge, understanding and insight appropriate to the study of language, using appropriate terminology and accurate and coherent written expression
(10 out of the 35 marks for the Unit; 10% of the final AS mark; 5% of the final A Level mark)
- **AO3:** know and use key features of frameworks for the systematic study of spoken and written English
(10 out of the 35 marks for the Unit; 10% of the final AS mark; 5% of the final A Level mark)
- **AO4:** understand, discuss and explore concepts and issues relating to language in use
(5 out of the 35 marks for the Unit; 5% of the final AS mark; 2½% of the final A Level mark)
- **AO5:** distinguish, describe and interpret variation in the meanings and forms of spoken and written language according to context
(10 out of the 35 marks for the Unit; 10% of the final AS mark; 5% of the final A Level mark)

What this module is all about

The aim of this module is quite straightforward: it is designed to lay the foundations for the study of English Language at Advanced Level. At first, this may seem odd; after all, you have studied something called 'English' or even 'English Language' throughout your school career, and English is probably your own mother tongue which you use confidently in a wide range of situations.

However, it is unlikely that the work you have done as part of your GCSE course has taken you very far towards the really careful, systematic study of your own language that is involved at A Level. For one thing, the range of language you study as an A Level student is much wider; although you study very little traditional 'literature', you do spend a lot of time looking closely at a great *variety* of written texts, and also begin to examine different kinds of *spoken* language in ways that may be new. Your GCSE English course will certainly have helped you become a proficient *user* of the language, but the emphasis of your A Level course is on turning you into a careful *student* of it.

The first AS module introduces you to ways of thinking about and discussing language that you may not have met before. The unit test will assess how effectively you have begun to apply these new ideas about language. It does this by presenting you with a range of examples of English in use, representing the huge variety of everyday language use, and by inviting you to discuss them in some depth.

Everything you subsequently do on your course is based, in one way or another, on these vital foundations.

Starting to explore

English is the language that you grew up with, and you have become skilled at using it in many situations. What's more, if you have committed yourself to studying it on your AS/A Level course, you've also probably proved to a GCSE examiner that you are rather good at reading, writing, speaking and listening.

The remarkable thing is just how automatic all of this has been. When composing that special letter of application for a job, or a tricky English assignment, we may be conscious of choosing our words carefully, but as native speakers we normally don't have to think very hard about the language we are using – there isn't time!

It's rather like learning to drive a car. At first, you'll probably find that it's difficult to co-ordinate the actions of steering, signalling, checking mirrors, changing gears, reading road signs and so on, but you soon stop thinking consciously about the complicated series of actions needed to get the car from A to B. What's more, most people become drivers without having to learn about the mechanics of the engine, or the intricacies of gearbox and transmission, or the fuel-injection system.

However, during your AS/A Level English Language course, as well as becoming a better 'driver' – developing your own skills as a user of English – you will investigate the workings of the language itself. You will become aware of the unconscious processes that are going on all the time when we use language, as we 'lift the bonnet' and examine just what makes language 'go'.

The 'science' of language study

You may not think of English as a very scientific subject, but in many ways A Level language work is rather like 'language science'. If you are taking a science subject, you will be familiar with certain methods of study such as:

- collecting and examining data (observing experiments, collecting specimens)
- describing, classifying and analysing data using diagrams, measurements and calculations
- testing different ideas about how things work.

These same activities are the basis of your English Language studies. The **data** can be found anywhere and everywhere – wherever the spoken or written word is used. You will learn how to describe language precisely and to classify it in many different ways, developing an appropriate terminology for the purpose. As in science, you will also consider possible explanations for your discoveries – even if you cannot expect to achieve absolute certainty or agreement in your answers.

The aim of your English Language course – and this book – is to help you develop an informed understanding of our language and to become an increasingly accomplished user of it. To achieve this, you need to become something of a linguistic investigator.

A question of language

ACTIVITY 1

C3.1a

Let's start by looking at the kinds of question that will drive our linguistic explorations forwards. The issues you begin to explore here underpin much of the work that you will do throughout your AS/A Level course.

The following language notes and queries arose from a series of interviews with English students. Read the queries and share with your classmates your first reactions to each one. Then, through discussion, try to reach agreement about an answer within your group.

After you have reported back to the class, compare your responses with the brief commentaries offered on page 64.

A ANN, 17

Why do people's accents, and even the words and phrases they use, vary so much – and is it true that some kinds of English are 'better' than others?

B MICHAEL, 19

Which came first, speech or writing – and which is more important?

C AYUMI, 16

When I'm at work I have to watch what I say and talk to customers in the way I've been trained to do. Out with my friends, it's different – we have our own set of words which we use all the time and if you didn't know them you probably wouldn't understand what we were on about half the time. Is this normal?

D GEORGE, 25

I saw a science fiction film in which instead of checking fingerprints, a computer could identify any human being just by analysing the way they talked. So, is it true that we have a sort of linguistic fingerprint – and would this also work with an extract of something which we wrote?

E KIBRIA, 22

What I don't understand when I look at Shakespeare's language, or even hear clips from old radio and TV shows, is why English has changed so much – and who makes it happen?

F JANET, 30

I always hated languages at school – we had to do French and German – and I always struggled with them. Now I've got kids of my own, I'm amazed by how easily they pick up English without really seeming to try! Why is my 4-year-old so much better at language than me?

Language all around us

The scope of English Language study at A Level is extremely wide. As explorers and students of language, you can start by making yourself aware of the sheer variety of the language that we consume or produce as a matter of routine. This variety will be the raw material for our investigations and explorations.

ACTIVITY 2 **C3.1a**

(a) Consider the four linguistic activities of listening, speaking, reading and writing. Using a large sheet of sugar paper, allocate each of them to one quarter of a circle, as in the figure:

In each quadrant, list as many examples as you can of different kinds of language activity in which you participate in a typical week. Aim to include at least half-a-dozen different activities in each quadrant.

For example, under 'Speaking' you might start by listing:

- on the phone to friends
- explaining the school/college day to parents
- social chat over lunch.

(b) Once you have listed your examples on the quadrants, **classify** them in any way you think is helpful. For example, you might describe both 'on the phone to friends' and 'social chat over lunch' as 'informal chat'. Here are some possible categories – but feel free to suggest your own:

Informal chat	Persuading someone to do something
Asking for information	The media – radio, TV, etc.
Using slang with friends	Making excuses or apologies
Listening to instructions	Being persuaded
Reading for facts	Using mobile phone and texting
Being amused or entertained	Making notes to remember work in class
Telling amusing stories to entertain	Making arrangements

After briefly presenting your findings to the rest of the class, compare your results with the commentary on page 65.

Keeping a language glossary

If you were embarking on a course designed to train you as an engineer, you would expect to learn a great deal of technical 'jargon'. Equally, A Level physicists or sociologists will acquire a working vocabulary of specialist terms unique to those disciplines.

The study of language has its own specialist vocabulary – a language for talking about language, you could say. Such a language is called a **metalanguage**. Throughout this book, you will be introduced to – and encouraged to use – the terminology needed for the precise description of different aspects of language. Remember, the Assessment Objectives require you to use 'appropriate terminology', so you need to make a point of learning and using this metalanguage as you go along. At the end of the book is a Glossary of most of the technical terms introduced – but it is a good idea to build up a personal language glossary of your own.

ACTIVITY 3

Even before you started your AS studies, you had a working vocabulary of the language we use to talk about language. Basic terms such as 'word', 'sentence' and 'paragraph' are all part of this vocabulary.

Take an exercise book and allow a couple of pages for each letter of the alphabet. List under each letter any language terms (such as 'word', 'sentence', 'full stop') that you already know. You'll probably be able to list many terms already.

As the course develops, add new terms, definitions and examples to each page as and when they arise.

You and your language: idiolect

One of our initial language queries raised the question of individual 'linguistic fingerprints' (see page 4). Indeed, our everyday experience suggests that individuals often have distinctive ways of using language, and the discipline of 'forensic linguistics' allows the positive identification of an individual (e.g. someone accused of a crime) by analysing closely a sample of his or her speech or writing. The term **idiolect** is used to define those features of language use which are unique to an individual. In this section we will try to define what makes up your own idiolect.

Of course, as your response to Activity 2 will have revealed, we all have the ability to vary our uses of language according to context. We can refer to this range of styles as our **language repertoire**.

Your language history and experience

As you look around your classroom, and listen to different members of the class speaking, you rapidly become aware that we all have our own, distinctive style of speech. So what has influenced and shaped this idiolect, this individual linguistic fingerprint which each of us reveals as soon as we open our mouths or put pen to paper?

ACTIVITY 4 **C3.1a**

(a) Look at the diagram on page 7. It represents some of the most important influences that are likely to have shaped your identity and your idiolect. In groups, try to agree on the order of importance of these influences, from 1 (the most influential) down to 8 (the least).

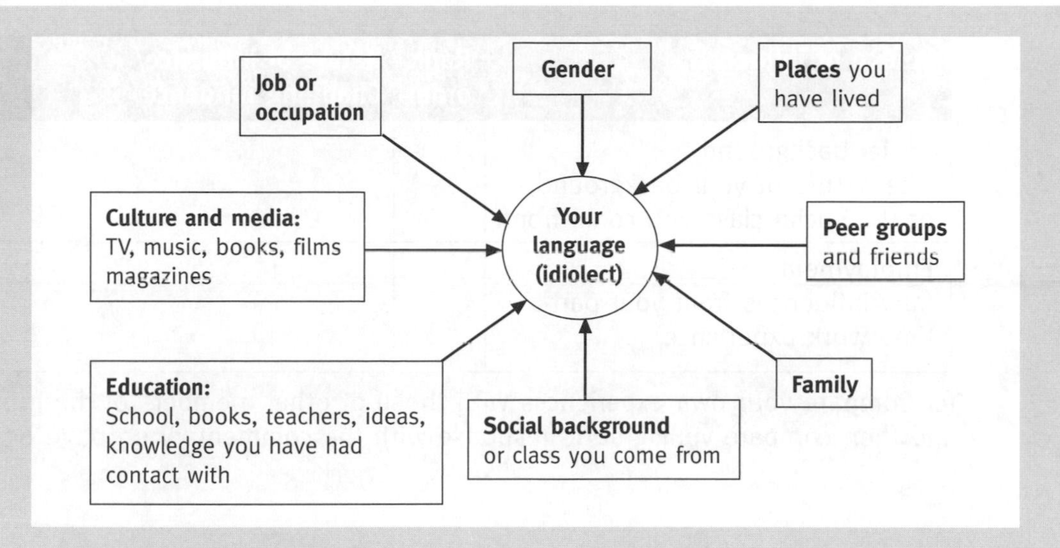

(b) For each of the possible sources of influence shown in the table, try to suggest the *specific* ways in which they have affected your personal language development.

As you consider each one, think about how it might have influenced:

- your accent
- your choice of words, phrases and slang
- your ideas about what is acceptable or 'good' English.

You should also think about how the *extent* of each influence may change as you get older.

Record your responses on a table similar to the one below:

Source of influence	Rank order	Nature of influence/ Changing influence
Your family		
Places you have lived		
Your education (Your school experiences, and the influence of teachers and what you have learned)		
Cultural influences (e.g. books, films, music, magazines and television)		
Your gender		
Peer groups (the various friendship groups you belong to)		

Source of influence	Rank order	Nature of influence/ Changing influence
Social background (the nature of your background, or the social class you come from)		
Employment (any influences from your part-time work experience)		

(c) Compare your own experiences with those of other members of the group, and then compare your group's response with the commentary on page 65.

Fitting in: language as a membership card

As we have noted, an important influence on the ways we use language is the social group or network we belong to. Of course, we all belong to many different groupings, so we develop different styles of language to suit the group we are with at any one time. All kinds of groupings — family, friends, workmates, football supporters, doctors, fans of a particular pop band — may develop distinctive uses of language that come to characterise them and indicate their identity. To join one of these groups we may have to learn its language — in other words, acquire its **sociolect**.

ACTIVITY 5

Start by listing the various social groups you belong to at different times. For example your family, your immediate group of friends, people who live in your town or region, people who share an interest with you, go to the same school or college, come from the same social background . . . Add some of your own.

Then ask yourself: *what is distinctive about the ways in which this particular group uses language*? The distinguishing features could include certain routines, rituals or patterns of interaction; a particular kind of vocabulary, 'buzz words' or slang; a particular accent or style of pronunciation.

Record your suggestions, then read the commentary on page 67.

Inclusion and exclusion

In many ways, a sociolect can act as a membership badge which proclaims the fact that you belong to, and identify with, a particular social group. If we go to live and work in a foreign country, to be fully accepted as a member of that community we expect to have to learn the language, customs and traditions. On a smaller scale, 'outsiders' who wish to join and be accepted by social groups may need to learn and adopt language features that characterise the group in order to fit in. This could mean a slight change in their accent, using a particular kind of vocabulary, or observing certain linguistic rituals.

However, we may be members of a group that doesn't want outsiders to join or to understand the meanings we are communicating to each other. In this case, the group may develop a language that almost becomes a code – a shared language that excludes those not 'in the know'.

ACTIVITY 6 **C3.1a**

Suggest how the distinctive **slang** or **jargon** associated with the following groups and activities has the effect of excluding those not 'in the know':

1. drugs slang used between dealers and buyers
2. medical terminology used between doctors as they discuss your condition
3. computer jargon
4. technical terms used by garage mechanics when they explain to you what has gone wrong with your car.

Language varieties: describing and classifying

Having reminded ourselves of the huge variety of language all around us, we now need to look more closely at a range of examples of language in use. Throughout your English Language course, you will be encouraged to collect and describe **data** – that is, specimens of speech and writing – and to explore ways in which these specimens can be compared with or distinguished from each other. We can compare this to the way a scientist – a zoologist, for example – might observe and collect specimens and classify them as mammals, fish, reptiles, etc.

In the examination for this unit you are presented with a collection of such language data or 'specimens', and asked to write in some detail about the different ways in which we can classify and describe them. The texts and activities in this section introduce you to the process of description and classification.

The word **text** is used throughout this book to describe any piece of language in either written or spoken form. Several of the texts are representations of spoken language. When a recording is made of speech and a faithful written representation of this recording is produced, the term for the resulting text is a **transcript**. This differs from a **script**, which is the term used for a piece of writing that is pre-written in order to be spoken, for example on a television programme.

Spoken language can be very different from writing, so when making a transcript it is usual not to use standard punctuation. Throughout this book the following **conventions** are used for transcripts:

- lower case is used throughout, except for names and the pronoun 'I'
- conventional punctuation marks such as full stops, commas, etc. are *not* used (we will consider the reasons for this when we look in detail at the nature of spoken language on page 20 below)

- short pauses for breath are shown as (.)
- longer pauses are shown by a number in brackets, e.g. (2), indicating the number of seconds the pause lasts
- a vertical line (/) indicates where two or more speakers speak at once
- square brackets and words in italics [*like this*] indicate actions or gestures
- underlining is sometimes used for stressed syllables, and CAPITALS for high volume
- [inaud] is used where speech is inaudible.

ACTIVITY 7

C3.1a, C3.1b

On the next page there are ten texts, A–J. In groups, agree how to organise the texts into groups of two or more, linking them by identifying some aspect that they have in common. You should suggest at least four or five groupings – more, if possible.

- Give each of your groupings a title that reflects what the texts have in common. You cannot use 'miscellaneous' or 'other' as a title.
- Include every text in at least one of your groupings.
- You may include the same text in two or more of the groupings.

Record your findings in the form of a table with these headings:

Linked texts	Group title	Features in common

Present and explain your findings to the class, then compare them with the commentary on page 67. This also provides details about the source of each text.

TEXT A

Right (.) you have a sheet in front of you (.) wait a minute I'll get you one (.) on it (.) have a look now please (.) on it (.) there's a list of the characters we looked at on Friday (.) look at the paragraph underneath (.) look at the paragraph underneath (2) what I want you to do please (.) is to ensure that you have a pen or pencil available to you (2) and that as we learn anything about any of the characters (.) you add any relevant information onto the sheet

TEXT B

There were times (.) if you felt in good fettle (1) we used to see who could hoy a ball furthest (3) it was a nice canny game an all but sometimes (2) windows used to get brocken (3) and another thing (.) in them days people were lucky if they had indoor netties (1) and it was bloody murder if you wanted to gan to the toilet in the middle of the neet

TEXT C

We joined the ship on Wednesday morning, the 10th of April, and had boat drill and proceeded at 12 o'clock. We called at Cherbourg and Queenstown. On Sunday it came in rather cold, Sunday afternoon. On Sunday night at about a quarter to 12, I was on the watch below and turned in, when there was suddenly a noise like cable running out, like a ship dropping anchor. There was not any shock at all.

TEXT D

Come live with me and be my love,
And we will all the pleasures prove,
That hills and valleys, dale and fields,
And all the craggy mountains yields.

TEXT E

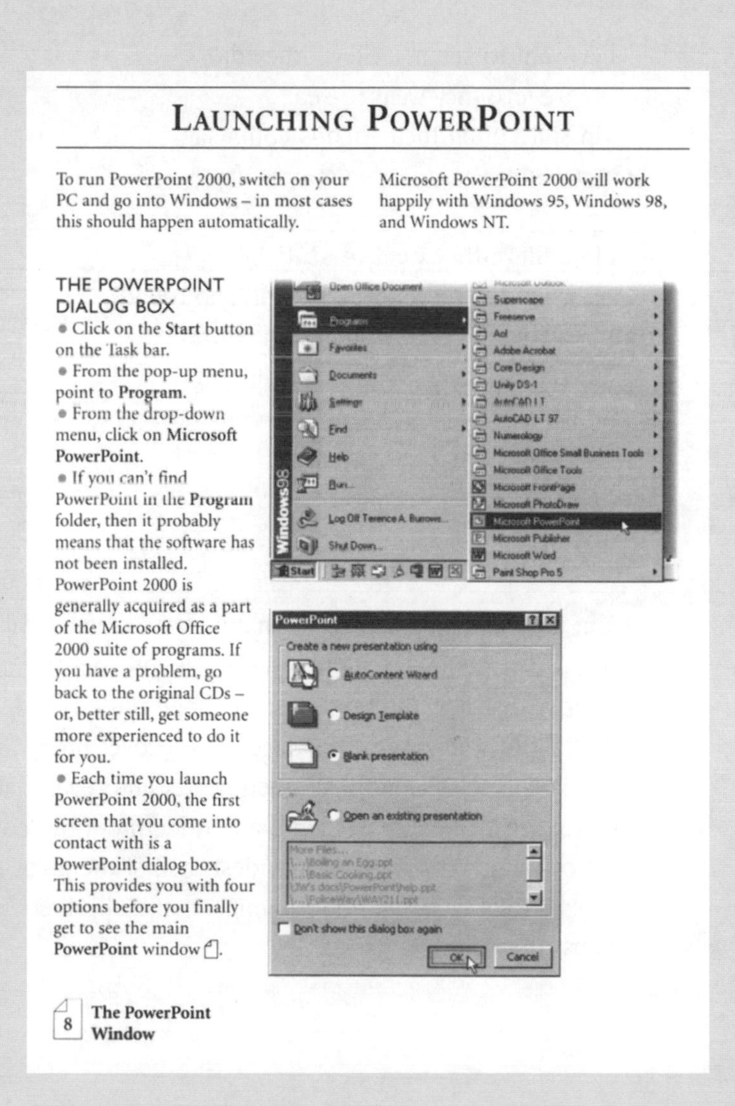

LAUNCHING POWERPOINT

To run PowerPoint 2000, switch on your PC and go into Windows – in most cases this should happen automatically.

Microsoft PowerPoint 2000 will work happily with Windows 95, Windows 98, and Windows NT.

THE POWERPOINT DIALOG BOX

- Click on the **Start** button on the Task bar.
- From the pop-up menu, point to **Program**.
- From the drop-down menu, click on **Microsoft PowerPoint**.
- If you can't find PowerPoint in the **Program** folder, then it probably means that the software has not been installed. PowerPoint 2000 is generally acquired as a part of the Microsoft Office 2000 suite of programs. If you have a problem, go back to the original CDs – or, better still, get someone more experienced to do it for you.
- Each time you launch PowerPoint 2000, the first screen that you come into contact with is a PowerPoint dialog box. This provides you with four options before you finally get to see the main **PowerPoint** window 8.

8 **The PowerPoint Window**

TEXT F

A: Tanya from West Shields on line 2 (.) hi Tanya
T: hi Alan
A: hello the best and the worst from you
T: the best for me was going to Canada (.) em (.) 4 years ago to see an adopted sister / I'd never met before
A: / right (.) which (.) which lump of Canada was it
T: er (.) Toronto and then I flew on to Winnipeg
A: oh great (.) I mean what's (.) you always get the impression that Canada's like just massive (.) this immense country / what's it actually like
T: / it is yeah

TEXT G

They went to sea in a Sieve, they did,
In a Sieve they went to sea:
In spite of all their friends could say,
On a winter's morn, on a stormy day,

In a Sieve they went to sea!
And when the Sieve turned round and round,
And everyone cried, 'You'll all be drowned!'
They called aloud, 'Our Sieve ain't big,
'But we don't care a button! we don't care a fig!
'In a Sieve we'll go to sea!'

TEXT H

From the beginning all men by nature were created alike, and our bondage or servitude came in by the unjust oppression of naughty men. And therefore I exhort you to consider that now the time is come, appointed to us by God, in which ye may (if ye will) cast off the yoke of bondage, and recover liberty. I counsel you therefore to bethink yourselves, and take good hearts unto you, that after the manner of a good husband that tilleth his ground, and riddeth out thereof such evil weeds as choke and destroy the good corn, you may destroy first the great lords of the realm, and after, the judges and lawyers, and questmongers, and all others who have undertaken to be against the common.

TEXT I

'Why, look yer 'ere,' said the miner, showing the shoulders of his singlet. 'It's a bit dry now, but it's wet as a clout with sweat even yet. Feel it.'

'Goodness!' cried Mrs Morel. 'Mr Heaton doesn't want to feel your nasty singlet.'

The clergyman put out his hand gingerly.

'No, perhaps he doesn't,' said Morel; 'but it's all come out of me, whether or not. An' iv'ry day alike my singlet's wringin' wet. 'Aven't you got a drink, Missis, for a man when he comes home barkled up from the pit?'

TEXT J

'You is not loving it?' the BFG asked innocently, rubbing his head.

'Loving it!' yelled the Bloodbottler. 'That is the most disgusterous taste that is ever touching my teeth! You must be buggles to be swalloping slutch like that! Every night you could be galloping off happy as a hamburger and gobbling juicy human beans!'

'Eating human beans is wrong and evil,' the BFG said.

Problems with classification

Although it is useful to try to categorise language in the ways suggested in Activity 7, as soon as we start to do so we encounter some problems. Perhaps you already found this when looking at the texts for the activity. Many of these texts are surprisingly complex, and it is important not to ignore these complications by fitting language into an over-simplified model.

The Unit 1 examination sets out to assess your ability to recognise and discuss some of these complicating factors. In the next activities we will explore some of them.

Mode – speech or writing?

It is not always easy to define a particular user of language as belonging exclusively to either of these categories. Some types of language may have elements of both modes in them. Text H from Activity 7, for instance, is part of a script which was pre-written in order to be spoken, whereas text I is an extract from a piece of writing – a novel – which tries to create the *illusion* of realistic speech by using accent and dialect features in its dialogue. Text D is clearly a written text, but *pretends* to be the poet 'speaking' to his lover.

We will investigate the distinctive characteristics of spoken and written language in more detail below (see page 20).

ACTIVITY 8

For each of the following examples (some from Activity 7), suggest ways in which they include elements of both spoken and written language. Compare your results with the table in the commentary on page 69.

Text	Problematic aspects
Text C: written record of testimony given to the *Titanic* enquiry	
Text J: extract from *The BFG*	
A politician's speech	
A job interview	
An episode of *EastEnders* A series of postings in an Internet chatroom	

What register?

One text may include several different styles of language, and so be impossible to define as being entirely 'formal' or 'informal' – it may have a 'mixed register'. Text G in Activity 7, for instance, features both reasonably formal, literary language such as 'On a winter's morn, on a stormy day' alongside the more informal 'Our Sieve ain't big . . . we don't care a fig!'

We will also see below (see page 19) that we need to think not just in terms of 'formal' or 'informal' language, but of a wide spectrum of styles.

Which audience(s)?

Texts may have more than one set of listeners/readers, and these different audiences may respond very differently to them. For example, the speaker of text B in Activity 7 (a Tyneside speaker reminiscing about his childhood) was talking only to his granddaughter – but he was also aware that she was taping the conversation for possible use in a language textbook, whose readers would be more interested in his dialect speech than in the content of the stories he was telling.

ACTIVITY 9

For each of the following examples (some from Activity 7), identify the possible multiple audiences and the different aspects of the text they may be interested in:

Text	Multiple audiences	Different meanings
Text D: 17th-century poem		
Text F: transcript of a radio phone-in		
Text J: extract from *The BFG*		
A women's magazine such as *Cosmopolitan*		

Compare your results with the table in the commentary on page 70.

Multi-purpose?

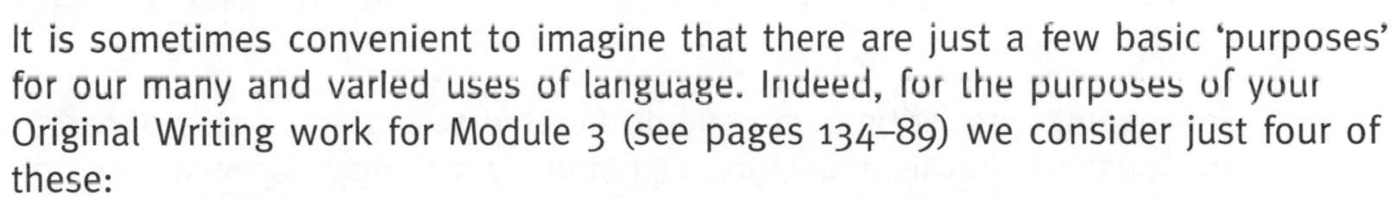

It is sometimes convenient to imagine that there are just a few basic 'purposes' for our many and varied uses of language. Indeed, for the purposes of your Original Writing work for Module 3 (see pages 134–89) we consider just four of these:

- language used to exchange **information**
- language used to **amuse** or **entertain**
- language used to **influence, advise** or **persuade**
- language used to give or receive **instructions.**

However, it would be a misleading over-simplification to suggest that all uses of language can easily be slotted into one or other of these categories.

ACTIVITY 10

For each of the language uses listed below (some from Activity 7), identify which (if any) of the above purposes apply. Where you think a text has more than one purpose, try to distinguish between **primary** and **secondary** purposes:

Text/language use	Purposes
Text B: transcript of Tyneside speaker	
Text D: poem	
Text F: radio phone-in	
Text J: *The BFG*	
A casual conversation with your friends	
A TV documentary about wildlife	
A tabloid news report about politics	

Compare your results with the table in the commentary on page 71.

Collecting your own data

ACTIVITY 11 **C3.1a, C3.1b**

Go back to the four headings you used to classify examples of language use on page 4: listening, speaking, reading and writing. For any one of these, collect your own examples of five or six of the uses of language you suggested there.

For reading and writing, you should be able to find examples of texts easily; for speaking and listening, you can start by making brief recordings of broadcast media. For examples of 'real' conversational speech you need to make tape recordings – but always follow the guidelines below:

Guidelines for recording and writing down 'live' speech:

- Seek permission from any participants before arranging to record conversations.
- Offer to wipe or destroy your tape if the participants object to the content afterwards.
- Let your recorder run for long enough to allow people to become less self-conscious about being recorded.
- Transcribe a short but accurate extract of what is on the tape.
- Don't censor or correct the speech – represent any pauses, hesitations and 'bad' language.

See page 10 for transcript conventions. Also use the examples on pages 10–13 as models for your transcripts.

Re-visit the commentary to Activity 7 on page 67, which introduces some important linguistic ideas and terminology. Then, for your five or six texts, repeat the linking/grouping exercise, copying onto A3 paper a table like the one below and using as many of the suggested categories as you can.

Use the table to explain:

- what your linked texts have in common
- how your linked texts in each category differ from each other
- any problems you have encountered in trying to categorise your texts.

Survey and classification of texts: reading/writing/speaking/listening				
Category	**Texts**	**What the texts have in common**	**How they differ**	**Problems of classification**
Purpose				
Audience				
Mode				
Register				
Variety				
Graphology				
Period				

Present your table and explain your findings to the class.

Genres

Genre is the term for each specific kind of text – either spoken or written – that seems to follow a distinctive pattern or set of conventions which become an agreed 'norm'. Some examples are offerered below:

Written genres		Spoken genres	
Fairy tales	Letters	Lessons	Jokes
Recipes	News reports	Phone calls	Apologies
Memos	Essays	'Chat-up' conversations	Consultations with a doctor
Advertisements	Horoscopes	Formal interviews	Answer-phone messages
E-mails	Horror stories	Shopping transactions	
Poems		Radio phone-ins	

ACTIVITY 12

C3.3

(a) As an example of a genre, let us consider the following recipe. As you examine it, tick off the genre conventions which apply:

Genre conventions: recipes

- ☐ usually have list of ingredients, itemised and quantified
- ☐ set out steps in a process, separated into short sentences/ paragraphs
- ☐ steps are itemised either with bullet points or numbers
- ☐ may sometimes miss out words and use an abbreviated note form
- ☐ may include some semi-technical vocabulary related to cooking
- ☐ sentences will usually consist of direct instructions
- ☐ sentences will include precise information about timings/ temperatures.

Macaroni with wild mushrooms

This dish packs a punch with a robust sauce of tomato and wild mushrooms. Some slivers of parma ham would also go well. You'll need a chunky macaroni, more like penne in size. You can find tomato salsina or sugocasa in Sainsbury's, but if this is unavailable, give some chopped tomatoes in juice a brief blitz in the food processor.

SERVES 4
40g/1½oz unsalted butter
1 tbsp groundnut oil
3 leeks, trimmed and thinly sliced
sea salt, black pepper
200g/7oz wild mushrooms, picked over, trimmed and sliced if necessary
100ml/3½fl oz white wine
150ml/5fl oz tomato salsina or sugocasa
1 small dried red chilli, finely chopped
200g/7oz chunky macaroni
chopped flat-leaf parsley
and freshly grated parmesan, to serve

BRING A LARGE PAN of salted water to the boil for the pasta. Heat 25g/1oz of the butter and the oil in a large frying pan over a medium heat. Add the leeks, season them and fry for 5-8 min, stirring frequently until soft and touched with colour at the edges. Remove them to a bowl, squeezing them with the back of a spoon to leave the fat behind.

MELT THE REMAINING BUTTER in the pan, add the mushrooms and fry, stirring frequently, until soft. Season them when cooked. If any liquid is given out, continue to cook until they're dry. Return the leeks to the frying pan with the mushrooms, add the wine and cook until well reduced. Now add the tomato salsina and the chilli and simmer for a min or two longer.

ADD THE PASTA to the boiling water when you are halfway through cooking the sauce. Give the pasta a stir to separate the tubes and cook until just tender. Drain into a sieve, leaving a little water clinging to the macaroni. Add to the frying pan and toss with the sauce.

TASTE FOR SEASONING and serve scattered with chopped parsley. Hand the freshly grated parmesan round separately.

(b) Choose half-a-dozen more genres from the table and collect/observe some examples of your own. Use a table with the headings shown below to present your summary of the distinctive features, or **genre conventions**, you find:

Genre	Examples/specimens	Genre conventions

(c) Experiment with your own writing by changing texts from one genre to another, referring closely to the genre conventions you have identified. Try one of these:

- Turn a recipe into a passage from a horror novel *or* a fairy story *or* the script for a TV cookery programme *or* an interview with the chef.
- Turn a news report into an apology *or* a poem *or* a fairy tale *or* a recipe.

Write a brief **commentary** in which you explain which genre conventions you have tried to adopt in your new text. See 'The commentary' in Module 3, Original Writing, on page 187.

The formality spectrum: register

If you looked in most people's wardrobes, you would probably find a wide variety of clothing suitable for different occasions: t-shirts and jeans for lounging around, rather smarter shirts, skirts and trousers for college or work, perhaps some overalls or other specific work-clothes, and the odd formal suit or evening dress for smart occasions.

We can compare our choice of language style to our choice of clothes – different levels of formality are appropriate for different situations, and we choose the style or **register** accordingly. If we get our selection wrong, the results may be comical or embarrassing!

ACTIVITY 13 — **C3.1a**

Consider the following versions of the same basic request and order them from the least formal (1) to the most formal (10). Try to identify the elements of each utterance that help define its level of formality, and note these.

- I was hoping you could let me borrow some money.
- I wonder if you might be so kind as to consider making me a small loan?
- Can I borrow a fiver?
- Could I perhaps borrow some money?
- Just gimme some bloody dosh!
- Please can I borrow some money?
- Lend us a fiver, can you?
- Could you possibly lend me some money?
- Gimme some cash, will ya!
- Would it by any chance be possible that you might be so good as to be of temporary financial assistance?

The results of the previous activity should suggest that we cannot speak just of 'formal' and 'informal' registers of English; it is much more useful to think of a *spectrum* of possibilities, as illustrated by the diagram below:

The formality spectrum

INFORMAL **FORMAL**

1 taboo 2 vulgarism 3 slang 4 non-standard dialect 5 colloquialism 6 informal SE 7 neutral SE 8 formal SE 9 very formal SE

NON-STANDARD ENGLISH **STANDARD ENGLISH**

1 Taboo language – swear words, or words that are generally considered to be deeply offensive and unacceptable.

2 Vulgarism – language which falls short of taboo but is nevertheless rather coarse and not normally used in 'polite' society.

3 Slang – a very broad term for many different uses of language which are not considered to be 'proper' or Standard English, but may be fairly widespread.

4 Non-standard (regional) dialect – words and grammatical constructions not considered to be 'good' or 'correct' Standard English, but which are confined to specific regions of the country. 'Fag' is a slang term widely used in the UK for a cigarette (although in the US it has a completely different usage). 'Tab' may be described as a dialect word, because its use for 'cigarette' is mainly restricted to parts of the north of England.

5 Colloquialism – another rather loose term, which literally means 'language as it is spoken'. This may be applied to some kinds of slang, or to the most informal language accepted as Standard English.

6–9 Standard English – informal, neutral, formal and very formal. Standard English (SE) is the term used for the vocabulary and grammatical constructions generally accepted as 'correct' English, but even here there is a spectrum ranging from informal (fairly casual language that stops short of slang or dialect), to neutral (the colourless, unremarkable language of 'normal' usage) to the formal and highly formal (such as legal language, for example).

ACTIVITY 14

Write an account of what you did on an ordinary day recently. Bearing the diagram and definitions above in mind, write three different versions of the same day using three different registers, as follows:

Version 1: Use a fair proportion of vulgarisms, slang, dialect (or even an occasional taboo word) to create a highly informal version of the account.

Version 2: Use informal and mainly neutral Standard English terms to produce a 'middling' account.

Version 3: Use formal and highly formal constructions to create an official-sounding version of events.

Write a brief commentary in which you identify some specific details which are different in the three versions, and which contribute to its overall register.

Speech and writing

An understanding of the relationship between spoken and written language is central to much of the work you will do in this course, and is also a key element of this module. Here are some of the questions we need to ask about speech and writing:

- Is writing just speech written down?
- Is writing more 'grammatical' than speech?
- When is it better to use one rather than the other?

To begin to answer these questions, look at some parallel pieces of data in the activity below.

ACTIVITY 15

C3.3

(a) Collect your own data by tape recording and transcribing a spoken response to one or more of the following situations. Also collect a considered, written response.

- Ask a partner to give you directions from your school/college to the town centre.
- Give a short account of how you spent your last summer holiday.
- Make a request to a friend to borrow an item or a sum of money.
- Persuade a reluctant friend to come with you to see a particular film (you could try doing this as a text message, also).

When you have collected your data, work through the following questions:

- What aspects of the spoken version are missing from the transcript you created, and what would they have contributed to the meanings the speaker was trying to convey?
- Is any of the content of the spoken account absent from the written statement? If so, what is missing, and why do you think it was omitted?
- Look at the ways the sentences are formed in both versions. What differences do you notice?
- Does the spoken version include unspecified references to people and places, using words such as *this*, *that*, *he*, *she*, *those*, *here* and *there*? If these are made more explicit in the written account, why do you think this is?
- How does the description of people, actions and events differ in the accounts?
- In general terms, what seems to be the difference between the style and register of the two versions, and what might account for this?

(b) Compare your findings with the following pieces of data. The first is a transcript of an oral account given by a witness to an accident, and the second is the written statement she subsequently produced. Apply the same questions to these and compare your analysis with the commentary on page 72.

Speech (transcript)	Writing (statement)
A: Did you see what happened B: Well (.) not really (.) er (.) I was just walking the dog like (.) you know (.) it was not long turned dark (.) and we'd been down the alley there and back (1) and (.) um (.) then then this car comes racing down here (.) bloody flying he was (.) so as I turned round there was this bloody great crash (.) you know tyres screeching and everything (.) so I turn around and there's black smoke pouring out where it had crashed like A: Could you see if anyone was hurt? B: Well (.) I was standing just over there (.) at the far end of them shops (.) and (.) and like I say (.) it was dark and there was all that smoke (.) and I just thought (.) he must have had it (.) had it like (.) you know	At approximately 8.30 last night I witnessed an accident involving a blue Ford Sierra on Abbey Road, Barrow. I heard the sound of a car approaching, apparently at some speed, before it braked suddenly and subsequently crashed into the wall near the junction with Dalton Road. Black smoke immediately began to pour from the vehicle, and I assumed that the driver must have been seriously hurt.

Characteristics and functions of speaking and writing

ACTIVITY 16

C3.1a

The previous activities revealed that there are some important differences between speech and writing, and the most important of these are summarised in the first column of the table below. These differences have implications for the ways in which we use language, either spoken or written, in a range of situations. The questions in the second column ask you to consider some of these.

However, as with other ways of classifying language, we also need to beware of over-simplifying the differences, and the third column invites you to question some of these distinctions more closely.

When you have worked through the questions, compare your responses with the commentary on page 73.

	Differences between speaking and writing	Questions	Problems
1	Speech conveys meanings using sounds which we combine into words, phrases and sentences, whereas writing uses visual signs and symbols (letters and punctuation) to represent these words.	Look again at a transcript of 'real' speech that you have recorded (or the ones on page 10 above). What happens if you try to 'punctuate' this	Our idea of what we mean by 'a sentence' tends to be based on what we have been taught about writing. So trying to describe speech in terms of 'sentences' can be tricky.

Differences between speaking and writing	Questions	Problems
The 'sentences' we speak are much less easy to define than the ones we are taught to punctuate with capital letters and full stops at school.	speech using the usual conventions of full stops, commas, etc?	However, it is *not* true to say that speech is 'less grammatical' than writing. If this were true, we wouldn't be able to understand each other!
2 Speech is an ability which seems to be acquired 'naturally', and without very much direct teaching; writing, on the other hand, has to be taught and learned. In the past many people who could communicate perfectly well in speech were unable to read or write.	Which aspects of the English writing system do you think are most difficult for someone who can already speak the language reasonably well?	As you will see in Module 6, Language Development (A2), this also can be something of a simplification of a controversial subject. In some important ways parents do seem to assist their children's spoken language development.
3 Much of what is communicated in speech comes from **paralinguistic** and **prosodic** features, and is closely linked to the immediate **context** in which it takes place (it is **context-bound**). Writing depends entirely on the words on the page, and is usually meaningful even to people who do not share the immediate context in which it was produced (it is **context-free**).	Which of speech or writing is most likely to reveal dishonesty or insincerity? Which would you prefer to use if you needed to deceive someone?	The **context** includes not just the time and place that the language is used, but also all the things the writer or speaker can assume about the people to whom he or she is talking or writing. With this is mind, perhaps you can suggest how even writing must always be 'context-bound' to some degree?
4 Speech is unplanned, and may include slips and mistakes of all kinds. Writing can be re-drafted: mistakes can be removed before the final version is seen.	When might it be desirable to use writing to avoid making unplanned slips?	When might spoken language be planned, semi-planned or even rehearsed? Which kinds of writing are spontaneous, and may include unedited slips and errors?

Differences between speaking and writing	Questions	Problems
5 Speech is momentary, unless taped, whereas writing offers a permanent record.	In what circumstances might you need to keep a record of a communication?	Writing can offer permanence, of course, but many kinds of writing are not designed to be preserved for long. These texts are sometimes called **ephemera**. Equally, some spoken language is intended to be recorded and preserved. Can you think of some examples?

ACTIVITY 17

Consider the following texts in the light of the suggested 'over-simplified' comments about speech and writing offered below. Discuss or write about how the examples illustrate problems with those comments.

Text description	Data	Over-simplification
Note left for builders working in a house while the owners are at work	Hi you two! Help yourself to the usual. Please leave key in the usual place when you've finished.	'Writing is always context-free, whereas speech is context-bound.'
(a) Recorded message left on a telephone answering machine (b) Note left in the kitchen	(a) *We're sorry that no-one is available to take your call right now. If you'd like to leave a message, please do so after the tone, and we'll try to get back to you as soon as possible. Thanks for calling.* (b) Just nipped out for a paper – back in 5. Tea in oven. xxxx	'Speech is informal, and writing is formal.'

Text description	Data	Over-simplification
Exchange between MPs in the House of Commons as recorded in *Hansard*, the official parliamentary record	**Mr Dennis Skinner (Bolsover):** Will my Right Hon. Friend ignore the bleating of the Liberal Democrats, who have been Euro-fanatics from the very beginning? Will he ignore the rants of the Shadow Chancellor of the Exchequer, who condemned the current Leader of the Opposition when they were uniting and dying over Maastricht? Will my Right Hon. Friend also keep finding excuses for not going into the euro? He has managed that for five years—good luck to him. **Mr Brown:** We will publish the assessment that we are making of the five economic tests. It is serious, detailed and rigorous, and the most comprehensive piece of work that the Treasury has done. It will look at all the relevant issues, as the five tests make absolutely clear, and the House of Commons will have the fullest chance to debate these issues.	'Speech is generally informal and temporary.'
Postings on an Internet chatroom site	**<alice in wonderland>** i see token has gone what a loser **<girl_thing>** hi all **<pipster>** NE girls wanna chat? **<lee1>** final score bolton 1-1 west brom **<IceColdEyeingUpAlexandra>** I hate this feeling I'm turning into Ally McBeal **<topdogg>** alice pm please **<furred_paw>** ello girl thing **<IceColdEyeingUpAlexandra>** its unseemly for a bloke **<alice in wonderland>** ok topdogg	'Speech and writing are separate systems and very different from each other. Texts are either one thing or the other.'

As you will see from the last example in the table above, new technology text types often have the properties of both speech and writing.

Standard English, slang and dialect

The extracts we considered at the beginning of this module included some examples of English that were clearly different from the 'standard' version we usually encounter in print. For example, in D. H. Lawrence's *Sons and Lovers* (text I on page 13), the speech of Mr Morel is represented in such a way as to suggest his broad Nottinghamshire accent and dialect. This is, of course, a piece of fiction. But what are Britain's regional varieties really like?

Let's hear a little more from the Sunderland man, aged 60, whose reminiscence about life when he was a child featured as text B on page 10. Some attempt has been made to reflect the more interesting pronunciations by using non-standard spellings.

when I was a bairn (.) many years ago (.) does tha want to know (.) grandma (.) that's mi mother (.) used to play bloody waar (.) when we used to come in on a night (.) and we'd all been plodgin (.) down in the bourn (.) that's a stream which is down near the beck (2) all our clathes were up the eyes in clarts (2) and mi ma used to say (.) you cannot ave any more money for any more ket this week (2) so (.) me and mi mates used to gan and clean pigeon crees out for the men who used to fly pigeons (.) when they come back they used to hoy them mebbies down in Bradford (2) they used to flee back (.) and we used to clean the cree out and he used to give us some money (.) to buy our own ket (4) what else does tha want to know (.) tha disn'y know when you're weel off you people (2) does tha want to know what we used to do for holidays (.) we used to get on a bus (.) and gan down to Seaborne about 7 mile away (2) nay Blackpools (.) nay Majorcas (.) nay bloody Ibizas (.) or bloody Tenerifes (.) we never had nowt like that (.) never thout on.

ACTIVITY 18 **C3.1a, C3.3**

Discuss and/or write an analysis of the Sunderland man's speech in which you identify the ways in which his language differs from Standard English. Then compare your findings with the commentary on page 74.

You might find it helpful to distinguish between *pronunciation* (as far as you can tell from the spellings), *vocabulary* and *grammar.*

Attitudes to accents and dialects

As you worked on Activity 18 you were beginning to make a distinction between two terms that are often confused. When focusing on the aspects of the speaker's pronunciation, you were looking at **accent**, whereas the vocabulary and grammar of a variety of language define which **dialect** it belongs to. The distinctive, educated and regionally neutral accent we used to associate with the BBC is known as **Received Pronunciation** (or **RP**), whereas the vocabulary and grammar of 'correct', acceptable English is called **Standard English (SE)**. Both SE and RP are rather special because they enjoy the prestige of being regarded as 'correct', 'good' or 'proper' English, and they are not native to any one region.

Attitudes towards other accents and dialects vary considerably. Some accents – often those such as Glasgow and Birmingham, associated with large urban areas – prove consistently unpopular and unglamorous, whereas others – such as the rural accents of the south-west of England or East Anglia – are perceived as 'quaint'. A third group of regional accents is highly regarded because the accents seem to combine friendliness with intelligence, which makes them ideal for companies seeking staff for large call centres. Attitudes towards dialects are equally mixed: many people are intrigued and charmed by the non-standard words of our regions, and fearful that we may be losing many of them, whereas others assume that speakers of dialects are either stupid or poorly educated.

This topic is covered in more detail in Module 2, Language and Social Contexts.

Preparing for the examination: Task 1, classification

In the Unit 1 examination you will be presented with a selection of data or texts and asked to examine them closely before carrying out two tasks. Each of the tasks carries an equal number of marks, and should take about half of the total examination time of 1½ hours, i.e. 45 minutes.

Here we will focus on the first of those tasks, which asks you to explore some of the many possible ways of comparing, linking, distinguishing and classifying different examples of language in use. The task is to 'discuss various ways in which those texts can be grouped, giving reasons for your choices'.

ACTIVITY 19

C3.3

Presented below is a set of texts similar to the range of texts you may find on the examination paper. Examine the texts carefully. Then work through the questions on page 31.

TEXT A

Nonsense Stories and Alphabets by Edward Lear

474 NONSENSE STORIES AND ALPHABETS

TO MAKE GOSKY PATTIES

TAKE a Pig, three or four years of age, and tie him by the off hind leg to a post. Place 5 pounds of currants, 3 of sugar, 2 pecks of peas, 18 roast chestnuts, a candle, and 6 bushels of turnips, within his reach; if he eats these, constantly provide him with more.

Then procure some cream, some slices of Cheshire cheese, four quires of foolscap paper, and a packet of black pins. Work the whole into a paste, and spread it out to dry on a sheet of clean brown waterproof linen.

When the paste is perfectly dry, but not before, proceed to beat the Pig violently, with the handle of a large broom. If he squeals, beat him again.

Visit the paste and beat the Pig alternately for some days, and ascertain if at the end of that period the whole is about to turn into Gosky Patties.

If it does not then, it never will; and in that case the Pig may be let loose, and the whole process may be considered as finished.

TEXT B

Transcript of an interview between a teacher (T) and her female student aged 17 (S), recorded in a sixth-form college in 2002:

T: right Gemma (.) let's have a look (.) how far have you actually got

S: well (.) I understood all about (.) you know (.) what we did in class

T: you mean the analysis we did of the speech

S: yeah (.) but (.) but I can't seem to do it with the homework

T: OK (2) have you got the framework (.) you know the questions we were using

S: yeah (5)

T: so first you need to read the whole of the passage OK

S: yeah

T: then start to ask yourself some (.) the questions on the sheet

---

TEXT C

The script of the opening of an episode of *Monty Python's Flying Circus*, first performed and broadcast on BBC TV in 1970, published by Methuen in 1989 in *Just the Words.*

A man in evening dress, sitting in a cage at the zoo.

Man *[JOHN]*: And now for something completely different.

Pan to show 'It's' man in next cage.

It's Man *[MICHAEL]*: It's

Animated titles.

Cut to studio: interviewer in chair.

[SUPERIMPOSED CAPTION: 'FACE THE PRESS'*]*

Interviewer *[ERIC]*: Hello. Tonight on 'Face the Press' we're going to examine two different views of contemporary things. On my left is the Minister for Home Affairs *[cut to minister completely in drag and a moustache]* who is wearing a striking organza dress in pink tulle, with matching pearls and a diamanté collar necklace. *[soft fashion-parade music starts to play in background]* The shoes are in brushed pigskin with gold clasps, by Maxwell of Bond Street. The hair is by Roger, and the whole ensemble is crowned by a spectacular display of Christmas orchids. And on my right – putting the case against the Government – is a small patch of brown liquid . . . *[cut to patch of liquid on seat of chair]* which could be creosote or some extract used in industrial varnishing. *[cut back to interviewer]* Good evening Minister, may I put the first question to you? In your plan, 'A

Better Britain for Us', you claimed that you would build 88,000 million, billion houses a year in the Greater London area alone. In fact, you've built only three in the last fifteen years. Are you a bit disappointed with this result?

Minister *[Graham]*: No, no. I'd like to answer this question if I may in two ways. Firstly in my normal voice and then in a kind of silly high-pitched whine.

TEXT D

Advertisement published in an American newspaper, the *St Louis Dispatch*, in 1912:

TEXT E

Transcript of a commentary on a rugby union match between England and New Zealand, recorded from BBC Radio 5 in 2002:

Commentator A: A great attacking position for England now (.) Dawson gets the ball spins it out (.) to Wilkinson (.) missed pass out to Greenwood (.) and he tries he beats the first tackle he's held up five metres from the line (.) England drive over the white jerseys are all there (.) out to Cohen who's on the right wing although he's the left wing (.) he's held up one metre from the line now the ball comes back (.) Dawson from the (.) right touchline out to Wilkinson swinging across (.) Grewcock in midfield drives (.) England'll get a penalty at worst anyway the referee (.) blows the whistle awards the penalty to England (.) back by the touchline (.) and good play indeed (.) by the English forwards

Commentator B: yes they're certainly taking an upper hand in this area they got that line out right Matt Dawson was so (.) he I don't think he'll oh he will take /

Commentator A: / oh he takes a short kick and oh he (.) th (.) Lomu touches it down but there was a body check there

TEXT F

HOME BUYERS' *Survey and Valuation*

Page 4 of 9

C7 Garage(s) and outbuildings
(Comment is restricted to important defects, likely to have a material affect on value. Inspection of leisure facilities, etc., is excluded.)

STONE BUILT LEAN TO CONSTRUCTION DETACHED SINGLE CAR GARAGE WITH CORRUGATED ASBESTOS SHEET ROOF - IT IS ADVISABLE THAT THE ASBESTOS BE REPLACED WITH SOME OTHER MATERIAL

C8 The site
(Only significant visible defects in boundary fences, walls, retaining walls, paths and drives are reported. Reference to potential hazards such as flooding and tree roots is included where these are readily apparent.)

AS NO PLAN OF THIS FAIRLY LARGE SITE WAS SUPPLIED BY SELLING AGENTS, WE HAVE ASSUMED BOUNDARIES AS PER THE ATTACHED COLOURED SECTION O.S. PLAN. ON THE SOUTHERN BOUNDARY IS A TIMBER PLANK FENCE WITH SQUARE TIMBER SUPPORTS WHICH WERE ORIGINALLY CEMENTED INTO THE GROUND THESE ARE ALL NOW LOOSE AND NEED RE-CEMENTING.
MOST OF STONE WALL ON EAST SIDE OF GARDEN AND TO REAR WEST COURTYARD SIDE IS COVERED IN IVY AND SHRUBS BUT AREAS NEED RE-POINTING. AREA OF DRY STONE BASE WALL IN PARKING AREA TO LEFT OF GARAGE IS IN POOR CONDITION

(Inspection covers within the boundaries have been lifted where visible and possible [except

TEXT G

The Boardwalk at Canary Wharf

★★★★★

Luxurious Serviced Apartments in London

More style, more space, more facilities, more independence and a great place to stay for one night or more

If you are visiting London, for business or pleasure, and you are tired of standard hotel accommodation, then take a look at our superb Boardwalk Suites. These stylish two bedroomed, fully serviced, luxury waterfront apartments are located in the fashionable Canary Wharf area and within 15 minutes of the new ExCel Exhibition Centre and London City Airport. Each apartment will sleep up to 5 adults in comfort, and is available for one night or more. Complete with terrific views across the marina to the Millennium Dome, the living room offers you the space to entertain guests in style. And with a well equipped kitchen, you can even eat in if you choose. But the truly amazing feature is the price, which is far less than the cost of similar hotel accommodation.

Special Offer

£189*

per night for 2 bedroom Marina Apartment which will sleep 5 people

*Minimum 2 nights stay or 3 nights for Easter and Bank Holidays. Subject to availability. Offer must be booked & occupied by May 31st 2001. Please quote LW2

So if you are planning a visit, on your own or with friends, give us a call and find out about our unbeatable value. We know we can exceed your expectations. Call now on:

020 7517 4777

LONDON MILLENNIUM SUITES
The Boardwalk at Canary Wharf

258-286 Boardwalk Place, Trafalgar Way, London, E14 5SH, England.
Tel: +44 (0) 20 7517 4777 Fax: +44 (0) 20 7517 4778
E-mail: info@millenniumsuites.com
Web: www.millenniumsuites.com

TEXT H

A review of a book about text messaging, *Text Me*, in *Craccum Magazine online*, 2002

4 thse of U wndrng wht 2 bi yr mble owng M8s/BF/GF 4 thr BDay, U hv fnd wht U R lkng 4 in a gr8 Pngwn bk clld TXT ME. Accrdng 2 th bk cvr it has 'al U need 2 knw re: txt mssgng'.

It tlls U hw 2 txt emotns _ hi-lites Nclude DLG n CLAB. U cn fite it out wth YR BF/GF via txt mssgs... LMA! MYOB! [:-(:@(Dnt wrry tho, U cn mke up by snding a VH or a @-,-'Ñ- Whn yr out U can qikly chck whr ppl R by txtng W@? and snd YR m8s an ETA if U'L B L8.

TEXT I

An extract from an article 'Au'd George: A Methody Pioneer' by A. Stanley Umpleby.

Au'd George war yan o'them strang-heeaded, rough an' riddy sooart o'men at wi used ti knaw up i't'deeals when we war lads, bud which seeam ti be dyin' oot fast. He hed neea eddication mich an' Ah sud doot if he ivver went ti skeeal aboon a twelvemonth. When he did gan t'skeealmaster used ti tell him he owt ti fetch a few hens wiv 'im ti gether t'cooarn up'at he scattered o't'fleear under his desk.

Here are some questions about the texts and the connections between them to get you started. Remember, as you explore the links between texts, it is important to cover *all* the texts, and use at least four different ways of linking texts together.

- Texts A and B might both seem to share the same **purpose** – giving instructions – but what is the *real* purpose behind text A? Which conventions of the **genre** of recipes is it using to create humour?
- Texts A and D both belong to an earlier **period** of history. In what ways do they reflect changes which have taken place in society and/or in language between then and now?
- Texts B and D both appear to be directed at a gender-specific **audience** – but in which of these is the gender aspect more significant?
- Several of the texts may have **multiple audiences** – which?
- Texts A and C are both designed to be **humorous** in the way they exploit recognisable conventions of specific **genres**. Which aspects of recipes and political interviews do they exploit for humorous effect?
- Several of the texts are written using a semi-specialised **register** which includes vocabulary appropriate to a particular topic. Which?
- Texts D and G are both adverts, and both therefore aim to persuade or influence. What similarities and differences do they have in the way they address their respective audiences?
- If you tried to define the texts by **mode** as belonging to either **speech or writing**, which texts would be most difficult to classify, and why?
- Texts H and I both differ from conventional Standard English. How would you describe and contrast the different **varieties** of English they represent?
- Jot down some more ways in which you can link or group the texts together.

You don't have long in the exam room to write up your ideas, so it may be useful to make a chart such as the one above as a starting point. You may also find it useful to use **Venn diagrams**, for example, to illustrate the ways some classifications overlap. The example below shows that you consider texts A and C to be purely informative, texts D and E to be purely entertaining, and texts B and F to have elements of both.

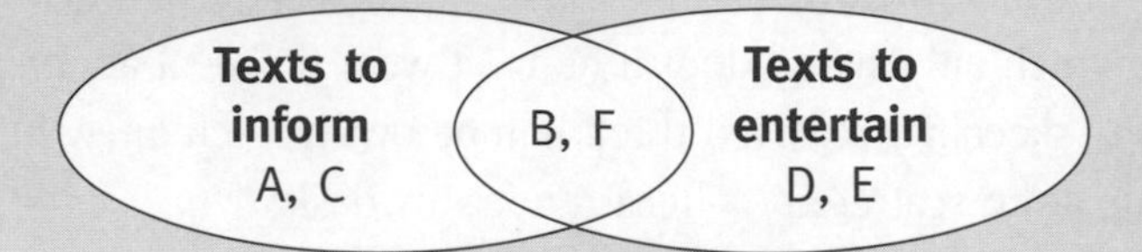

Whatever notes you use, it is vital that you communicate in clear, fluent English to the examiner these things:

- You are aware that language use can be classified in many different ways.
- You can apply this knowledge effectively to the specific texts in front of you. Don't just generalise: discuss the texts specifically and precisely, using the appropriate linguistic terminology.
- You are aware that the danger of classification is over-simplification. The paper is likely to include texts which are not easy to categorise in a straightforward way. You need to discuss these along the lines of the exercises above (see pages 22–25).

It is unlikely that you can do all of this in an answer of less than two or three pages.

Now have a go at writing your answer to this exercise, in about 45 minutes. Then compare your attempt with the sample answer in the commentaries (see page 74).

Describing language in detail: stylistic analysis

So far in this module, we have concentrated on ways of comparing, contrasting and classifying texts. The previous section has introduced some essential ideas and terms used in language studies, and the first task of the Unit 1 examination tests your ability to apply these ideas flexibly and sensitively by making links and distinctions between texts.

This section examines how we **analyse** in detail the ways language is used in a text, and how we explain why or how the **contexts** of these texts have contributed to their distinctive styles. This is what the second part of the Unit 1 examination paper is about. In it, you have to carry out a more detailed study of three of the texts (including one of the transcripts of spoken texts). This kind of activity is known as **stylistic analysis.**

Using frameworks

In stylistic analysis we cannot rely on being able to spot key features by chance. As linguistic scientists and investigators, we need to look systematically at language, asking a methodical series of questions as we investigate it.

This is what is referred to in the Assessment Objective 'know and use key features of frameworks for the systematic study of spoken and written English'.

When we consider why, and how, a particular piece of language has come to be written or spoken the way it has, there are two sets of questions to answer:

- What has influenced the writer or speaker to produce the text?
- How can we describe the distinctive style of this particular text?

Our work so far means that we have already begun to answer the first question. To answer the second question, we need to think of language in terms of different 'levels' or 'frameworks'. At each level (or within each framework) there are a number of questions we can ask – and try to answer – about the style of language in a particular text. In the remainder of this module, we will explore each of these more fully.

ACTIVITY 20 C3.3

The table below sets out some of these key questions and adds a 'key terms' column to flag up important linguistic terminology for later reference. Make yourself familiar with this framework and its key questions; it is the basis of much of the work that follows in this module. Later sections and activities explore it more fully. Once you are familiar with it, you can use it to define the key stylistic features of any text you come across.

(a) Study the examples drawn from text D (page 11), 'Come live with me and be my love'.

(b) Choose any of the other short texts we have considered in this module so far. Try to answer the key questions for your chosen text and write up your responses as a short essay.

Key question	In other words . . .	Example: Text D	Key terms for future study
How is the text organised?	Does it have a clear beginning/middle/end? Is it a list? Is it a series of steps?	Starts with an invitation . . . will lead to the promised result – pleasures.	discourse structure

Key question	In other words . . .	Example: Text D	Key terms for future study
What does it look like on the page?	Is it set out in columns? Paragraphs? Verses? Are its sections numbered or titled? Does it include panels of text or diagrams? Does it use different typefaces, type sizes?	A verse of short, regular lines.	form; layout; graphology
What kinds of sentences does it use, and how are they constructed?	How many sentences are statements? Questions? Commands? Exclamations? Are the sentences long, short or a mixture? Does their construction seem basic or complicated? Does the text use complete, 'correct' sentences or some abbreviated ones? Are there examples of unusual word order?	A command, followed by a promise or prediction. Mainly 'normal', but some unusual word order ('we will all the pleasures prove').	sentence function/ length/ structure
What kinds of vocabulary and phrases does it use?	What proportion of the words convey facts or opinions? Is the language emotional or detached? Does it seem personal or impersonal, simple or sophisticated, formal/neutral/informal? Does it include words that belong to a particular subject or theme? Or words that are specialist, technical, literary or old-fashioned? Are there any non-standard or regional expressions? Is language being used in its literal sense – or does it use similes and/or metaphors and other expressions?	Personal words ('you' and 'we'). Quite simple words ('come') with parts of the country landscape ('hills', 'dales', etc.). 'Prove' used in a different, old-fashioned sense.	colloquialism; slang; archaism; jargon; dialect; metaphor; figurative language; idioms; register; semantic fields; word classes

Key question	In other words . . .	Example: Text D	Key terms for future study
What is distinctive about the spellings or sounds used?	Is the text generally orthodox, or are there examples of unusual spellings or punctuation? Does the speech have a non-regional ('BBC'), 'posh' or regional accent? Are there any noticeable patterns in the sounds/spellings?	Rhyme at the ends of lines. Regular rhythm.	orthography; received pronunciation (RP); rhythm; alliteration; assonance
What meanings does the text have? Does it mean what it says? How can it be interpreted?	What is the actual meaning? Is there an implied or 'hidden' meaning?	Does the writer wish to marry his intended lover? What does he mean by 'pleasures'? Has the meaning of the word 'prove' changed since the poem was written?	semantics; pragmatics; denotation; connotation

Language framework: discourse structure

What do we mean by the *structure* of a piece of language? After all, we can usually recognise what holds everyday objects together: a building, for example, generally consists of a set of foundations, and an interconnecting series of load-bearing walls, beams and girders. Well, just as different buildings – houses, churches, stadiums – have different structures, so uses of language have their own distinctive structures.

This means looking at these key questions:

- How does it start?
- How does it finish?
- What is the sequence of sections involved in the middle?

There are many different ways in which texts and speech can be organised and constructed, but some common structures do occur frequently. You will certainly be able to recognise and identify examples of these. Let's begin by looking at some examples of spoken texts.

Discourse structure in speech

Although we may not be aware of it at the time, how we use spoken language in familiar everyday situations is also structured in particular ways. When we participate in these situations, it is as if we have learned to expect that they will follow a predictable but unwritten 'script'.

For example, many phone calls may follow a similar pattern to the one analysed below:

Example	Structural element
A: 324667. B: Oh hello. Is that Mr Jim Harrison? A: Yeah, speaking. B: This is Hayley Jones – you may remember we met some time ago. A: Yes, of course.	*Exchange of identification of parties*
B: How are you? I hope I'm not calling at an inconvenient time. A: No, no, not at all. I'm fine. How are you? B: Oh, pretty good. I'll tell you why I'm calling. Its about those books you ordered a while ago.	*Small talk, leading to identification of purpose of call*
B: We were just wondering if you'd received our invoice for the goods, and when we might expect to receive your payment? A: Ah yes. I have it in front of me, actually. Thanks for that. You should be receiving our cheque over the next couple of days.	*Main business of call*
B: Oh that's good, Mr Harrison. We'll look forward to hearing from you then. Thanks for your help. A: Not at all. If you'll excuse me, I've got someone waiting on the other line.	*Winding up, perhaps including a summary of what has been said, and a reason to close the conversation*
B: Of course. Goodbye now. A: Bye. Talk to you soon.	*Exchange of goodbyes*

Activity 21

For each of the following speech situations, describe the stages the conversation is likely to go through – in other words, its typical discourse structure. Keep asking how such discourse typically begins, develops and concludes.

- Making a confession/admission.
- Asking for a favour.
- A doctor's appointment.
- Chatting someone up.

We will consider other important aspects of the structure of conversation later (see 'Analysis of conversation', page 58 below).

Discourse structure in writing

ACTIVITY 22

There are many different kinds of written texts, but many of them may follow one or other of the set of discourse structures suggested below. Add your own examples to the ones given.

Structure	Examples	Your examples
Non-sequenced **lists** Stepped or sequenced **lists**	Shopping lists Instructions	
Logical **arguments** (Because of A, this leads to B, and the conclusion C)	Persuasive articles or newspaper editorials	
Problem/anxiety–solution structures	Adverts may establish a problem – spots – and go on to provide the solution – a brand of skin cleanser	
Desire–fulfilment structures	Similarly, advertisers (or politicians) may invoke a desire before offering to provide its fulfilment in the shape of their product or party	
Analysis and explanation (**X** has happened: what follows works out why and how it did so)	Essays and formal reports	
Narrative accounts	News reports; short stories	

Telling stories: narrative structures

Of course, stories, or narratives, are not confined to written texts; we tell many different kinds of stories in various situations, whether we're gossiping with friends about what happened at the weekend, telling a joke, reading a bedtime story or writing a report of a scientific experiment. However, when we start to look for the structure of stories, some common patterns begin to emerge.

Many stories establish a situation, introduce an element of disequilibrium, reach a crisis and finally resolve the problem, returning to a position of stability. Some, like news reports, give all the essential details first then elaborate on them. Others, like detective stories, withold the key details until the last page.

Activity 23

Think about the examples of narratives suggested below. For each of them, try to define what their structure is.

- Joke: Three prisoners are captured in the war, and are about to be executed. They are asked what they wish to have for their last meal. The first asks for a pepperoni pizza, which he is served and then taken away. The second requests a filet mignon, which he is served and then also taken away. The third man requests a plate of strawberries. The captors are surprised: '*Strawberries*?' 'Yes, strawberries.' 'But they are out of season!' 'I'll wait . . .'
- Personal anecdote: you tell your friends about something that happened to you at the weekend.
- Excuse provided to teacher about non-completion of homework. Do you give the ending – 'I haven't done it' – at the start, or do you make it your punch line?
- A fairy story or nursery rhyme.
- A typical episode of *EastEnders*.

Language framework: layout, form and graphology

At the level of discourse structure, we are concerned with the inner construction of discourse in different contexts. By contrast, at the level of form and layout, we are interested in those features that contribute to the shape and (in writing) appearance of a written text. Such features are collectively referred to as the **graphology** of a text.

The following questions all relate to the total impact of a text on the page:

- Is it arranged in columns, paragraphs, blocks or continuous text?
- Does it feature diagrams, pictures or other visual elements?
- What typefaces, type sizes and styles (such as *italic* or **bold**) does it use?
- What impressions do any of these features create, for example about the tone or structure of the text?
- How does the **context** of the text (where, when and why the piece was produced) help explain these distinctive features?

Activity 24

(a) Look again at texts D, F, and G from the set of texts on pages 29–30. Use the questions above to compare and contrast the graphology of these texts.

(b) Find a typical example of each of the following kinds of texts, and then answer the questions above to define their graphological features:

- message in a greetings card
- tabloid newspaper report
- formal business letter from a company
- informative leaflet for the general public
- magazine aimed at an early teens readership.

(c) Now consider the following versions of the same summons to appear at a magistrates' court to answer a criminal charge. What different 'messages' are being conveyed by the different typefaces? Which are the most and least appropriate typefaces?

1

You are hereby summoned to appear at Newtown Magistrates' Court on Tuesday, February 13th at 10.30 am to answer charges that on November 14th, 2002, you did wilfully commit an act of disorderly conduct.

2

You are hereby summoned to appear at Newtown Magistrates' Court on Tuesday, February 13th at 10.30 am to answer charges that on November 14th, 2002, you did wilfully commit an act of disorderly conduct.

3

You are hereby summoned to appear at Newtown Magistrates' Court on Tuesday, February 13th at 10.30 am to answer charges that on November 14th, 2002, you did wilfully commit an act of disorderly conduct.

4

You are hereby summoned to appear at Newtown Magistrates' Court on Tuesday, February 13th at 10.30 am to answer charges that on November 14th, 2002, you did wilfully commit an act of disorderly conduct.

The forms of spoken discourse

At first the 'forms' of spoken discourse may be less obvious. What we mean by the 'form' of a spoken text can be summed up in a few simple questions:

- Who typically are the participants?
- What are their roles in relation to each other?
- In what circumstances does the conversation usually take place?
- What kinds of thing do the speakers usually say to each other?
- Are there any 'rules' which seem to limit what can and cannot be said or done in this situation?

ACTIVITY 25

Let's try applying these questions to some common types of spoken language. Complete the missing sections in the table to describe the forms of these examples:

Question/ discourse type	Job interview	Classroom lesson	Live TV football commentary	Formal meeting
Who takes part?	One or more employers and an interviewee		Main commentator and an 'expert' adviser	
What are the usual circumstances and context?	An office or other room on business premises	A classroom in a school or college		A committee room or similar, with members sitting round a desk/table
What are the roles of the speakers? What kinds of thing do they say?		Teacher leads, asking questions, evaluating answers, giving instructions and explanations, and maintaining discipline		Chair manages the meeting, taking it through the agenda, and maintains orderly discussion

Language framework: the grammar of the text

Sentences: length, construction and function

When we start to break down language into smaller units than the whole of the text, at the level of the sentence we begin to look at those aspects of language that people think of when they use the word **grammar**. This includes areas of language study known as **morphology** (see page 43 below) and **syntax.** The term **syntax** is used when discussing the ways sentences are put together by placing words in a particular order.

Length

However, perhaps the first and easiest way of distinguishing how sentences are used in a particular text is to comment on their *length*.

Some texts may use predominantly short sentences – like this children's story, *Floppy the Hero*, by Roderick Hunt:

> A fire engine went by. There was a fire. Everyone ran to see. 'Get back,' said a fireman. A barn was on fire.

It is not only writers for children who deliberately keep their sentences short. Writers of instruction manuals, such as text E (page 11) may break down their information into small units, as in:

> * Click on the Start button on the task bar

Construction

Very short sentences are also, by definition, simply constructed. For this reason it is easy to confuse length and complexity. In fact, even longer sentences can still be relatively simple. Consider these two sentences, of identical length (48 words):

> **A** It was a nice canny game an all but sometimes windows used to get brocken and another thing in them days people were lucky if they had indoor netties and it was bloody murder if you wanted to gan to the toilet in the middle of the neet.

> **B** Not having had prior knowledge of the events which were about to unfold, and being possessed of the mistaken assumption that his way in the world was to be one of unimpeded progress, Michael was ill prepared for the news with which he would be greeted that morning.

Although of identical length, the sentence in text A strikes us as *simpler* than that in text B because of the ways in which it joins together its various parts (mainly using 'and' and 'but' to string them together). Text B, in contrast, uses more grammatically complex ways of linking the sentence elements together ('not having had', 'with which he would be'. . .).

The stylistics framework also reminds us to ask whether a text is written using complete, 'correct' sentences, and whether it uses any examples of unusual word order. Our usual notion of what constitutes a 'complete' sentence is based on written language; in speech, utterances like 'Hi Alan' and 'It is', which are technically not 'complete sentences', are very common. Such sentences are sometimes called **minor sentences**. Some written texts may also use an abbreviated or note form in the interests of economy.

As for word order, we may often find unusual examples in poems. Look back at pages 10–13, and in particular text D on page 11, 'The Passionate Shepherd to his Love' – the poet writes 'we will all the pleasures prove' rather than 'we will prove all the pleasures' – and text G on page 12, 'The Jumblies' ('In a Sieve they went to sea' following the more usual 'They went to sea in a Sieve'). Writers – and speakers too – may choose to vary the usual word order for many reasons.

We shall investigate sentence structures and syntax in more detail in *A2 English Language*: Module 4 Language Investigation, and Module 6 Language Development.

Function

Another relatively simple way of describing the kinds of sentences used in any piece of discourse is to ask what job or function they are most commonly carrying out. Here is one framework that identifies four sentence functions:

- The most common sentence type is the statement or **declarative**. This can be a statement of fact, an event, a feeling, an opinion or a prediction.
- Another type of sentence is the question or **interrogative**.
- A third type is the direct command, or **imperative**.
- The **exclamation** is a rarer type of sentence. Exclamations can include very short utterances, such as 'Great goal!'.

ACTIVITY 26

(a) Go back to any of texts we looked at earlier (see pages 27–31). For any of these, count the instances of each sentence type occurring in the extract, then use a pie chart or bar chart to record your findings. For example, text A (the teacher's instructions) consists of a mixture of declaratives and imperatives:

Declaratives	Imperatives
You have a sheet in front of you There's a list of the characters we looked at on Friday *What I want you do is to . . .	Wait a minute I'll get you one Have a look now please Look at the paragraph underneath . . . ensure that you have a pen or pencil available . . . add any relevant information

*This is debatable. This utterance is in some ways an imperative, but by putting 'what I want you to do is . . .' at the start, in effect the teacher turns it into a long declarative.

The resulting pie chart might look something like this:

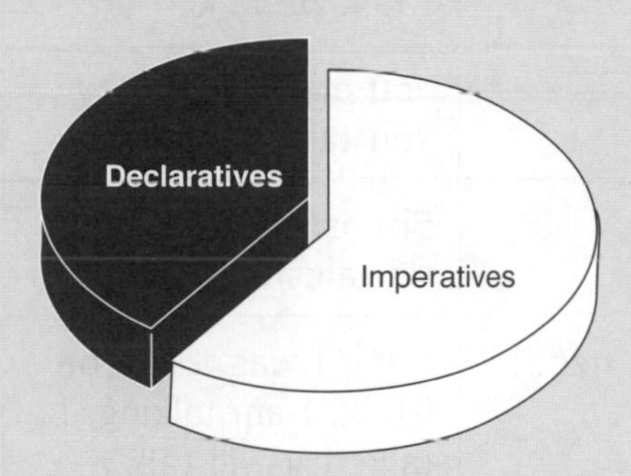

(b) For any of the following types of text, try to predict the proportions in which you will find the four kinds of sentence:

- a manual for a piece of computer software
- a TV advertisement
- an interview with a celebrity in a magazine.

Now find some examples of these kinds of texts and count the numbers of each sentence type to test your prediction.

(c) Finally, try to explain *why* the texts should have more of one type of sentence than another. Think about the purpose and subject matter of the texts, their **context**.

Word formations: morphology

Grammar is not just about word order, or syntax; it is also about the way we change the forms of individual words according to the job they are doing in a sentence. This aspect of grammar is known as **morphology.**

Many words in English are made up of two or more meaningful elements.

For example, in the sentence above, *words* = *word* + *s* (more than one), *meaningful* = *meaning* + *ful* (turns the noun *meaning* into the adjective *meaningful*). These units of meaning are known as **morphemes**.

Many words take on a different from, or grammatical function, by changing one or more of their morphemes. *Happy* can become *unhappy*, or *happiness*, and *cipher* can become *decipher*, *deciphers*, *deciphering* or even *undecipherable*. Some other words may change their form completely – *sing/sang*, *woman/women*, or *is/was*, for instance.

It is the rules of grammar, or morphology, that decide how and where we make these changes to words. For example, with **verbs**, whether we use *is*, *are*, *be*, *was* and *were*, or *talk*, *talks*, *talked* or *talking*, depends on:

The **person** it refers to	I am/we are I talk/we talk	**1st person singular/plural**
	You are You talk	**2nd person singular and plural**
	She is/they are He talks/they talk	**3rd person singular/plural**
The **tense** that is needed	I am, I was, I will be I talk, I am talking, I talked, I will talk	**Present, past or future**

One of the ways in which dialects differ from Standard English is in the patterns of these variations. A speaker of one dialect may say *I were* and *you was* rather than *I was* and *you were*.

Nouns usually change to show whether they are singular or plural (*box/boxes*, *child/children*) but there are exceptions – *sheep* and *deer* do not change.

The forms of words may also change according to their meaning and **word class** (see below), as in *consume*, *consumer*, *consuming*, *consumption*, or their position in a sentence (*She likes me, I like her*).

ACTIVITY 27

Look again at text J, the extract from *The BFG*, on page 13. This text includes some examples of unusual morphology, where the giants seem to be getting their grammar and words mixed up.

For each one, try to explain how it differs from Standard English:

Example	Comment
You is not loving it?	
The most disgusterous taste . . .	
. . . that is ever touching my teeth	

Compare your comments with the commentary on page 76.

Language framework: words and phrases (lexis)

The **vocabulary** of a language includes all the words available in it. **Lexis** is the term used for the vocabulary chosen for a text. As the number of questions included in the stylistics framework (see pages 33–35) suggests, at this level there is always a lot to observe.

It is useful here to be able to describe accurately different kinds of words and the jobs they do in a sentence, as well as their meanings. **Word classes** provide one traditional framework for doing this.

Let's look again at the eye-witness testimony from the *Titanic* (Text C, page 11). The following words from the extract have something in common:

We (x2)	morning	Cherbourg	it	I	cable
ship (x2)	April	Queenstown	afternoon	watch	anchor
Wednesday	drill	Sunday (x3)	night	noise	shock

All of these words are involved in various kinds of naming. As such, they all belong to the word class of **nouns**. We can subdivide this class like this:

Word class description	Function	Examples
proper nouns	names of specific places, months, days, people	Cherbourg, Queenstown, April, Sunday
concrete nouns	names of objects	ship, cable, anchor
abstract nouns	names of feelings or ideas	shock
pronouns	substitutes for names of people and things	we, it

Let's look now at these words from text E, 'Launching PowerPoint' (page 11):

run	switch	should happen	click
point	can't find	means	Is

These are words belong to the class **verbs**. This class is sometimes misleadingly referred to as 'doing words', but this is unhelpful; the most frequently used verbs in English are *be/is* and *have/has*, which do not describe actions of any kind. Other verbs define states or feelings (e.g. *I love you*).

Now consider the function of these words from text I, *Sons and Lovers* (page 13):

dry wet nasty

These words all add descriptive information about the noun to which they refer. So Morel's *singlet* (a concrete noun) is variously referred to as *dry*, *wet* and *nasty*. This places these words in the class of **adjectives**, which qualify or provide additional information about a noun.

Now look at the word *gingerly* from the same passage. This is also descriptive, but it does not describe an object – it describes the action of putting out a hand. It therefore belongs to the class of **adverbs**, which provide information about a verb (usually how, where or when it occurs).

These major word classes are the ones likely to be most useful in stylistic 'finger-printing'. They are listed along with **prepositions** and **conjunctions** in the table below.

Principal word classes

Word class	Function	Subclasses	Examples
Nouns	name specific people, places, times; things; feelings, ideas	proper; concrete; abstract	London, Tony Blair, Christmas; jelly, rocks, anorak; happiness, equality
Pronouns	substitute for or refer to nouns	personal; impersonal possessive	I, me, you, s/he, it, we, they; my, mine, your, his, hers, its, yours theirs
Adjectives	provide additional information about nouns	factual; opinionative	blue, steel, six; awful, excellent
Adverbs	provide additional information about verbs	manner (how); time (when); place (where)	quickly, unpleasantly; then, now; here, everywhere
Conjunctions	join phrases together within a sentence	co-ordinating; subordinating (these terms are explored in *English Language A2*)	and, but, so; because, although, despite
Prepositions	define positions and relationships		in, on, between, against, over, under

ACTIVITY 28 **C3.1a**

Look back at some of the short texts you collected for Activity 11 on page 16. For any of these texts, identify and highlight examples of each principal word class. Make a list of these items on separate pieces of paper – one each for nouns, verbs, adjectives, adverbs, conjunctions and prepositions – in the order in which they appear in the text.

Give the lists one at a time to a partner, and for each one invite them to predict the nature of the text on the basis of the listed words. At the end, discuss which word class enabled your partner(s) to identify the type of text most easily, and why this might be.

Using word classes within the stylistics framework

If we return to the key questions listed in the table on pages 33–35, we can now use word classes systematically as a means of investigating some important aspects of language use. The table below indicates how the study of word classes in a text can help answer these questions:

Key question	Word class investigation
How much of the text conveys facts and how much conveys opinions? Is the language emotional or detached?	1 The most obvious words to look at are the adjectives and adverbs. Ask whether they convey factual or emotional or opinionative details about the noun or verb they describe. 2 However, nouns and verbs can be just as revealing. Compare, for example: (a) 'The soldier moved away' (b) 'The deserter fled' and (c) 'The hero retreated'.
Does the text seem personal or impersonal?	We can usually answer this question by looking at the pronouns. There are three aspects to consider: 1 Does the writer or speaker draw attention to himself or herself by using 'I' (the first person singular)? 2 Does the writer or speaker use the first person plural ('we', 'our'), and if so, who does it include or refer to? 3 Does the speaker or writer use 'you' (the second person) to address readers or listeners directly? If the answer to all three of these questions is 'no', then we can safely describe the language as impersonal.
Is the text formal/neutral/informal? Is it simple or sophisticated? Does it include words that belong	Here we are considering the register of a text. Nouns and verbs are likely to be central, but consider adjectives and adverbs too. Even

Key question	Word class investigation
to a particular subject or theme, or that are specialist, technical, literary or old-fashioned?	conjunctions and prepositions (such as 'therefore', 'hitherto') can help mark out a text as rather formal.
Are there any non-standard or regional expressions?	This is a matter of the dialect of a text. Most written English is in Standard English, though some writers (like D. H. Lawrence in text I, from *Sons and Lovers*) may try to capture regional speech on paper. Spoken discourse is much more likely to include dialectal variations, which may use alternative nouns and verbs for everyday items and actions. And there may be other differences from Standard English – such as unusual plurals ('childer' for 'children', etc.) or different present and past tenses (such as 'I were', 'you was'). See the section on slang and dialects in this module (page 26).
Is language being used in its literal sense – or does it use similes and/or metaphors and other figurative expressions?	Although single words may be metaphorical – 'You're such an angel!' (noun), or 'I've got to scoot!' (verb), for example – we often need to consider whole phrases here. English makes deliberate use of similes, metaphors and other expressions to convey meanings more vividly, but bear in mind that the language also contains many everyday words and phrases that are idiomatic (their meanings cannot be guessed from their literal sense).

Language framework: sounds and spelling

The study of sounds is called **phonology**; the term for spelling is **orthography**. As we began to see earlier (see 'Speech and writing', pages 20–25), the relationship between the sounds of spoken English and the way we write the language is complex. There are only about 44 basic sounds in English; these basic building bricks, from which everything in our language is ultimately constructed, are called **phonemes**. Unfortunately, we have only 26 letters in our alphabet to represent these – so our spelling system can never be entirely straightforward.

By using pairs of letters (or **digraphs**) such as *sh-* and *ch-* to represent single phonemes, a standard spelling system has evolved over several centuries which makes the 26 letters of the alphabet capable of expressing many sounds, but we are all too aware of many inconsistencies – think of *rough, bough* and *cough*, *no* and *know*, or *cyclists* and *psychologists*. Some phonemes in English do correspond fairly reliably with the written alphabet: the letter 'd', for instance, does usually express the sound *d* – though even here the letter may be used singly ('dog') or in a pair ('ladder') to represent the same sound.

Another oddity is that the most common vowel sound in English does not have a letter associated with it, and is expressed using a huge variety of spelling combinations. Say aloud the vowel sound represented by the letters in bold in each of the words below:

b**a**nana undeni**a**ble nat**ura**l rubb**er** cust**ar**d

In each case, depending on your regional accent, you will probably be making a short rather abrupt sound, something like 'uh'. This surprising little vowel is, in fact, the phoneme linguists call **schwa**.

Standard and non-standard spellings

Some texts may include non-standard spellings for various reasons. For example, historical texts may include unusual spellings of otherwise familiar words that reflect changes in language over time; and a flick through your local Yellow Pages can also reveal how some organisations (such as Kwik-Fit) deliberately alter spellings to grab our attention. This is also a favourite technique among pop and rock bands.

ACTIVITY 29

(a) For each of the categories in the table below, collect six additional examples of variant spellings. Try to suggest exactly how the alternative spelling affects the way you respond to the name of the company or group.

Cafés and restaurants	Card shops	Groups and bands
The Koffee Kup Brewers' Fayre Donut Magik	Cards 'r' Us Kelly's Kards Wishing U Well	The Beatles Boyzone

(b) Now look again at text I in Activity 19, 'Au'd George: A Methody Pioneer' (see page 31). Here the writer has deliberately departed from Standard English spelling to capture the Yorkshire accent. Read the text aloud, then 'translate' the text into Standard English/Received Pronunciation, noting which features of the Yorkshire accent it is designed to capture, and any differences from Standard English grammar.

An example is provided on page 50.

Non-standard spelling	Feature of Yorkshire accent
Au'd George war yan o' them	Old George were (SE = was) one of them (SE = those) This indicates different vowel sounds from the RP '**o**ld' and 'w**e**re' and the absence of 'l' and 'f' in the forms of *old* and *of*
rough an' riddy sooart o' men	
up i't'deeals	
dyin' oot fast	
Ah sud doot	

Phonology in writing

Although it may seem like a contradiction in terms, we can sometimes observe noticeable patterns in the way particular sounds are used in written texts. This may be because such texts are actually designed to be heard, or read aloud, or simply because of the effect they produce as we 'hear' them inside our heads when we read.

These **phonological** patterns may include:

- rhythm
- rhyme
- **alliteration** (*Peter Piper picked a peck of pickled peppers*)
- **onomatopoeia** (*pop*, *sizzle*, *splash*).

Of these, perhaps the most difficult to write about is **rhythm**. We can see how rhythm works at its simplest by looking again at text G (page 12), 'The Jumblies'. Musicians are used to talking about the beats in a passage of music; similarly, with verse we can usually feel where the natural 'beat' of the language falls.

ACTIVITY 30

Work through the activities suggested alongside 'The Jumblies' in the table.

Text	Activity/commentary
They **went** to **sea** in a **Sieve**, they **did**,	1 Read these lines aloud and note how the 'beat' falls on the syllables

Text	Activity/commentary
In a **Sieve** they **went** to **sea**: In **spite** of **all** their **friends** could **say**, On a **win**ter's **morn**, on a **storm**y **day**, In a **Sieve** they **went** to **sea**!	in bold. These beats are usually referred to as **stresses** in verse. What sort of pattern begins to emerge? 2 You'll see that there seems to be a pattern of 4-3-4-4-3 stresses in the lines, but that the 'three-beat' lines seem to have an invisible pause built in. Just as in music, where silent beats are marked with a rest, in rhythmical verse the pauses are built into the rhythm.

ACTIVITY 31

Gather some samples of the types of texts shown in the table below. Identify the specific linguistic sound effects used and write them in the second column. In each case, try to explain how the effect makes the text achieve its purpose for the intended audience.

Data/texts	Sound effects used (alliteration, rhyme, rhythm, onomatopoeia, etc.)
Advertising slogans/jingles	
Children's verse	
Tabloid news headlines	

Language framework: semantics and pragmatics

The study of how meanings are created is called **semantics**. Here, we will briskly consider some of the main areas for exploration within this framework and suggest some related activities.

One way of thinking about how the vocabulary of English is organised is to group related words into **semantic fields**. This is, in effect, what a thesaurus does. Some examples follow:

Semantic field	Examples
happiness	joy, pleasure, delight, ecstasy, contentment
red	crimson, vermilion, scarlet, burgundy, cherry
motor vehicles	car, bus, truck, lorry, motorbike, moped, scooter
drinking vessels	cup, mug, glass, beaker, tumbler

Within each semantic field, some words may appear to be very close in meaning – they share a similar **denotation**. However, they may differ in subtle ways; some may have a more positive or negative feeling about them, for instance, or have different associations, or be used in different contexts or registers. Another way of saying this is that they have different **connotations**. This is why it is sometimes said that there is no such thing in English as a perfect pair of **synonyms** (words identical in meaning).

ACTIVITY 32

Explain the differences in the following sets of near synonyms, in terms of their differing connotations:

Sets of synonyms	Differences
my house/my home/my pad/my place	
fat/plump/big-boned/obese	
cheap/inexpensive/bargain/economical	

Use a thesaurus to examine other similar sets, and to make your own distinctions between individual words within them.

Euphemisms and dysphemisms

In many areas of meaning, the semantic field includes items which allow us either to avoid stating precisely what we mean, or the reverse – to put it extremely bluntly. Consider these various ways of telling you that you've lost your job:

You're sacked	You've been made redundant	We're downsizing	You're being shown the door
You're fired	You've got the chop	We're releasing you	You are surplus to requirements
I'm letting you go	You're being given your cards	Your services are no longer required	You're being thrown on the scrapheap

Some of these seem to avoid facing the unpleasant reality – 'we're downsizing' or 'we're letting you go' (as if you really wanted to leave anyway!). Such polite or evasive words and phrases are known as **euphemisms**. On the other hand, phrases such as 'being thrown on the scrapheap' or 'got the chop' seem to be designed to maximise the brutality and emotional shock. Such terms are known as **dysphemisms**.

Literal and figurative language

As the previous exercise has revealed, euphemisms and dysphemisms seldom use language literally, and often include colourful figures of speech and metaphors. So it is not just poets and writers of English literature who use similes and metaphors. On the contrary, ordinary everyday speech – and not just euphemisms or dysphemisms – is full of expressions which are not intended to be taken literally and which are based on metaphors. For example, some of the most common expressions to be heard at the moment include sayings derived from football, such as 'a level playing field', and 'moving the goalposts'.

The closer you look at everyday speech, the more of this metaphorical, or **figurative**, language you find.

ACTIVITY 33

(a) Many common expressions in everyday use are based on metaphors, but they are so familiar that we take them for granted. List – and look out for – examples of these two:

- using something 'high' to represent good, and something 'low' for bad – such as 'I'm on cloud nine', 'She's down in the dumps'
- representing life is a journey – such as 'You're on the right track', 'He's gone off the rails', 'What's the next step?'.

(b) Sometimes the use or accidental misuse of literal and figurative senses can be comical. Here, for example, are some quotations attributed to sports commentators in the collection of gaffes known as *Colemanballs*.

For each of them, explain how the humour arises in terms of literal and figurative meanings.

'Colemanball'	Comment
'He says he'll walk away from the game when his legs go.' (Anon)	
'And Seaman, just like a falling oak, manages to change direction.' (Attributed to John Motson)	
'Dean Headley has left the field with a back injury . . . more news on that as soon as it breaks.' (Attributed to Pat Murphy)	

What we really *mean: pragmatics*

We have begun to see that the meanings people attitubute to language are not always predictable from looking at the surface meaning of words. We have also seen that there may be many different ways of conveying similar meanings. What's more, even relatively innocent-seeming conversations about the weather, or your favourite music, or what you did at the weekend, may have a 'hidden agenda', or as actors and drama students might call it, a **sub-text**. The study of the meanings people actually intend and understand is called **pragmatics**.

ACTIVITY 34

(a) Let's look again at the transcript of the interview between teacher and student which we met on page 28. Alongside the text below are some prompt questions relating to the possible sub-text, or pragmatic meanings, implied by the situation. Answer the questions, and try re-creating the scene according to the answers you suggest.

Text	Possible sub-text
T: right Gemma (.) let's have a look (.) how far have you actually got	Could the teacher be implying some criticism of the student here with her question and the word 'actually'?
S: well (.) I understood all about (.) you know (.) what we did in class T: you mean the analysis we did of the speech	Does the student answer the question directly? If not, why not? Could she be anxious not to appear 'thick'?

Text	Possible sub-text
S: yeah (.) but (.) but I can't seem to do it with the homework	Why doesn't she just say 'I can't do it'? Or could the student just be using 'can't seem to' as an excuse for not having done the work?
T: OK (2) have you got the framework (.) you know the questions we were using S: yeah (5)	Does the teacher accept that the student has a problem? Or could she suspect this is just an excuse? Would this be reflected in how she says this?
T: so first you need to read the whole of the passage OK S: yeah T: then start to ask yourself some (.) the questions on the sheet	How patient is the teacher? How far will her paralinguistic and prosodic features convey her real feelings about the student and the situation?

(b) To observe pragmatics in action, try role-playing the following situation in groups of three, with A and B as participants and C an observer.

Student A: You had an argument with Student B yesterday, and you wish to make up. You want to be friends again, and you believe that the argument was just a 'blip'. You see Student B working and decide to use the excuse of wishing to borrow a set of notes for a lesson you missed, in order to make contact.

Student B: You had an argument yesterday with Student A, whom you have always privately disliked. As you see him/her approach, your stomach churns – you just don't want to know. You will be reasonably polite.

Both A and B: You must not refer directly to the argument you had, or to any aspect of your relationship. Confine yourself to discussing the question of the lesson missed, and the borrowing of notes.

Student C: Observe to see how the sub-text, or pragmatic meanings, of this apparently ordinary interaction are shown.

Putting it all together

Stylistic analysis of texts

In the Unit 1 examination, the second task on the paper asks you to analyse in some detail the use of language in three of the texts you are given. The question is usually phrased in such a way as to ensure that one of these texts will always be a piece of spoken language.

This task requires you to apply the linguistic knowledge you have gained so far to the analysis of the texts by:

- **selecting** their distinctive features for discussion – you won't have time to discuss every detail of the texts
- applying **some** of the language frameworks to each text – not all the language frameworks will be relevant or useful to any one text
- using the appropriate linguistic **terminology**
- relating the stylistic features of the texts to their **contexts** (where, why and when they were produced).

The basic question is, as always:

How does this text use language and how is this related to the context in which it was produced?

ACTIVITY 35

C3.3

This is an approach which you should be able to apply to most of the short texts you are likely to meet in the exam. We will use text C (*Monty Python's Flying Circus*) from Activity 19 (see page 28) as an example.

Step	Example
First reading: During your first reading of the text, try to answer these basic questions, jotting down your responses in rough: • Who is its audience? • What is the text saying to its audience? • What is the text doing to its audience? • What, in general terms, do you think is the intended impact of the text on its audience?	This text has several audiences. At first, the audience was the actors and director who would enact it as a performance. Then its audience included all the original viewers of the programme. Now, in published script form, its audience may be people simply reading it as a text. The text is clearly designed to entertain and amuse the viewers/readers, but some parts of it are designed to instruct the technical director where to point the camera.
Select and apply the frameworks: How does this text use language? Decide which of the frameworks is most useful for this text: Discourse? Pragmatics? Grammar? Phonology? Lexis? Semantics?	On the page there are two types of text – dialogue and stage directions. It may be useful to comment on how these are distinguished lexically, graphologically and grammatically. Most of the humour results from the style of language used (register, lexis) and the plays on words and meanings (semantics and pragmatics). It is a parody of a certain kind of discourse (TV political programme).

Writing your analysis: now write up your analysis. It's good to start with a very brief summary of your answers to the 'what?' questions. You can comment on the text bit by bit as you go along, but it may be better to use the framework as a way of organising your analysis into five sections.

Remember: keep relating the features you describe to the **context** of the text.

See the commentary on page 76.

Analysing spoken texts

One of the texts you analyse in the second part of the Unit 1 examination will be the transcript of an example of speech. You can apply a similar approach to the analysis of transcripts, provided you also remember to apply, where relevant, the discoveries you have made about the nature of spoken language.

ACTIVITY 36

Let's consider text E, the rugby commentary, which we first looked at on page 29. Use the prompts below to start to focus on how language is used in this extract, before writing up your analysis as in activity 35.

Context:

- What are the functions of this kind of radio commentary?
- How might it differ from a TV equivalent?
- What can the speaker take for granted in his audience?
- In what ways would prosodic features be important in the delivery of this commentary?

Transcript	Prompts
Commentator A: <u>A great attacking position for England now</u> (.) Dawson gets the ball spins it out (.) to Wilkinson (.) <u>missed pass out to Greenwood</u> (.) and he tries he beats the first tackle he's held up five metres from the line (.) England drive over the <u>white jerseys</u> are all there (.) out to Cohen who's on the right wing although he's the left wing (.) <u>he's held up one metre from the line now the ball comes back</u> (.) Dawson from the (.) right touchline out to Wilkinson swinging across (.) Grewcock in midfield drives (.) England'll get a penalty at worst	What kind of 'sentences' are these? List the verbs used. How often? How fast? Which tense? Which semantic field? How does he avoid repeating 'England'? Overall, which lexical items seem to assume that listeners have at least a basic understanding of rugby? How often does the speaker pause at sentence boundaries?

anyway the referee (.) blows the whistle awards the penalty to England (.) back by the touchline (.) and good play indeed (.) by the English forwards	At what points in a sentence *does* he pause? → What proportion of the text consists of proper nouns? Relate this to the text's context and function.
Commentator B: Yes they're certainly taking an upper hand in this area they got that line out right Matt Dawson was so (.) he I don't think he'll oh he will take /	→ Here we move from description/ narration to evaluation. How does the brief break in play affect the kinds of thing the commentator(s) can say?
Commentator A: / oh he takes a short kick and oh he (.) th (.) Lomu touches it down but there was a body check there	→ What seems to be the function of Commentator B? Why does A feel he needs to interrupt?

Analysis of conversation

The most interesting thing about talk is how we interact as social beings. After all, we use language not just to exchange information but also to negotiate our social relationships.

We have already explored ways in which the **discourse structures** of certain conversational situations typically follow a recognisable pattern. For instance, an encounter with friends may start with a greeting and some small talk, move to anecdotes about what you've each been doing, and end with excuses for leave-taking ('Well, must be going . . .', etc.) followed by repeated 'bye', 'see you', 'take care', 'be in touch', or other similar phrases (see page 36 above).

ACTIVITY 37

C3.1a

We need also to consider the factors that determine the ways people talk to each other in a particular situation. In groups, discuss how each of the following factors might influence the part you play in a conversation, and the vocabulary, expressions, tone of voice and accent you use. Take into account the cultural expectations that would apply to each:

- the **place** where a conversation occurs (at home, in class, at a party, in church, at the workplace . . .)
- who else is present (friends, family, teachers, workmates, boss . . .) and your **relationship** with them
- the **purpose** of the conversation (social chat, job interview, buying/selling, asking a favour . . .)

Now compare your responses with the commentary on page 77.

A framework for analysing talk

We have already applied a systematic method to the stylistic analysis of a written text (see pages 33–35). Now let's try something similar for speech, but starting from a slightly different set of questions:

Key question	Explanation
Who seems to lead the talk?	This means looking closely at how the talk moves on as each speaker takes their turn. These alternating turns are referred to as **adjacency pairs**. In some situations, the pattern may be obvious – a teacher or a police officer may ask all the questions, for example.
Who says what gets talked about?	The ability to influence the subject or **agenda** of a conversation is usually a sign of personal status or dominance. In formal talk, the agenda and who controls it (or **topic management**, as this aspect of talk is known) may be obvious; in informal situations, where may topics may be covered, we need to look more closely at whose subjects get talked about and whose don't.
Who talks most?	Always a key question, but the answer to this question will not always lead us to the dominant speaker. Sometimes, the most powerful person needs to say very little.
Who interrupts? Who backs down?	This is usually an interesting question. If someone is easily interrupted this may be a sign of low status, whereas the right to speak uninterrupted is often an indicator of conversational dominance.
Who gets to comment on what people say?	In classrooms, teachers routinely say in response to students 'Good answer', 'Well done', or 'That's right' (or their opposites). However, when a teacher asks a particularly searching question, students seldom say 'Good question, sir/miss'. The right to make judgements about what other people say is often a sign of status or power.
What are people trying to do to other speakers? . . . Or, what do people really mean?	As we have seen (see 'Semantics and pragmatics', pages 51–55 above), we do not always say exactly what we mean, or

Key question	Explanation
	mean exactly what we say. What seem to be the actual meanings either intended, or understood, by the participants in the conversation? What is being implied? What is the **sub-text**?

ACTIVITY 38

(a) To put this framework for analysing conversations into practice, we'll look closely at the piece of spontaneous speech we saw earlier as text F (page 12). It was recorded from a late-night radio phone-in.

Re-read the transcript with this first, basic question in mind*: What do you notice about the way this conversation works and the language used by each speaker?*

Then re-read the data, applying each of the questions in our framework.

(b) Compare your notes with those made by a student, reprinted in the commentary on page 77.

(c) Now try analysing text B, the conversation between a teacher and her student printed on page 28, in a similar way.

We will return to more analysis of talk and pragmatics in Module 2, Language and Social Contexts (see page 79).

Preparing for the examination: Task 2, stylistic analysis

Having spent half of your time on the grouping and classifying task (Task 1) you will have just 45 minutes left to demonstrate your skills of stylistics analysis. In that time you have to choose **three** of the given extracts (one of which must be a spoken text) and write a brief but detailed analysis of them, identifying their distinctive linguistic features and relating these to the contexts of their production and reception.

Here are some key points to remember:

- Judge your time carefully. You can afford to spend only about 15 minutes on each text.
- Write clear, precise English and use the appropriate linguistic terminology to define precisely the language features in front of you. This fulfils Assessment Objective AO1.
- **Don't** just note features mechanically. **Always** try to relate the specific stylistic feature to some aspect of its context (who, why, where and when).

- **Don't** make negative points (e.g. 'there are no questions in this text') unless there is something really unusual about them.
- **Don't** try to apply every framework (discourse, grammar, lexis, etc.) to every text. There isn't time and not all the frameworks are always relevant. Select the most interesting aspects of language to discuss in each case.
- For higher grades, **do** make sure you discuss some of the more 'difficult' frameworks – discourse structure, grammar or pragmatics – in relation to at least one of your texts. Answers which are limited to lexical and grammatical features tend not to receive the highest marks.

Do you know your language terms?

ACTIVITY 39

Test your knowledge of some of the basic linguistic concepts and terms introduced in this module by completing the following passage, inserting the appropriate words. Check your answers on page 78.

We began by exploring the varieties of language all around us. One way of classifying these is by purpose: for the purposes of the Original Writing part of the course we considered four of these – to entertain, to inform, to instruct and to [1] ___________. We discovered, of course, that many kinds of writing and speech do not fit easily into this simple categorisation.

There are many other ways of classifying language use. One is to define whether the text is in the spoken or written [2] ___________, but even here, some kinds of language (like texting, or chatrooms) embody characteristics of both. Some uses of language can be distinguished in terms of their formality. Of course, we have to be careful not just to assume that language is either 'formal' or 'informal'. There is a whole spectrum of formality, moving from the most vulgar language considered to be unacceptable or forbidden ([3] ___________), through to the kind of unofficial, colourful language which is used throughout the country but is not regarded as 'proper' English ([4] ___________), to the variety of English vocabulary and grammar accepted as 'correct' ([5] ___________) in its 'neutral', formal and highly formal forms. In this way we can define what we call the [6] ___________ of a text. This may also refer to the words, or [7] ___________, which relate to a specific topic area or subject. We may also come across the language varieties of different regions of the country. We distinguish between the pronunciation that is part of regional speech by calling it an [8] ___________, whereas the words and grammar which distinguish this from Standard English we define as [9] __________. It is often interesting to consider texts as examples of distinctive kinds of language use which have recognisable features or conventions ([10] __________), and it is always important to bear in mind the readers or listeners for whom the text is being produced – in other words, the [11] __________.

When we start to analyse precisely the distinctive style of a text, we need to consider a number of different aspects of language, and use a number of different [12] __________. We can consider, for example, the way a piece of language is organised and constructed; how it begins and ends, and what happens in the middle. Here we are analysing text at the level of [13] __________. Then, for written language, there is the physical presentation of the text on the page, or [14] __________.

The study of grammar usually consists of two areas; the way that sentences are constructed and words arranged in a particular order is covered by [15] __________, and the way that words are formed, and the changes we make to them according to their job in a particular sentence, is a matter of [16] __________.

For example, we say 'I write' but 'she writes' according to whether we use the [17] __________ or [18] __________ person of the verb. We can also think about the kinds of sentences used. One way of classifying different sentences is to define their function. Some sentences ask questions ([19] __________), others give commands ([20] __________), others simply present statements ([21] __________), while some are outbursts or comments ([22] __________). Some sentences, in fact, are not really sentences at all by the usual definition, but may consist of only one or two words. Such sentences are called [23] __________. sentences. Different kinds of texts may have different proportions of each type of sentences.

In the past, people used to talk about 'parts of speech', whereas nowadays we refer to word classes. Words like *pen*, *grass*, *automobile*, *disagreement* and *David Beckham* are all [24] __________. We can subdivide this big class: *pen, grass* and *automobile* are all objects in the real world, so they are known as [25] __________. *David Beckham* is the name given to a well-known person, so this is a [26] __________, whereas *disagreement* is an idea or feeling – in other words, an [27] __________. Then there are so called 'describing words', which are usually attached to these to provide different kinds of information. These may describe colours, or qualities, or factual details – they are all [28] __________.

Traditionally, the definition of a [29] __________ is a 'doing' word. However, this is misleading; the most common one is 'is' or 'be', followed by 'have', and many of these words describe states or feelings rather than actions. Extra information about these words is given by [30] __________, which will tell us something about how, where or when this is going on. These, then, are the four principal word classes, but of course there are others: words like *I*, *you*, *he*, *him* and *she* ([31] __________), words like *with*, *and*, *but*, *because* and *so* ([32] __________) and words like *on*, *in*, *under*, *beyond* and *after* ([33] __________).

Breaking language down even further can lead us to think about the sounds of English – this is the study of [34] __________. English is made of 44 basic vowel and consonant sounds called [35] __________. However, when we talk we usually don't just depend on these, as our gestures, eye contact and body language (or [36] __________ features) and our intonation, speed of speaking and the ways we stress our words ([37] __________ features), all play an important part in communication. This is why so much speech seems to be less meaningful if you are not present when and where it is spoken – in other words, it tends to be [38] __________ – __________.

We have also looked at how words themselves convey meanings. The study of this aspect of language is called [39] __________. The meanings of words are complex; two words in a similar [40] __________ field may appear to have similar meanings or be [41] __________ of each other, but the chances are that even though they may share a similar denotation (*house* and *home* can both refer to the building in which you live), they clearly have different feelings and ideas associated with them – in other words, they have different [42] __________. One of the most interesting topics here is the difference between language that means exactly what it says, used literally, and language that works like a kind of metaphor – in other words [43] __________ language. We don't always say exactly what we mean in English; we might sometimes say we are going to powder our nose when we mean something else (that is, use a [44] __________). At other times, we might create coarse humour by being more blunt than is usually polite, which is a [45] __________. Indeed, in many contexts, the meanings we intend, or the meanings people understand, may not be immediately obvious just by looking at the words they use. There may sometimes be a hidden meaning or intention – what drama students and actors might call a sub-text – to the most innocent uses of language. The study of this area of language is known as [46] __________.

Commentaries

Activity 1

A: There are many reasons why there is so much variation in English. If we go back over a thousand years or more, 'English' was not a single language but included a number of related German dialects brought to this country by invaders from the region of present-day Germany (you will study this aspect of English next year, for Module 6, Language Development). These ancient differences produced many local variations, and until the twentieth century many local communities and their **dialects** remained relatively isolated. Even today, communities may take pride in retaining distinctive voices that express their character and identity – this is the subject of one of the sections in Module 2, Language and Social Contexts ('Dialects of the British Isles'). It is true that the version of English used in the media and taught in schools (**Standard English**) is often seen as 'correct', but this can be a controversial issue, as we'll discover later.

B: Speech certainly comes before writing in children's language learning, as it has throughout the history of human society. Spoken language is fundamental to our personal and social lives, yet in our society it often seems to be valued less (by our educational and examination systems, for example) than writing. However, although traditional English courses have often been based on the study of literature and the printed word, your AS/A level English Language course pays at least equal attention to the various forms of talk. You will study speech and writing throughout the course, and the relationship between the two is an important aspect of Module 1, Introduction to the Study of Language.

C & D: The situation described by Ayumi in text C is one that we all recognise. Each social situation we find ourselves in tends to produce its own distinctive forms of language. As we move from one place to another and assume different roles, we adopt the language of the particular social group to which we belong.

Nevertheless, as individuals we may still retain our personal linguistic 'fingerprints', so the science fiction scenario suggested in text D is really not as far-fetched as you might imagine. Although skilled performers like Rory Bremner can produce striking impressions of individuals' voices, the precise combination of tone, pitch, volume and expression that make up an individual's speech can be as distinctive as a fingerprint (see the discussion of **idiolect** on page 6). Furthermore, we have individually distinctive features in our writing, too. The science of **forensic linguistics** has enabled the identity of texts to be established in law, leading to confirmation of the authorship of anonymous letters or poems, and even to the conviction of criminals on the basis of their writing.

E: There is no doubt that every language continually changes, just as the people and the societies that use it continue to evolve. It is easy to see how such changes – for example the development of technology – can bring about changes in vocabulary, but English has developed in many other ways too. As Kibria's question indicates, when we look at old written texts we notice all the *thee's*, *thou's* and strange word order, and see that the **grammar** of English has changed in some ways; and when you hear old BBC news broadcasts or the soundtracks of old films you know that even pronunciation seems to have changed. This kind of change does not happen as a result of someone making a decree or passing a law; however, people who have influence, power or authority in society may be more likely to affect the process of language change. This topic is one of the two major areas covered by Module 6, Language Development.

F: Janet's experience of learning languages is certainly not unusual; most of us find learning a second language far more difficult than acquiring our own mother tongue. This is because we are seldom in the position of infants, totally immersed in the language; neither do we have the same motivation to learn. As children, learning to communicate is vital to our every need. Besides, many British people are deterred from learning a second language by the widespread use of English across the world. It also seems to be true that our receptiveness to new languages and our ability to learn them decline as we grow older. You will study language acquisition in depth as part of Module 6, Language Development.

Activity 2

You will probably have recorded a wide variety of language usage under each of the four quadrants. In practice, of course, speaking and listening tend to overlap in many situations, but you should still have been able to identify plenty of different contexts for each of the four language activities. Of course, there is no single best way of classifying language in use. In this exercise, you may have decided to categorise according to the purpose or **function** of language in a given situation (exchanging information, asking questions . . .), the nature of the situation itself (formal or informal, family/school/workplace . . .) or the language **medium** (phone, Internet . . .). You might also have considered the **style** of language you would actually use (for example slang, polite, etc.). These are just some of the many valid ways of classifying language – we will go on to consider others, and to collect these types of classifications systematically.

Activity 4

Your parents – or anyone else closely involved in your upbringing – were your earliest and, for much of your pre-school life, your main influences. They provided you with much of the 'data' on which you based your earliest guesses at how English works. You probably imitated not just the words and phrases you heard them use, but also their **intonation** patterns and accents. At an early stage, you may also have learned notions of what was acceptable or unacceptable usage in terms of 'good' or 'bad' English, or swear-words considered **taboo**. However, once you started going to school, the linguistic influence of your parents and family probably diminished steadily as they competed with many other and increasingly powerful factors in your life. In your A2 course, you will go on to study in some detail the processes of early language acquisition and the role that parents have in this.

More controversial is the question of how your general **social background** or **class** may have affected your language. There does seem to be a relationship between your social class and some aspects of language use (e.g. accent), and in the past some researchers have suggested that pupils from poorer backgrounds have more restricted language use. However, this is a highly controversial area. Similarly, the question of **gender** has been the subject of much recent interest, with some research indicating differences between the way men and women use language. These are topics which you will study in more depth in Module 2, Language and Social Contexts.

Your education will certainly have had a major influence on your language development, introducing you to many new words and encouraging you to develop your language skills throughout your educational career. Teachers may also have been strong influences in developing your sense of what is 'correct' or 'acceptable' English – though despite years of such influence, outside the classroom you probably still use language in ways they may disapprove of! More generally, your encounters with different subjects and ideas will certainly have contributed hugely to the expansion of your language.

However, in school, the linguistic influence of groups of **friends** is soon likely to outstrip that of either parents or teachers. Your need to be accepted by your peers is likely to have led you to use similar speech to the friends you most wish to be like – so your accent may have become more like your friends' than your parents', and your speech may have begun to include the playground **slang** or swear-words that parents and teachers tried in vain to discourage. Some groups may develop slang words unique to them, or share particular catch-phrases which become 'buzz words'.

The **places** where you lived may have influenced you in ways that you were entirely unaware of at the time. The most obvious aspect of your speech, one that may reveal your geographical origins, is your **accent**; this term is used to describe the way you pronounce the sounds of English, and the distinctive **intonation** patterns that accompany your speech. You may also use words, phrases and unusual grammatical constructions characteristic of a region, collectively known as **dialect.** If you have moved from one place to another you may have adjusted your speech, consciously or unconsciously, to fit in with your new surroundings and, as a result, significantly changed your accent/dialect.

TV, music and other **media** no doubt became an increasing influence as you got older. Phrases adopted from the Australian English of *Neighbours*, or the street slang of 'gangsta rap', may have started to feature in the vocabulary of you and your friends. This is likely to affect accent and grammar, too; phrases borrowed from such sources may include non-standard constructions and pronunciations.

As you grow older, you encounter a new set of linguistic influences when you enter the world of **work**. The way you are obliged to use language when serving burgers, selling shoes or talking with fellow workers on a building site may involve you with a kind of **jargon**, a different kind of slang, or speaking in an accent slightly different from your usual one. To start with, this influence may not extend far beyond your workplace, but as adult life progresses it is likely to have an increasingly strong effect on your individual language use.

Activity 5

Your **family** may well have some words which are used in ways that outsiders might not recognise, perhaps because they arose from incidents in the past or other aspects of family life. Many families have rituals that involve certain phrases being said at certain times (such as birthdays and Christmas). Everyone's examples will be different.

Your immediate group of **friends** may have certain favourite 'buzz words' or slang, or use swear-words in particular ways. You may be influenced by catch-phrases from favourite films, TV programmes or music, which you subsequently introduce into your conversation. There may even be a favoured accent – and newcomers to the group may end up altering their speech in this direction in order to fit in.

People who live in your **town or region** will share some aspects of accent and pronunciation, as well as some dialect vocabulary and non-standard English grammatical constructions. People who share a particular interest and people who do the same job are most likely to share a specialist vocabulary or technical **jargon** that is specific to the interest or job.

People from the same **social background** may also share some linguistic features. The relationship between the **social class** we belong to and the accent, dialect and style of our speech is a complex and often controversial one which is covered in more detail in Module 2, Language and Social Contexts. In general, people from working-class backgrounds do tend to use a higher proportion of regional accent/dialect features than those from professional or middle-class backgrounds.

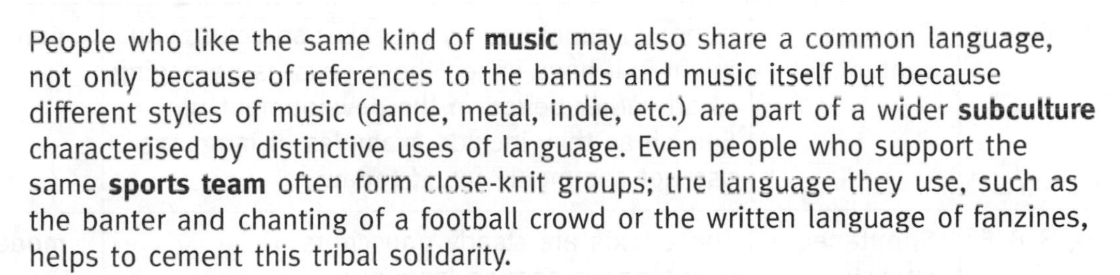

People who like the same kind of **music** may also share a common language, not only because of references to the bands and music itself but because different styles of music (dance, metal, indie, etc.) are part of a wider **subculture** characterised by distinctive uses of language. Even people who support the same **sports team** often form close-knit groups; the language they use, such as the banter and chanting of a football crowd or the written language of fanzines, helps to cement this tribal solidarity.

Activity 7

The extracts are:

A: Transcript of a recording made during an English lesson in a secondary school.

B: Transcript of a Tyneside speaker reminiscing about his childhood in conversation with his granddaughter of 17.

C: The evidence of an eye witness given to the US enquiry into the sinking of the *Titanic* in 1912.

D: Extract from 'The Passionate Shepherd to his Love', a poem by Christopher Marlowe, written in the late sixteenth century.

E: Extract from T. Burrows, *Creating Presentations*, published by Dorling Kindersley.

F: Transcript of a radio phone-in programme.

G: Extract from 'The Jumblies' by Edward Lear, 1871.

H: Quoted from a speech attributed to John Ball, co-leader of the Peasants' Revolt, 1381.

I: Quoted from *Sons and Lovers* by D. H. Lawrence, 1913.

J: Extract from *The BFG* by Roald Dahl, 1982.

How you decided to group sets of texts will have depended on which aspects you chose to focus on – and of course, there are many possible ways of doing this. The table below exemplifies some of these; note especially the **key concepts and terms** used to define each category.

Linked texts	Group title	Features in common	Key concept /term
C & G	Disastrous sea voyages	Both texts are about sea voyages which end badly! Here we are thinking about the subject matter or **topic** of the texts	**topic**
A & E	Instructions	Both of these texts are designed to convey sets of instructions.	**purpose**
D & H	Persuasion	These texts, on the other hand, are designed to be persuasive. In both cases, we are focusing on the **purpose** or function of the texts to define them.	
D, G & H	Previous centuries	Although separated by roughly 500 years, you might still have linked these texts as belonging to an earlier **period** in the development of English as they include examples of language use not commonly found today.	**period**
A, B & F	Spontaneous speech	These texts are clearly transcripts of spontaneous spoken language.	**mode**
H, I & J	Scripted or fictional speech	These texts include either scripted or fictional representations of speech.	
C, D, E & G	Written texts	On the other hand, these texts seem to be examples of written language. In all three cases, we are focusing on whether the text is in speech, or writing – this is the **mode** of the text.	
A, B, G & J	Young audience	These texts seem to be directed at 'young', i.e. non-adult listeners or readers.	**audience**

Linked texts	Group title	Features in common	Key concept /term
		These texts seem to be directed at significant gatherings of people.	
A & H	Addressing a group of people	These are examples of one-to-one conversations.	
B & F	One-to-ones	In each case we are thinking here about the **audience** of the texts.	
B, G, I & J	Non-standard /regional language	These texts all include examples of language (either **slang** or **dialect**) which is not regarded as 'correct' Standard English. This is a question of the **variety** of English involved.	**variety**
C, D & H	Formal language	These texts all use language with quite a high level of formality – a matter of the **register** of the texts.	**register**
B, C, G, I & J	Stories/ narratives	These texts all tell stories of one sort or another.	**genre**
D & G	Verse/poetry	These texts are written in verse. Here we are classifying the texts according to their **genre**.	
E & J	Illustrations	These texts both use illustrations as well as words to communicate. In other words, we are looking at their lay-out and physical presentation on the page, or **graphology**.	**graphology**

Activity 8

Text	Problematic aspects
Text C: written record of testimony given to the *Titanic* enquiry	This is a record of witness testimony. The witness will obviously have spoken this but it is likely to have been planned, rehearsed or even written first. Then it has been recorded and written down as the official court record.
Text J: Extract from *The BFG*	Like text I, this is a written text which includes the representation of fictitious speech. As a story intended for children, it may also be received by some children as a story read aloud.

Text	Problematic aspects
A politician's speech	Few politicians will risk speaking 'off the cuff' without planning or preparation. Many speeches will be written – possibly by someone else! – and delivered via a script or an autocue.
A job interview	This is an apparently spontaneous conversation – but the questions posed by the interviewer are likely to have been planned and written down beforehand, and the answers by the interviewee may have been rehearsed.
An episode of *EastEnders*	Although we experience this as 'natural' speech, this is, of course, an illusion: these are actors who have memorised the words written down by scriptwriters.
A series of postings in an Internet chatroom	In one sense, this is writing – we communicate using written words – but in another, we behave as if it is speech and conversation.

Activity 9

Text	Multiple audiences and different meanings
Text D: 17th-century poem	Is the poem *really* intended to be for the poet's lover? If so, its other readers – us, and anyone else interested in poetry – are cast as eavesdroppers on an intimate moment. Of course, 21st-century readers may not have been in the poet's mind when he wrote the poem, but 17th-century ones probably were.
Text F: Transcript of a radio phone-in	Tanya was speaking to the DJ – but would also have been aware of the much wider audience listening to the show. This may have made her rather nervous, or certainly limited the kinds of thing she felt she could say.
Text J: Extract from *The BFG*	The audience for the story appears to be primarily children – but it is their parents who may initially skim through, select and buy the book, which they might not do if they considered it unsuitable. It may also be the adults who read the book to, or with, the child, and they may respond to it in a different way.
A women's magazine such as *Cosmopolitan*	Supposedly aimed at a female audience, many women's magazines attract casual male readers, whose interests and responses to what they read may be very different from the primary audience.

Activity 10

Text/language use	Purpose
Text B: transcript of Tyneside speaker	The speaker may be trying to amuse, or even educate (give information to) his granddaughter, though in the context of a language textbook, the purpose of the text may be to give an example of a specific regional dialect.
Text D: poem	On the face of it, the poem is persuading the poet's lover to be his 'love', but this may be a fiction, like a pop song; it is primarily to amuse or entertain its readers.
Text F: radio phone-in	The purposes of the different speakers are different; Tanya is presumably trying to amuse or entertain the DJ, while the DJ is hoping to use Tanya to entertain the audience. Perhaps Tanya is also giving information, but in the hope of some reward or a prize.
Text J: extract from *The BFG*	Stories like this are primarily to entertain and amuse children, but with many children's stories there may be a less obvious, more educational purpose or 'moral' behind the story.
A casual conversation with your friends	Do any of our four purposes really fit here? To 'amuse' is certainly one of the intentions, but perhaps the primary purpose is not covered by the purposes suggested – that is, simply to reinforce social relationships. As we shall see in Module 2, Language and Social Contexts, this is a vital function of language.
A TV documentary about wildlife	There may be several things going on here. Perhaps the primary purpose of the programme makers is to inform, but they know that if it is not also entertaining, few viewers will watch it. There may also be an underlying persuasive intent, if programme makers hope that viewers will be more likely to support animal charities or be sympathetic to animal welfare causes after watching the programme.
A tabloid news report about politics	It is debatable whether many tabloid news stories are primarily to inform or to entertain. Clearly they try to do both, but some types of story (e.g. politics) may have more of an informative content than others (e.g. scandal/showbiz stories). However, there may also be a subtle persuasive element, as the political bias of many papers is often reflected in the way they report political stories.

Activity 15

(b)

- Some features missing from the transcript are the speaker's facial expressions, hand gestures and body language (these physical aspects, which contribute to the meanings of speech, are called **paralinguistic features**). Also missing are the actual sound and tone of her voice (this includes the way her voice moves up and down as she speaks – the **intonation**), the stress placed on particular words, and the tempo of the speech. These aspects of the way our voices and manner of speaking add to our meanings are referred to as **prosodic features**. Their absence makes it difficult to judge the speaker's mood, attitude and feelings about the events she describes.

- The elements of the spoken account most obviously missing from the written statement are the hesitations and **fillers** that occur in spontaneous speech. These may be verbal ('you know', 'like') or non-verbal ('er', 'um'). The written statement also avoids the digressions (the witness's dog-walking) that appear in the spoken version.

- The spoken version seems to consist of long continuous sentences that include breath pauses and the words 'and' and 'so'. These are called **compound sentences**. Sentence boundaries are generally less clear in speech – it is not always easy to say when one sentence stops and the next starts – so it is usual to indicate pauses in transcriptions using (.) instead of conventional punctuation.

- The inexplicit or **deictic references** work in speech because the speaker and the listener both have knowledge of the places referred to. This is often a significant aspect of speech – many of its meanings are closely tied up with the context in which the words are spoken. Thus we refer to meanings which are **context-bound**. In writing we cannot expect our readers to share the same context, so our meanings need to be explicit and **context-free**.

- In her spoken account, the speaker tends to sensationalise events, describing the car as 'racing' and the smoke as 'pouring'. At some points, the speaker uses the present tense – 'this car comes racing down', 'so I turn around and there's black smoke pouring out' – even though the events are in the past. This is a common feature of spoken narratives – it is as if the speaker is bringing events alive by re-enacting them in the present.

- The spoken version contains an example of regional, non-standard grammar ('them shops') and several colloquial expressions like 'bloody great crash' which have been replaced in the written version, making it generally more formal and precise.

Activity 16

1 You might be able to apply some kinds of punctuation quite easily – such as marking questions with a question mark. You may decide to use commas to mark some of the pauses in your speech, but these do not necessarily occur at the places you would normally use commas in writing (between clauses). The major problem is likely to be deciding where sentences begin and end (**sentence boundaries**). In speech, we may produce either long, rambling sentences loosely connected by 'and', but', 'so', etc., or very short utterances which don't constitute sentences at all.

2 You may identify the English spelling system as an obvious source of difficulty because it is not a consistent representation of the sounds of the language. As adult writers, you may also take lots of things for granted which you once had to learn – such as the alternative forms of upper and lower case letters, and the fact that we write from left to right and top to bottom. It also follows from the discussion above that learning to construct acceptable sentences and punctuate them is a major challenge.

3 *Question:* Most people report that it is easier to be deceptive in writing, because you can control everything you put down on paper. Speaking face-to-face, too many of those tell-tale paralinguistic features seem to be beyond your control – avoidance of eye-contact, nervous fidgeting or sweating palms may give you away.

Problem: All writers make some assumptions about their readers. A note you leave for the milkman – 'None today please' – may mean very little if transplanted from the doorstep where you left it, and the meanings of texts written in the past may be so rooted in the times they were produced that they have little meaning for us today.

4 *Question*: In situations where they are nervous, or where their words are likely to be given extreme attention – a speech at a friend's wedding, for example – many people prefer to have the security of a written script, which they have prepared and edited.

Problem: Even when you cannot easily have a script with you, it may be that you have mentally 'rehearsed' what you are going to say – when making an apology, or a difficult request, or breaking some bad news, for example. On the other hand, many people seem to be much less careful about checking text messages and e-mails for errors, treating them almost like a form of spontaneous speech.

5 *Question*: There are many different contexts in which we need to keep records – notes in a class, details of financial transactions, and so on. In these situations writing is vital. Writing also enables us to pass on knowledge to others, preventing us from having to re-invent and re-discover things every generation!

Problem: Many texts such as tickets, wrappers and packaging, text messages and even e-mails are not designed to be kept for long; on the other hand, anyone who has to make a speech or be interviewed in the presence of a journalist or a tape recorder may be aware that their spoken words may achieve some kind of permanence.

Activity 18

Pronunciation. It is difficult to tell from a transcript exactly how a speaker sounds. On the basis of the imperfect information presented here, you would probably note the shortened *mi* for 'my' and some extended vowel sounds (*waar* for 'war' and *weel* for 'well'). He also pronounces 'no' more like the Scottish 'nae'.

Vocabulary. The speaker's vocabulary includes a number of words we do not recognise as Standard English. Amongst these, 'bairn' is commonly used in the north of England and in Scotland for child; 'clarts' to mean mud is rather less common, and is restricted mainly to the north-east of England. 'Bourn' and 'beck' are two alternatives for small streams, while 'ket' in the north and east can refer to snacks or sweets. Oddly, the same word can also mean rubbish in parts of Cumbria and Yorkshire! 'Gan' for go is common throughout the north-east, whereas 'hoy' is rather more limited to the Tyne and Wear region. (*Source*: Upton, Sanderson and Widdowson, *Word Maps: A Dialect Atlas of England*, Croom Helm, 1987.)

Grammar. As far as grammar is concerned, you may have been surprised to find that the speaker generally uses Standard English constructions. The exceptions mainly concern the verb 'do' and its use in the formation of the question 'does tha want to know' (Standard English 'do you want to know') and the negative statement 'tha disn'y know'. There is also an example of what linguists call a **double negative** construction in the phrase 'we never had nowt' (Standard English 'we didn't have/never had anything') – a feature of many regional dialects – and a non-standard prepositional phrase in 'on a night' (Standard English 'at night').

Activity 19

One way of grouping the texts is according to their purpose or function. For example, text A and the teacher in B both appear, at first glance, to be giving instructions. Texts C, E, F, H and I seem to be giving or exchanging information, whereas texts D and G are both primarily persuasive. However, if we look more closely, this method of classifying the texts becomes problematic. For example, texts A and C may resemble instructive or informative texts but in fact are designed to create amusement and to entertain. Text E (the sports commentary) may be designed equally to entertain and to inform, just as the book review (text H) may be designed to influence, and therefore persuade, its readers.

Another way of looking at the texts is according to the time they were produced. Texts A and D are from the 19th/early 20th century, and this is reflected in several ways. We no longer measure foods by 'pecks' or 'bushels', and modern sensitivities may prevent people finding the references to the beating of a pig particularly funny. Fashions, too, have changed, and the style of the corset advert is very different from lingerie adverts of today.

We can also consider the audiences of the texts. Texts B and D are both directed specifically at a female audience, but whereas B is a one-to-one consultation, D is published in a newspaper and is thus aimed at a much wider readership.

Some other texts seem to assume that their audience understands the semi-specialised register which they use. For example:

A (cooking)
E (rugby union)
F (houses)
H (text messages).

However, some of the texts may have multiple audiences, each of which will respond differently to them. Text A, for example, may have been written originally to amuse Victorian children, but may now be read by adults curious about the work of the writer, Edward Lear. Text C was originally a script, intended first for actors to perform, then for a TV audience to see, and only later published for a different set of readers to read on the page.

The texts represent a wide variety of different genres. We have two adverts (D and G) but these are very different in terms of their contexts, intended audience and style. Texts B, C and E all seem to involve dialogues of two or more people, but they are also quite different. B and E are transcripts of spontaneous speech, though a commentary on national radio is clearly a very different genre from a private discussion between a teacher and student. Text C appears to be a dialogue but is, of course, a script written for performance. Something texts A and C have in common is that they both exploit recognisable conventions of their specific genres – recipes and political interviews – for comic effect.

Another way of linking the texts is acording to their mode. Obviously, in the form in which we see them now, all of them are written down. However, texts B and E are transcripts of spontaneous speech, the meanings of which would have depended not just on the words transcribed but also on prosodic, paralinguistic and contextual factors for their full impact on their listeners. Texts A, D, F and G on the other hand were designed and produced as written texts, with D, F and G including important graphological elements (either in terms of illustrations or layout) to help them convey their meanings. Other texts are more problematic; as already noted, C is a written text produced to be enacted as speech, whereas text I uses non-conventional spellings to create the illusion of the sounds of Yorkshire dialect, as if it were being spoken rather than written.

In terms of the varieties of English used, most of the texts use Standard English, though as we have already seen, texts A and D include words which may no longer be as commonly used as they once were. Texts H and I both differ from conventional Standard English. Text H is a new form of abbreviated language which emerged with the introduction of text-messaging technologies, whereas I represents a much older dialectal form of English that is rooted in the past. It may even be the case that text-messaging is a form used mainly by younger mobile phone users, whereas some regional dialect use is more confined to older speakers.

Activity 27

Example	Comment
You is not loving it?	In Standard English we would say 'Don't you love it?' or perhaps 'You don't like it'. The giant is not changing the word order to make the statement into a question, and is using an inappropriate tense – the present tense ending in *–ing* (the present *continuous*, or **progressive** tense) would not be used with the verb *love* here.
The most disgusterous taste . . .	He means 'disgusting', but instead of using the ending –ing to form the adjective, he uses –erous. A similar ending is sometimes used for this purpose, of course, as in *disastrous*, *numerous* and *dangerous*.
. . . that is ever touching my teeth	Here, as in the first example, he uses the present continuous tense where in Standard English we would say *has ever touched*, a tense called the **present perfect**.

Activity 35

This text has several audiences. At first, the audience was the actors and director who would enact it as a performance. Then its audience included all the original viewers of the programme. Now, in published script form, its audience may be people reading it as a text. The text is clearly designed to entertain and amuse the viewers/readers, but some parts of it are designed to instruct the technical director where to point the camera. Overall, there may be another intention to mock politicians or the kinds of political discussion programmes on which they appear.

TV viewers will probably recognise the conventions of another type of TV programme, with its predictable format, title sequence and 'talking head' introducing the piece to camera. This is the typical discourse structure of serious political discussion programmes. The piece is funny because all of this looks and sounds serious, but what follows is not.

The words of the dialogue are distinguished graphologically from stage directions as they are presented in different styles of type (mainly italics), and also distinguished grammatically, as they are not in complete sentences (e.g. *Cut to studio*). They also include technical lexis which the director/cameraman would understand (*cut*, *pan*, etc.) but which the more general audience for the programme may not.

The humour of the piece partly comes from the register of one context – a fashion show – being used in an entirely different context – a serious political interview. Both of these registers are fairly formal, with their own specialised vocabulary. It is the juxtaposition of these two registers that is funny. We have 'Minister for Home Affairs' and 'views on contemporary things' clashing with 'a striking organza dress in pink tulle'. Both registers include fairly technical lexis (e.g. *tulle*) specific to their topic. The 'fashion' register uses many descriptive adjectives – *striking*, *organza*, *brushed*, *gold*, etc.

Much of the humour in the text can be discussed in terms of pragmatics and semantics. First, there is the huge contrast between the 88,000 million, billion houses promised and the three actually built; then the interviewer's polite question, 'Are you a bit disappointed?' seems to be very mild, as the intention of such a question would obviously be to completely ridicule the minister. Finally, the joke at the end of the text depends on the double-meaning of 'two ways'. Usually we expect that it means 'looking at it from two points of view' but it turns out that the minister means it literally, by changing his style of speaking.

Activity 37

Some **places** certainly seem to limit the range of roles you can take and the things you can say. You may have discussed the differences between the way you act in your own home and when visiting someone else's. As a 'host' in your own home, you may assume more of a leader's role with a group of friends; in church you are unlikely to feel it appropriate to tell a certain type of joke to the person next to you; at work, especially if you are involved with the public, you are likely to behave with more attention and respect towards complete strangers than you would in other situations.

However, when the question of where you are is combined with who you are with, and your **relationship** to those people, the limitations become even clearer. You may have thought about **gender** – how an all-male, all-female, or mixed company influences the way you talk. Equally interesting is the question of relative **status** – whether, in any particular situation, you seem to enjoy a dominant role (with younger brothers and sisters, or with friends, perhaps), whether you are more or less equal to your conversational partner, or whether the situation places you in a subordinate role (say, in the classroom, with parents or at work). In each case, the different role you play determines whether you ask questions, crack jokes, use formal or colloquial language, or make an effort to soften your natural regional accent in the interests of formality.

Where the **purpose** of talk is very clearly defined – for example, a customer buying a CD from a music shop – the exchange becomes very predictable. Interviewers ask questions to find the best person for the job, stand-up comedians tell jokes to make us laugh, and doctors ask us questions to diagnose an illness. We would be surprised if any of these people digressed from the style of language that their situation requires.

Activity 38

Student's notes

The talk begins with the DJ cueing in the caller. This places him 'in charge' of the interview. He also uses her first name, assuming some familiarity and informality, and an informal greeting. Tanya replies, using the same informal greeting, but allows the DJ to continue to take the lead with what sounds like a catch-phrase but is also her next cue. Tanya replies, echoing the DJ's words, coming straight to the point but with some hesitation – perhaps as a result of nervousness?

The DJ attempts to interrupt – a bit rude? Broadcasters often try to do this. But Tanya carries on. When she has finished, the DJ now succeeds in getting in his question. Humorous, informal use of 'lump'. Repeats 'Canada'.

Again, some hesitation from Tanya, before a straight reply. The 'lead' in the talk is the DJ. The DJ offers a comment on Tanya's answer – makes her feel good? Like a teacher? False start – personal comment to suggest has shared interest. Phrases next question.

Tanya offers agreement – supportive – but slightly overlaps, forcing the DJ to repeat part of question.

Activity 39

1	persuade	12	frameworks	24	nouns	36	paralinguistic
2	mode	13	discourse	25	concrete	37	prosodic
3	taboo	14	graphology	26	proper noun	38	context-bound/ dependent
4	slang	15	syntax	27	abstract noun	39	semantics
5	Standard English	16	morphology	28	adjectives	40	semantic
6	register	17	first	29	verb	41	synonyms
7	lexis	18	third	30	adverbs	42	connotations
8	accent	19	interrogatives	31	pronouns	43	figurative
9	dialect	20	imperatives	32	conjunctions	44	euphemism
10	genre	21	declaratives	33	prepositions	45	dysphemism
11	audience	22	exclamations	34	phonology	46	pragmatics
		23	minor	35	phonemes		

This module counts for **35%** of the AS qualification, or **17½%** of the total A Level marks.

ASSESSMENT OBJECTIVES

The skills and knowledge you develop in this module, which will be tested in the examination you take at the end of it, are defined by the examination board's Assessment Objectives. These require that you:

- **AO1:** communicate clearly the knowledge, understanding and insight appropriate to the study of language, using appropriate terminology and accurate and coherent written expression
(5 out of the 35 marks for the Unit; 5% of the final AS mark; 2½% of the final A Level mark)
- **AO3:** know and use key features of frameworks for the systematic study of spoken and written English
(10 out of the 35 marks for the Unit; 10% of the final AS mark; 5% of the final A Level mark)
- **AO4:** understand, discuss and explore concepts and issues relating to language in use
(10 out of the 35 marks for the Unit; 10% of the final AS mark; 5% of the final A Level mark)
- **AO5:** distinguish, describe and interpret variation in the meanings and forms of spoken and written language according to context
(10 out of the 35 marks for the Unit; 10% of the final AS mark; 5% of the final A Level mark)

What this module is all about

Links with Module 1

In the previous unit, you started to understand the variations in the ways that English is used all around us. You also learned that there are different ways of describing and analysing language use, and began to apply a number of analytical frameworks to this task. These methods of analysis are the basic tools which you will continue to use as you extend your explorations of language throughout both the AS and A2 English Language courses.

As you study this module you will often need to review the relevant material first covered in Module 1, as indicated by the symbol

In particular, we will continue to use the following key concepts and frameworks to explore how social context affects language use:

discourse	the ways in which the content of a text is structured and organised
pragmatics	the ways in which social messages/relations and implied meanings are conveyed in language
semantics	the ways in which meanings are communicated in language
grammar	all aspects of the structures and functions of a language
lexis	the range of vocabulary available to speakers of a language
phonology	the vocal aspects of language, such as intonation, rhythm, pace, volume and stress in spoken English
graphology	all aspects of the visual appearance and presentation of written texts

What's new about Module 2?

Social contexts

The emphasis in Module 2 is even more strongly on the social contexts of language – how our uses of language are related to the way we live and develop relationships with others. To look more closely at this relationship, we will focus on a number of themes prescribed by the examination board; in each case, you will still be developing your skills of linguistic analysis and description of texts (both spoken and written), but you will be doing so in relation to some specific contexts in which language is used. *The main theme of Module 2 is that the meanings of any spoken or written text can be understood only by fully considering the particular social contexts in which that text is produced.*

This means thinking about:

- *who* produces it – in terms of their identity, role, status and position in society
- *why* it has been produced – in terms of its intended (and sometimes unintended) meanings, and the purpose(s) writers/speakers bring to the text
- the *relationship* between the author/producer and the receiver/audience, their relative status and power, and their attitudes towards each other
- the *place and time* in which it was produced
- the ways in which different forms and media of communication affect and constrain what we say and write.

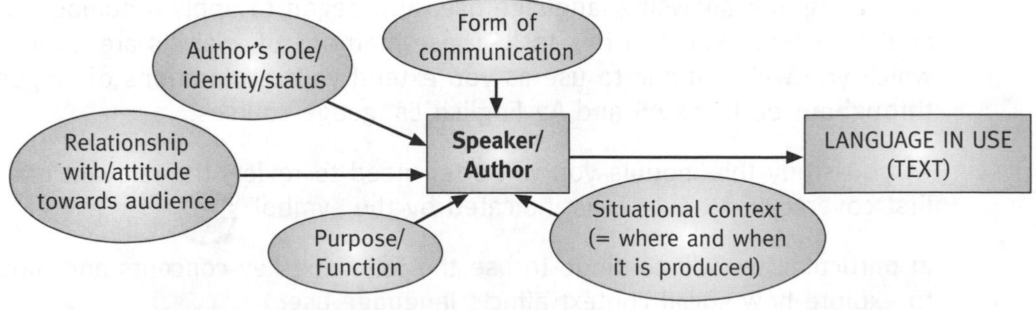

Social contexts shape the language we use

In this area of language studies we try to answer a basic but far-reaching question: How does our use of language reflect the way we live in our society?

The Unit 2 examination topics

There are **five** key areas for investigation that can appear in the AQA B Unit 2 examination, but only **three** of them will be specified for examination in any one year. You will be required to answer questions on **two** of these.

These areas are:

Language and power	The study of how language in use may reflect differing kinds of power in society, and how it can be used to exert influence and control
Language and occupational groups	The study of the distinctive ways in which people sharing a common profession or occupation use language to communicate between themselves and with others
Language and gender	The study of the ways in which our uses of language may be influenced by our gender, and linked to the way men and women are viewed in society
Accents and dialects of the British Isles	A study of the ways in which the use of English varies in different regions, and our attitudes towards these variations
Language and technology	A study of the ways in which the forms of communication technology (such as telephones, television or computers) affect the ways we use language in those media

How many topics to study?

Although you only have to answer **two** questions in the examination, there are many good reasons to study **all three** of the topics prescribed in any one year:

- There is only **one** question per topic on the exam paper – if you only studied **two** topics you would have no alternatives in the exam room.
- As you will discover, all of the topics overlap with one another; studying one will also help develop your understanding of the others.
- In particular, many of the ideas relating to **Language and power** underlie the other topics too – so it's even worth studying this when it isn't being examined as a set topic on the paper.
- All of the topics will provide important foundation material for your A2 course, and will also give you plenty of ideas for your Language Investigation (ENB4) if you carry on with the A2 course.

Ideas from language study, investigation and research

If you look closely at the weighting of the different Assessment Objectives for

Modules 1 and 2, you will see that AO4 – 'understand, discuss and explore concepts and issues relating to language in use' – carries more weight in this module.

In order to fulfill this objective, you will be asked to study several different kinds of 'texts' or 'data', and to respond to them in the exam.

These may include:

Data (Primary)	Examples of **actual written and spoken language (as transcripts)** as used in everyday practice relating to the specified topic
Attitudes	Accounts and discussions of language use reflecting people's ideas and **attitudes** about language (e.g. letters or articles about the specified topic in newspapers and magazines)
Texts	**Representations** of language relating to the specific context in the media and literature (e.g. the attempt to suggest dialect in cartoons, adverts or novels)
Academic studies	Academic **research** carried out into aspects of language use (e.g. surveys)

We have already introduced (see page 2) the idea of becoming a kind of **language scientist**. That is to say, gathering 'specimens' of data, examining them closely, and trying to explain how they 'work'.

But scientists do not work at random, or in a vacuum; they usually set out to answer a specific question, or test a theory which other scientists have proposed. They do this by taking care to collect appropriate samples of data and carry out analysis. Sometimes their findings confirm what others have thought, and sometimes scientists make a discovery that appears to contradict the established theories. In either case, they approach their data with an open mind.

As you study each topic in this module you will need to:

- develop a 'scientific' approach to the study of language, as outlined on page 2
- explore a variety of language data and learn about some existing ideas and research
- recognise some of the difficulties and limitations in language research
- carry out some small research projects of your own. This means collecting some data – either recording and transcribing speech, or collecting examples of appropriate written texts – and analysing them thoroughly in the light of the ideas you'll study and/or discuss in class (this will also help to prepare you for the language Investigation (ENB4) on the A2 course)
- be open-minded in applying these ideas and theories to new data.

A note on using ideas from language study and research

'Research' comes in two varieties:

- *Primary research* includes the systematic gathering and analysis of language data by **yourself** and **your fellow students**.
- *Secondary research* means looking at the ideas and findings of others, including your fellow students and contributors to textbooks and the Internet.

It is important, throughout this module, to bear the following points in mind:

- approach published research with caution: much of it may be based on old material in contexts very different from your own
- analyse the data in detail, and apply the appropriate **analytical frameworks** accurately – this remains a key Assessment Objective (AO3).
- little credit is given in the exam for simply reproducing material from notes or textbooks or 'name-dropping' references to well-known academic studies
- credit ***is*** given for making relevant **connections** between the data in front of you, the ideas about language you have developed on the course and other investigations/research you have carried out or are aware of (AO4)
- never try to make the data 'fit' any ideas you bring to it; always be open-minded.

And watch out – the data/text set in the examination may actually contradict some of the 'established' ideas and your own preconceptions!

The activities and material suggested in this module will help to get you started; however, it is important that you pursue your studies well beyond the limits of this book – please note the suggestions for further research and reading.

After exploring some of the broad issues involved in this module, we will focus on all five of the topics that are set in rotation for the Unit 2 examination. Your teacher will advise you which of these are set for examination in the year you enter it.

Starting to explore

The next two activities help you begin to ask the kinds of question you will be investigating later in the module.

ACTIVITY 1

We all vary our language according to the social context we are in at any one time. We can call this variation in an individual's use of language his or her **language repertoire**.

(a) Read the following brief pen portrait of Charlotte Johnson, aged 34.

Charlotte was brought up on the outskirts of Manchester and attended her local comprehensive school before studying Business at Birmingham University. Her parents have lived all their lives in the north of England; her father was a factory worker, her mother a shop assistant. Eight years ago Charlotte married Ray, an accountant from Essex whom she met at university, and they now live in London with their twins Emma and Jack, aged seven. She is the Personnel Manager at a local retail computer and software store, which involves being part of the store management team and dealing with staff recruitment, training and appraisal. In her spare time she enjoys playing squash, and occasionally she manages to meet up with a couple of her old school friends who also live and work in London, though as a busy working mum she relies heavily on her mobile phone and laptop computer to keep in touch with people.

Discuss your responses to the following questions:

- how might the way Charlotte uses language (both speaking and writing) vary in the course of a typical week, according to context: at work, with her friends, with her parents, at home?
- what factors might influence these variations?

Compare your responses with the commentary on page 159.

(b) Now let's consider how some data demonstrates the influence of social contexts on language in use.

First, remind yourself of the questions we used in Module 1 (pages 59–60) for analysing talk. Now apply these questions to the following transcript of a conversation. The caller (C), a 40-year-old male, is ringing the Customer Services department of a large company and, after being cut off once and then put on 'hold', has been put through to an employee (A) at the call centre.

Develop your analysis by suggesting the ways in which the following contextual factors may be influencing the way the two speakers are using language:

- the fact that it is a telephone, rather than face-to-face, conversation ('Language and technology')

- the role and style of speaking that A will have been trained to use by the company ('Language and occupational groups')
- the fact that C has already made several attempts to call the company (situational context)
- the fact that both speakers are male ('Language and gender')
- any differences in their accents and dialects ('Accents and dialects of the British Isles')
- the different underlying pragmatic intentions and meanings of the two speakers. ('Language and power')

A: [Edinburgh accent] good morning (.) you're through to XX Customer Service and my name's Adam (.) how may I help you

C: [RP accent] ah, hello (.) it's about a redirection request that seems to be causing a few problems

A: I see sir (.) could I take your customer reference number please

C: yeah (3) it's 543 (.) 986 (.) 674 (.) PY

A: (4) that's (.) Mr Brown

C: that's correct

A: of 57 Jackson Avenue

C: that's it

A: and what seems to be the problem sir

C: well to be honest I'm getting a bit fed up having to explain the same thing over and over again (.) I've tried three times now to get this sorted out but // it seems to be impossible to arrange a simple

A: // oh

C: redirection without (.) // well (.) spending hours and hours trying to get through

A: // mm

A: I'm very sorry to hear that sir (.) can I just confirm a few details and I'm sure I'll be able to sort things // out for you

C: // I've already given my name, number and shoe size to the last person I spoke to before getting cut off

Compare the results of your analysis with the commentary on pages 159–60.

ACTIVITY 2

Another productive approach is to look at the different kinds of discourse that take place even within a specific organisation, such as a college. The following set of data was recorded/collected in a number of different circumstances within a college in the course of a typical week.

(a) For each of the extracts/transcripts, identify examples of ways in which the social factors listed might have influenced the language used within each language framework. You could use a table such as the one below to record your findings for each piece of data.

Data ________________ Context ________________

Social frameworks	Language frameworks					
	Discourse Structure; turn-taking patterns	**Grammar** Standard or non-standard English Variations in sentence construction and word order (syntax)	**Semantics and pragmatics** Literal or figurative meanings Any pragmatic meanings implied	**Lexis** Degree of lexical formality/ informality Non-standard English or technical words	**Graphology** Layout, font type, graphic design	**Phonology** Accent Prosodic features: tone, timbre, tempo and intonation
Situation: Where and when						
Who: identity, status, role or position						
Relationships: Relative status, power and attitudes						
Intentions: Purposes which writers/ speakers bring to the context						
Form of communication: the medium or technology being used						

TEXT A

Transcript of answering-machine message on the main college switchboard:

Voice: [female, bright and friendly sounding, RP with hints of local (North West) accent]

thank you for calling Newton Sixth Form College (.) if you know the extension number you require please dial it now (.) for adult education enquiries please dial two six o (.) to leave a message on the answerphone please stay on the line

---

TEXT B

Extract from transcript of an internal telephone conversation between a teacher (A) and a technician (B):

A: hi is that Dave
B: yeah speaking
A: oh hi (.) it's Paul over in the LRC room (.) sorry to bother you er it's just that I seem to have a problem with my e-mail account
B: yeah
A: it's telling me it doesn't recognise my log-on ID
B: oh yeah (.) you're not the first [laughter] we've got one or two problems on the network // at the minute
A: network // oh right
B: and we're on the case (.) are you on Outlook or just the web-based e-mail
A: just the er web-based (.) you know the ordinary one
B: have you got Outlook
A: um I I don't think so (.) I mean I usually just // you know I don't actually use it that much
B: // OK you you might have to come out of e-mail and try from another machine (.) or you could try to re-boot

---

TEXT C

Teacher's comments on a student's English Literature assignment:

> A pleasing effort, Julie, which covers a good range of relevant details. The discussion of IVii hints at some awareness of the dramatic potential of the scene – remember your AOs! – but still needs more detailed examples. Some improvement here in the general standard of expression (AO1!) but do watch your punctuation. Keep up the good work – well done!

Compare your findings with the commentary on pages 160–1.

(b) Carry out your own data-gathering exercise, either in your own educational institution or more interestingly in another type of institution to which you have access, collecting a range of different spoken and written texts, and perform a similar analysis.

Remember:

If you are recording conversations for language investigation, *always* gain the permission of all the participants beforehand. It is best to draft a standard letter outlining the circumstances and purposes of the recording you wish to make, and ask all participants to sign it.

As you have seen already, there are many questions to ask about how our use of language is related to social factors and contexts. These questions often overlap, but for the purposes of this module, we can sum them up under five headings:

- How does language in use reflect the status/position of individuals/groups in society and their attempts to influence, persuade or direct others? (See the 'Language & Power' section below.)
- How do members of a particular occupation/profession use language to communicate with each other, and with the wider public? (See the 'Language and occupational groups' section below.)
- How might any differences between men's and women's roles in society, and our attitudes towards them, be reflected in language use? (See the 'Language and gender' section below.)
- 'How does English vary in different parts of the British isles and how are these variations represented and perceived? (See the 'Accents and dialects of the British Isles' section below.)
- What is distinctive about the way language is used in different media/technologies, and how do these technologies affect and constrain the way we communicate within them? (See the 'Language and technology' section below.)

Language and power

Language and power: a key topic

- many of the ideas explored in this section are also central to the other topics in this module
- you are advised to study this section even if **Language and power** is not one of the examined topics when you take the ENB2 paper.

Whenever groups of people gather together, create organisations or interact, we quickly become aware that some people are able to exercise more influence and authority than others. Indeed, a great deal of 'ordinary' interaction and language use seems to be concerned with trying to exercise influence over others – getting them to do things, to think things, and to feel things. In situations or organisations where we are aware of clear differences in status, such as in the family or at work, we may take for granted these inequalities in influence and authority and the various uses of language they produce. However, even among groups of apparently 'equal' friends or workmates, the language we use may also reflect the constant negotiation for position and influence which is the stuff of so much social interaction.

ACTIVITY 3

Let's consider how far this is true for some of the groups you belong to. For each of the groups listed below – or any others you belong to – order the members of the group in terms of their status or influence within it:

- your family
- the group of friends you socialise with most
- people at your place of work.

Power and influence may be enjoyed by certain individuals (the Prime Minister, your mother or father, the head teacher, a media boss such as Rupert Murdoch), by groups of people (a trade union, a pressure group, the police), or even by entire nations (the United States, Russia).

ACTIVITY 4

C3.1A

(a) In a group, try to agree on a list of the five most powerful individuals and groups of people in Britain. Then try to agree which of the following enjoy more power and influence in our society in general terms:

- white people, or people belonging to other ethnic groups
- men or women
- business managers, or those working for them
- people who help run the media (TV and newspapers), or people who buy or subscribe to media products
- people in the north of Britain, or people in the south.

Explain your views to your class before comparing the outcomes of your discussion with the commentary on page 161.

(b) It is worth distinguishing between the terms power, status, authority and influence. Try to define the differences between these – use the prompts below to develop your ideas:

- Which of these derive(s) from the professional or official position a person holds in society?

- Which of these arise(s) from the personal respect given to them by other people?
- Is it possible for a powerful person to have low status – and vice versa?

Whatever conclusions you reached in Activity 4, you will have started to ask where power, status, etc. come from. You may have considered the relative importance of:

- individual strength of personality: such as that possessed by the extrovert 'leader' of a group of friends
- profession or occupation: a police officer has power because of the uniform, not because of who s/he is
- social class or background: how far might someone from a well-off family or with a good education have some advantages?
- gender: men may still have more influence than women in many areas
- ethnic origins: white British people may still enjoy more power than people from Asian, Caribbean and other non-white backgrounds
- wealth and economic power: rich people may be able to exert their power in all sorts of ways
- political power: politicians clearly enjoy the power to shape policies and pass laws.

With all this in mind, we must now turn to the raw material of our study – language – and begin to explore the ways in which these inequalities of power and influence are reflected in the English we use. In general, we can observe this working in two ways: the use of language by powerful individuals or groups to enforce their authority (known as **instrumental** power) and the use of language to exert influence and persuasion (or **influential** power).

Language and power in action: analysing conversation

It will be helpful first to review the material covered in Module 1 on 'Analysing talk' – see pages 59–60 – and 'Pragmatics' (page 54).

Talking to each other seems so natural that we could easily assume that conversation is a random, unstructured business. However, we have already seen in Module 1 that different kinds of conversations follow different patterns, and that what we can say in different situations is limited by context, purpose and audience.

Perhaps the most obvious structural feature of everyday speech is that we usually take turns to talk. Of course, there are occasions when someone interrupts, or is cut short, or starts to talk at the same time as someone else, but on the whole talking is a fairly orderly business. Even when disagreement is being expressed and tempers are frayed, we tend to observe this basic rule of conversation: turn-taking.

The most basic unit of conversation is the **adjacency pair.** This is when one utterance – 'Have you been drinking?' – is immediately followed by an appropriate response – 'Certainly not, officer'. Although we are not consciously aware of them, there seem to be rules that limit the kinds of response that we can make to any utterance, depending on the situation. In some contexts (e.g. a social chat) the question 'Have you been drinking?' may be an innocent enquiry; in others (e.g. having been stopped in a car by a police patrol) it could be seen as an accusation. In this case, it could be followed by a denial (as above) or a confession – 'Yes, I'm afraid I have' – or, if you were feeling bold, a counter-question or accusation – 'What makes you say that?' Other responses are possible, but these are potentially provocative – 'What if I have?' (challenge); 'Get lost!' (insult/command) – or just impossible or insane: 'Yellow', 'One hundred and sixty', or 'That's my hamster'.

Some utterance types					
Greeting	Enquiry	Request	Instruction	Challenge	Accusation
Confession	Denial	Excuse	Insult	Answer	Valediction *(saying goodbye)*
Agreement	Disagreement	Declaration	Apology	Acknowledgement	Information

ACTIVITY 5

For each of the following openings, suggest the kinds of response that are most likely to complete the adjacency pair. The first one is provided as an example:

- 'That's a nice top' (observation)

Possible responses: 'Thanks!' (acknowledgement); 'I got it in the sales' (information); 'Yes it is, isn't it?' (agreement); 'Do you think so?' (disagreement)

- 'Can I have a word with you?'
- 'Can I help you?'
- 'Leave me alone!'
- 'How do you plead? Guilty, or not guilty?'

Of course, most conversations consist of a series of many adjacency pairs in which the response to one pair becomes the start of the next:

'How are you?'
'Fine thanks. And you?'
'Been better . . .'

1st pair: Greeting/enquiry and response ('How are you?' / 'Fine thanks. And you?')
2nd pair: Return enquiry and response ('Fine thanks. And you?' / 'Been better . . .')

In extended talk, we move from turn to turn with little conscious effort – but we take our cues to speak from a number of clues provided by the current speaker. We then take our turn – or 'seize the floor' – until the next person's turn.

ACTIVITY 6

In groups, try to identify the types of cue that enable us to seize the floor. Think about:

- visual cues (does a speaker give us a sign?)
- phonological cues (does something happen to the speaker's voice?)
- syntactic clues (can we tell from a speaker's sentences when she or he is coming to an end?).

Compare your suggestions with those in the commentary on pages 161–2.

In conversation, as well as recognising when we can take a turn, we must also choose what kind of utterance it is appropriate to make at any given time – it is clear that underlying 'rules' operate here, too. The way these rules might work in practice is likely to vary according to social contexts and relationships. One way of understanding this is to think of everything we say as having both a surface meaning and a social (**pragmatic**) function. Take this simple exchange:

A: How are you doing?
B: Not bad, thanks. Yourself?
A: Ay, not bad. Bit nippy out, though.

The surface meaning of A's first utterance is clear enough – it seems to be an enquiry about B's health or well-being. However, in many situations – as in this example, which occurred in the corner shop where B regularly stopped to buy sweets and newspapers – the social function of the utterance is to establish a pleasant, social relationship and to create an opportunity for some informal interaction. B's reply similarly has a meaning and a function; the meaning is vague and non-committal, but at least by replying appropriately B signals a willingness to develop the relationship. If B had stopped with 'Not bad, thanks', failing to initiate the next adjacency pair and leaving A to ask the next question, the pragmatic meaning might have been: 'I'm happy to respond to your friendliness and I'm not going to be rude, but I have no particular wish to converse as I'm in a bit of a hurry'. However, the 'Yourself?' that B adds has the effect of putting the ball back in A's court, equalising the conversation in terms of the willingness to participate.

This kind of small talk is sometimes called **phatic** talk; its function is mainly social rather than to carry out a particular transaction. In many informal and social situations, much of a conversation may be phatic, but in other situations this may not be the case. We often discover that running beneath the surface of our conversations is a whole set of functions and intentions that may be quite different from the surface meanings of our utterances. These underlying meanings may reveal as much about power and status relationships as the surface meanings of the dialogue. In drama and theatre, actors call this aspect of conversation the **sub-text**; in linguistics, the study of these underlying meanings and social functions is called **pragmatics**.

ACTIVITY 7

(a) Think of a typical visit to a GP's surgery. If the doctor greets you with the words 'How are you?', how might the meaning and function of this question differ from the casual enquiry of the corner shopkeeper?

(b) Now consider another familiar situation, in which the conversation goes like this:

A: I was just wondering if you fancied coming over tonight (.) you know (.) for a drink and that

B: (3) well (.) I'd like to but (.) I've really got to stay in tonight (.) I've got that history essay to hand in tomorrow

A's surface and pragmatic meanings are both reasonably clear – to ask the question 'Do you want to come over?', and to explore the extent to which B is interested in him or her. Suggest why A does not simply say 'Do you want to come over?', or even 'Do you fancy me?'

B's reply is very revealing. The meaning is clear: the answer is 'no', and for a good reason. What do you think is the function of the pauses, the hesitant 'well', and the excuse offered?

Compare your interpretation with the commentary on page 162.

Grice and his Maxims

Under the broad heading of 'The Co-operative Principle,' The linguist H. P. Grice tried to define the various guiding principles, or **maxims**, that we unconsciously tend to observe and expect as we construct conversations by moving from turn to turn. He maintained that when a conversation is working normally, we tend to assume that:

- what we say will have something to do with what has just been said (the maxim of **relevance**)
- what we say will be neither too long nor too short (the maxim of **quantity**)
- what we say is likely to be true (the maxim of **quality**)
- what we say is likely to be clear and meaningful (the maxim of **manner**).

Of course, these maxims can be broken, and often are – people lie or ramble on, people can be unco-operative, unclear or obscure. But when this happens, according to Grice, we are able to 'read between the lines', or become aware that there is something 'abnormal' about the conversation. So, for example, if someone only replies to our questions with the briefest of responses (and thus breaks the maxim of quantity), we begin to infer that s/he may dislike us, or feel uncomfortable or unwell, or have a secret to hide, or whatever.

Analysing talk: summary

When examining conversational data, it is helpful to use a systematic framework that reminds you of the different questions to ask at different linguistic levels. This approach will also help you to achieve one of the Assessment Objectives: to 'know and use key features of frameworks for the systematic study of spoken and written English'.

Conversation: applying an analytical framework

Element	Key question	Techniques and strategies
Pragmatic framework	How does the dialogue reflect social relationships and implied meanings?	Turn-taking patterns, agenda and topic management, speakers' forms of address to each other, politeness strategies, phatic talk and implied meaning. Focus especially on the social function of utterances rather than surface meaning
Grammatical framework	What grammatical structures does each speaker use, and with what effects?	Sentence types, lengths and structure; use of Standard English or non-standard features; non-fluency features such as slips, false starts and repetitions
Semantic framework	What kinds of meaning does each speaker contribute?	The most frequent utterance type of each speaker – question, command, joke, confession, etc.
Lexical framework	What kinds of vocabulary does each speaker use?	Register; degrees of formality, colloquiality, topic specificity; factual or emotional content; personal or impersonal style; literal or figurative expressions; status and discourse
Phonetic/ phonological framework	What are the vocal characteristics of speakers and what are the effects of those characteristics?	Intonation, stress, tempo, rhythm and pauses (if this information is available)

Power in practice: classroom language

The classroom is a good place in which to start to examine the pragmatics of everyday conversational discourse, and the ways in which power is reflected in language use. In a classroom, the powerful position of the teacher is reflected in the unique set of rules that seem to control the kinds of conversations taking place. In most schools, these conversations tend to follow clearly defined patterns, and reflect the purpose of the interaction (education/instruction), the context (pupils in a class with a teacher) and power relationships (the teacher has more power than the students).

Many teacher/student interactions may follow a pattern such as the one below.

Example of classroom discourse	Commentary
T: First let's recap a few points from yesterday. What are the various social contextual factors that we thought influenced the way we use language? S1: The situation. T: Yes, of course, the situation – but what does that mean? Can you unpack that a little for us, John? S2: The place and the time. T: Good – let's take them one at a time. How might the physical location we're in affect language?	Teacher starts by announcing the **agenda** and then initiating the talk with a question. The question may be open (inviting a wide range of responses) or closed (allowing only a limited set of possible answers). In either case, the question is designed to test/extend/challenge the students, and is therefore different from the majority of questions we may ask in other contexts. The students respond with an answer. If no response follows, the teacher may re-phrase the original question. The teacher will usually give some evaluative feedback on the response, reinforcing it by repeating it or re-phrasing it in his or her own words. The teacher will then try to move things on, either by pressing the student(s) to provide more detail, or by asking the next question. The teacher has the power to nominate individual students, or allow voluntary responses. This will usually be by first name; by contrast, students are usually expected to address the teacher by 'sir', 'miss', 'madam' or title. The unequal (or **asymmetrical**) power relationship is also reflected in: • the differences between the kinds of question teacher and students are allowed to ask (could a student challenge a late teacher with 'where have you been?') • the power of the teacher to remind students of the rules of discourse ('stop talking/don't answer back!') • the right to expect to be listened to, sometimes for quite lengthy 'turns' • the control of the agenda – by cutting short any distractions or interruptions • the possible use of irony, sarcasm and humour to make a point.

There are many ways in which you could study classroom language; a few possibilities are offered below. They all involve gaining permission to tape-record part of a lesson and transcribing a section. You may be able to refer to the outcomes of your investigation (and those of your fellow students) in the Unit 2 examination.

- Compare the techniques used by two different teachers to manage the same class.
- Compare the way the same teacher manages classes of different age groups.
- Focus specifically on the way different teachers get a lesson started, phrase questions or evaluate student responses.
- Compare the frequency with which different teachers nominate or accept answers from male or female pupils, and/or examine the forms of address used towards them.
- Focus on how pupils/students try to exercise power for themselves by infringing the normal 'rules'.

Power in practice: other conversational contexts

ACTIVITY 8

(a) Consider a typical family conversation around the meal table. Suggest how the status/power of a family member is reflected in the amount of talking he or she is permitted to do before being interrupted or told to be quiet.

(b) In many social contexts, the right to ask questions and expect truthful answers is an indicator of power. Suggest some examples.

(c) In the following two situations, the respondents' refusal to give a meaningful answer (to a question to which they know the answer) is potentially provocative. Suggest why, referring to Grice's maxims (see page 93) as appropriate.

Teacher: 'What's your name?'
Pupil: 'Why?'

Policeman: 'What's your name?'
Young man: 'Mickey Mouse.'

(d) The right to pass judgment on other people's utterances is another sign of power or status. If you ask a stranger for directions, listen encouragingly, and then respond with 'Very clear directions. Well done!', you may provoke an unpleasant reaction. Suggest why.

(e) Conversational patterns are affected not only by differences of social status and power, but also by differences in the personal status of participants. To explore this idea, let's look at a conversation recorded during an evening meal at a house where a group of middle-aged friends have gathered. Use the framework of questions introduced on page 94 to analyse the conversational relationship of participants A and B:

A: this head (.)
B: oh (2)
A: heads have to be able to understand (.) // the kids that they're dealing with
B: // mm
A: don't they (.)
B: yeah
A: I mean if they're going to do a good job they have to be able to understand the background (.) the problems that the kids they're dealing with have got and //
B: // yeah
A: and (2) being (2) prejudging this bloke // it seems
B: // well that's all we can do because he didn't give anything of himself did he
A: (.) he didn't (3) it wasn't (1) I think what they should have done the day before was they should what they did with the em when the candidates came in for the em (1)
B: // deputy's job
A: // yeah they should have they should have had a programme of people for them to talk to
B: mm absolutely

Now compare your analysis with the commentary on page 162.

Language and the professions

It is sometimes said that professional people have power in society. Members of the legal, medical, financial and other professions tend to command respect from the rest of us, and exercise considerable power in their specialist areas. Some writers have suggested that some of the ways in which these groups use language can help to preserve and apply their power over non-specialists:

- They may use shared specialist language or **technical jargon.** This can function as a kind of code which excludes those outside the profession.
- This use of specialist language may even have the effect of intimidating outsiders and non-specialists.
- Outsiders may think that they tend to patronise non-specialists to preserve the 'mystique' of group membership.

We will pursue these ideas in more detail in the section devoted to the topic 'Language and occupational groups' (see page 104)

To take one example, the variety of the written language in which the law of the land is communicated and enforced is, in one sense, the most powerful kind there is. Yet it can seem an impenetrable and alien variety of English. Some protest that this specialist, codified and often impenetrable jargon must be designed to exclude ordinary people and keep lawyers in business!

However, it can also be argued that the peculiar characteristics of legal language can be explained by its peculiar context, history and function, as we will see below.

Activity 9

After studying the following text, which is the introductory page of a life assurance policy, identify your own examples of each of the features given in the table below, and note their contextual explanation.

Whereas the Person Assured named in the schedule hereto has effected the assurance herein described with **The Standard Life Assurance Company** hereinafter called the Company and whereas the Person Assured has delivered to the Company as the basis of this assurance the proposal and declaration referred to in the schedule:

Now this policy witnesseth that in consideration of the payment to the Company of the first and all subsequent premiums as provided herein the Company will pay the benefits stated in the said schedule to the Person Assured or to the executors, administrators or assigns of the Person Assured or as otherwise stated in the said schedule upon proof satisfactory to the Directors of the Company of:

(1) the happening of the event or events on which the benefits are to become payable as specified in the said schedule,

(2) the title of the claimant or claimants, and

(3) the correctness of the date of birth of the Life Assured stated in the said proposal and declaration unless previously admitted by the Company:

And it is hereby declared that the Person Assured is a member of the Company in accordance with and subject to the regulations of the Company and that this policy is subject to any conditions and provisions endorsed or written on this and any following page of this policy.

In witness thereof and by the authority of the Board of Directors of the Company these presents are executed at Edinburgh on the date of signing shown on the said schedule.

Language feature	Contextual explanation
Includes many lexical features with a specialist meaning, including terms derived from French or Latin.	Legal documents are not intended for general readership, but as communications from one expert to another. The presence of French- and Latin-derived terms reflects the historical importance of those languages in law – an accident of the distant past when the triumphant French-speaking Normans developed the basis of our legal system after their invasion of 1066

Sentences tend to be long, with many qualifying clauses and relatively little punctuation	Ambiguity must be avoided at all costs; there must be no room for different interpretations
Pronouns tend to be avoided in favour of repeated reference to specific names	Again, there must be no doubt about who or what is being referred to at any given point, hence the constant re-defintion and qualification and clarifcation of terms. Terms used to refer to people and organisations are precisely defined
May include abbreviated references to articles of law or relevant 'precedents'	Again, documents are intended to be shared between professionals who share the same legal knowledge, rather than by lay people
Includes some words from a highly formal register (e.g. hereinafter, thereof) which are now seldom found outside the legal context Similarly, some grammatical forms (e.g. third-person singular verb endings in -eth) are used, which are not Standard English	Legal documents have been written to an established formula over several centuries. As such, they have become almost immune to the changes that have taken place in language outside the legal context

Language and politics

Politics is also an area where language is used to exert power and influence. We will consider below (see page 102) how politicians can use a range of techniques to make their speeches effective; it is also interesting to examine what happens when a politician, intent on getting his or her message across, confronts a political interviewer whose job is to challenge and attack. Here are some suggestions for investigations you can carry out in the field of political discourse.

- Tape and transcribe your own selection of political interviews on programmes like BBC2's *Newsnight* and Radio 4's *Today* programme. Use the analytical framework on page 94, and/or an alternative such as Grice's Maxims (see page 93), to analyse the techniques of the interviewers and the ways that politicians try to deal with them.

- Tape any TV discussion programme such as *Trisha*, BBC 1's *Question Time,* or even *The Jerry Springer Show.* Use the analytical framework to examine how the chair keeps control of the discourse, and how panel members and members of the audience all try to exert influence and power in the discussions.

Activity 10

This role-play activity provides an opportunity to test some of your discoveries about language and power in practice. You will first need to transfer the 'Situation' and 'Power' cards shown below to plain cards.

(a) In pairs, pick one of the Situation cards. Each describes a situation involving two people in a potentially asymmetrical power relationship.

(b) Agree who will play each of the two roles described on the card.

(c) Each player now draws a Power card without disclosing its contents. This card allocates a power level from 1 (the most powerful) to 4 (the least powerful). Note the types of language use appropriate to your role.

(d) Enact the role-play accordingly.

(e) Show the role-play to the rest of your class or group. They should try to identify the power rating of each player and support their judgments by referring to characteristics of the language used.

Situation cards

Child/teenager asking a parent for permission to stay out late at a party	Police officer interrogating suspect about a burglary	Boss congratulating employee on good work as part of an annual appraisal interview
Employer interviewing candidate for a job as a waiter	Teacher telling off a student for recent poor behaviour	Customer complaining to shop assistant about faulty goods recently purchased
Barrister in court cross-examining witness in a trial	Judge on *The X Factor* evaluating a contestant's performance	Teacher praising student for good work

Power cards

<table>
<tr>
<td>

Power 1

Use formal Standard English but with an RP-ish accent

Speak in a deep tone of voice

Talk slowly, pausing before and sometimes during each sentence

Use technical, educated or sophisticated vocabulary

Lead the conversation – choose and change the topic

Interrupt frequently. Don't allow your partner to finish sentences

Comment often on the quality of your partner's responses

Ask direct questions abruptly and aggressively

Never use hedges if giving instructions/asking questions

Avoid politeness strategies

</td>
<td>

Power 2

Use fairly formal Standard English but with a soft local accent

Speak with a fairly low pitch

Talk quite slowly, sometimes pausing before speaking

Use some technical, educated or sophisticated vocabulary

Lead the conversation – choose and change the topic

Interrupt your partner once or twice

Make an occasional comment on the quality of your partner's responses

Ask direct questions quite abruptly

Use minimal hedges if giving instructions/ asking questions

Use basic politeness markers such as *please* and *thank you*

</td>
</tr>
<tr>
<td>

Power 3

Use Standard English but use your natural regional accent

Use a middling pitch

Talk at a moderate speed

Treat your partner as an equal – if you wish to use first names check with them first that this is acceptable

Avoid technical and highly sophisticated vocabulary

Use some hedges, apologies/other politeness strategies

Qualify your opinions with phrases like *I might be wrong*

Interrupt once or twice but apologise for doing so

Allow your partner to lead the conversation sometimes

Only give way sometimes if interrupted

Give some supportive feedback when the other person is talking

Use some hedges when giving instructions or asking questions (*Would you mind ...*)

</td>
<td>

Power 4

Use quite a lot of non-standard dialect and accent features

Speak in a higher voice than normal

Talk rapidly

Address your partner formally, using their full title or sir/miss/madam

Use lots of vague, non-technical language and verbal fillers like *sort of, like* and *you know*

Use lots of hedges, apologies/other politeness strategies

Always qualify your opinions with phrases like *I might be wrong* or *I'm really not sure about this*

Don't interrupt and wait until invited to speak

Give way straight away if someone interrupts you

Give lots of supportive feedback when the other person is talking

Wait your turn – and say as little as possible without ever appearing rude or uncooperative

</td>
</tr>
</table>

Persuasion and rhetoric

Another important aspect of our exploration of language and power is how it can be used to persuade, influence, convince, inspire – and even intimidate. In this section we ask what makes a particular text powerful in any of these senses, an area of language study which is sometimes referred to as **rhetoric**.

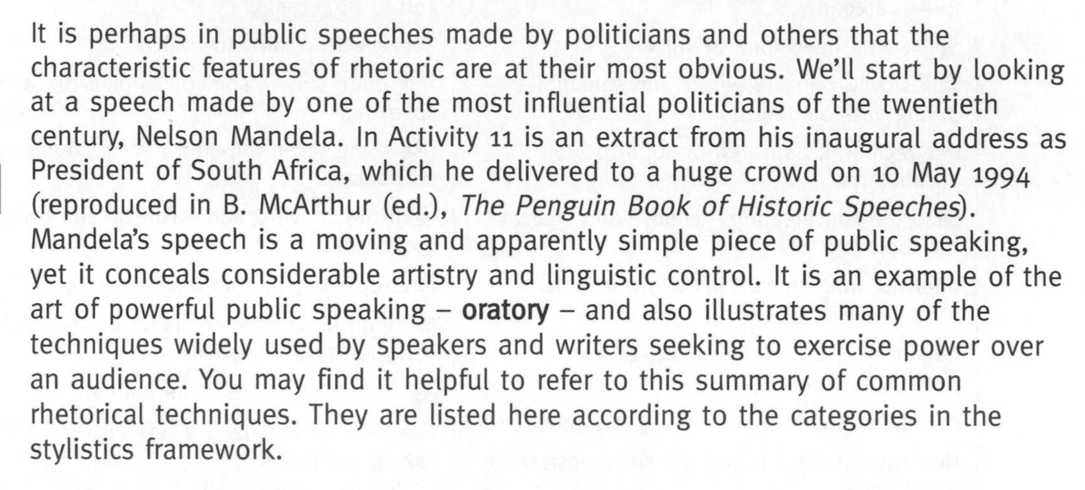

It is perhaps in public speeches made by politicians and others that the characteristic features of rhetoric are at their most obvious. We'll start by looking at a speech made by one of the most influential politicians of the twentieth century, Nelson Mandela. In Activity 11 is an extract from his inaugural address as President of South Africa, which he delivered to a huge crowd on 10 May 1994 (reproduced in B. McArthur (ed.), *The Penguin Book of Historic Speeches*). Mandela's speech is a moving and apparently simple piece of public speaking, yet it conceals considerable artistry and linguistic control. It is an example of the art of powerful public speaking – **oratory** – and also illustrates many of the techniques widely used by speakers and writers seeking to exercise power over an audience. You may find it helpful to refer to this summary of common rhetorical techniques. They are listed here according to the categories in the stylistics framework.

The power of language: some common techniques

Discourse structures	*Problem-solution:* the speaker convinces the audience that they have a problem, then provides a solution *Desire-need-fulfilment:* the speaker convinces the audience that there is something they need or desire, then promises they can have it if . . .
Sentence structures	*Lists and repetition:* Groups of three Parallelism – repeating sentences with similar structures ('Let there be . . . Let there be . . . Let there be . . .') Contrasts and opposites Rhetorical questions
Lexical choice	Pronoun use Direct address (second person: you) Personal authority (first-person singular: I) Unity and bonding (first-person plural: we) Figurative language (metaphor, simile, personification) Emotive language Humorous language Factual support and authority, or citation of other authorities
Sounds and spellings	Alliteration Rhythmic patterns and repetitions

ACTIVITY 11

Try to define those features of the following speech by Nelson Mandela that contribute to its power and impact on the listeners. Look in particular for any patterns (such as different kinds of repetition or contrast) used to express and shape the ideas effectively. It will be helpful to review the framework for stylistic analysis outlined in Module 1 (pages 33–35), and some of the linguistic terminology introduced there.

Today, all of us do, by our presence here, and by our celebrations in other parts of our country and the world, confer glory and hope to newborn liberty. Out of the experience of an extraordinary human disaster that lasted too long, must be born a society of which all humanity will be proud. Our daily deeds as ordinary South Africans must produce an actual South African reality that will reinforce humanity's belief in justice, strengthen its confidence in the nobility of the human soul and sustain all our hopes for a glorious life for all.

The time for the healing of the wounds has come. The moment to bridge the chasms that divide us has come. The time to build is upon us. We pledge ourselves to liberate all our people from the continuing bondage of poverty, deprivation, suffering, gender and other discrimination. We are both humbled and elevated by the honour and privilege that you, the people of South Africa, have bestowed on us, as the first president of a united, democratic, non-racial and non-sexist South Africa, to lead our country out of the valley of darkness.

We understand it still that there is no easy road to freedom. We know it well that none of us acting alone can achieve success. We must therefore act together as a united people, for national reconciliation, for nation building, for the birth of a new world. Let there be justice for all. Let there be peace for all. Let there be work, bread, water and salt for all. Never, never and never again shall it be that this beautiful land will again experience the oppression of one by another and suffer the indignity of being the skunk of the world. Let freedom reign. The sun shall never set on so glorious a human achievement! God bless Africa! Thank you.

Nelson Mandela, 10 May 1994

Now compare your analysis with the commentary on pages 162–3.

In Module 3 you will find more examples of persuasive writing, together with suggestions for your own writing activities that will allow you to try putting some of these techniques into practice.

The language of power in the media

Many of the techniques used by politicians are equally evident in other forms of persuasion with which we are more familiar. In the media, for example, we are bombarded by advertisements, publicity campaigns, news bulletins, articles, editorials and letters which, in different ways, use language to persuade us of their authority and truth.

As part of your preparations for the Unit 2 examination, you should carry out some detailed investigations of these kinds of texts.

ACTIVITY 12 **C3.1b, C3.3**

Here are some suggestions for possible investigations of the power of persuasion in practice. Each involves gathering some data, analysing it closely, and writing up or presenting your findings to your class.

(a) Gather a selection of advertisements for a variety of rival products, and compare them in terms of their use of powerful or persuasive language. (Remember to check your analysis against the stylistics framework.) Make a presentation of your findings to the class.

(b) Compare the language techniques used by advertisers.

(c) Compare adverts for comparable products (e.g. toiletries or cosmetics) aimed at male and female audiences. This links usefully to some of the issues raised in the 'Language and gender' section below.

(d) Collect two editorial pieces from different newspapers on the same topic and the same day. Carry out a stylistic analysis of the texts, examining closely how they each use language to persuade and influence readers.

(e) Collect some examples of letters written to the correspondence page of your local newspaper. Examine the ways in which writers have attempted to make their language powerful.

Language and occupational groups

Whenever a group of people with a shared interest or area of expertise gets together, it is almost inevitable that they develop distinctive ways of using language. There may be technical, specialised or slang terms which outsiders perceive as 'jargon', characteristic ways of talking to each other and ways of referring to things that form part of their common knowledge and familiarity.

If this is true of people with a shared hobby or recreation – football fans, film enthusiasts, music lovers, train spotters, and so on – how much more is it true of those who share a common trade or profession and work alongside one other? This aspect of Unit 2 will consider the distinctive ways in which language is used in these professional and occupational contexts, asking three key questions:

- What forms does specialised occupational language take?
- What are the purposes and effects of these uses of language?

- How do various occupational groups communicate with members of the public who are their customers/clients?

In order to answer these questions, we will need to gather and scrutinise examples of:

Data (Primary)	such as transcripts of talk in occupational/ professional situations, between colleagues and with the public, written texts such as official correspondence, training manuals, job descriptions and the like.
Attitudes	such as letters and articles about professional jargon and the uses and abuses of language in the workplace.
Texts	such as fictional representations of work situations and scripted dialogue in TV programmes,
Academic studies	such as surveys or summaries of observation and research.

ACTIVITY 13

If you have worked part-time or otherwise, take a few moments to share your experiences and observations of some of the linguistic 'practices' at your place of work. You should consider:

- any specialised terminology you had to learn, and why this is essential
- ways in which colleagues address one other, and their seniors and juniors within the organisation
- any training you may have received in terms of how you should talk to customers/clients, and how you have had to adapt your 'normal', or non-occupational, language use
- any 'in-house' slang that you have found yourself adopting when talking with other employees.

Compare the outcome of your discussion with the commentary on page 163.

Defining the job: job descriptions

If your eye has been caught by the job advert, and it has succeeded in tempting you to find out more, you may send for an 'application pack', which is likely to include a more detailed definition of exactly what the job involves. This is called a job description; it defines the various duties and responsibilities of the post.

Unlike the original advertisement, there is no real persuasive purpose to this document. Instead, it may be used as a way of assessing you in the job and appraising your performance.

Activity 14

If you have a part-time job, or know someone who has, you will probably be able to examine some examples of 'job descriptions' defining employees' responsibilities. (The Human Resources section of an organisation may be willing to let you have a sample.)

Using the prompts under the following language frameworks, comment on the way your job description tries to define the duties involved.

Graphology/ Discourse	How do the graphological features of the text assist clarity of interpretation, and reflect the organisation of the text?
Lexis/ Semantics	To what degree are the lexical and semantic fields of the text specific to the occupation involved? Try to comment on the range of verbs used to define duties, and the use of adjectives and/or adverbs to qualify or specify these duties.
Pragmatics	Are there any possible areas of ambiguity or differences of interpretation in the definitions of duties?
Grammar	What is distinctive about the sentence types used in the text?

Learning the trade – and the jargon

We've filled in the forms, survived the interview and got the job. What usually follows will be some basic training or 'induction' before being let loose alongside colleagues. Whatever the job, part of 'learning the ropes' will inevitably involve becoming familiar with the 'in-house' language – a way of talking that may be specific to the occupation, or to that particular workplace, or both (see Activity 13). This will involve:

- the way you talk to your colleagues
- the way you talk to your superiors and subordinates
- the way you talk to your customers/clients.

We'll consider what this means in practice by examining transcripts of three different kinds of conversation within a single workplace – a hospital.*

*I am very grateful to Prof. Ron Carter of Nottingham University for granting permission to use these extracts, which originally appeared as part of the Language In the National Curriculum project.

ACTIVITY 15

Examine the transcript below. Here, a consultant is accompanied by a group of student doctors as he visits one of the patients on his ward. The group of trainees gathers around the patient's bed whilst the consultant explores his case with one of the students.

Focus your analysis on three key areas:

(a) The way in which the conversation reflects the occupation, relative status and roles of the consultant and student.

(b) The distinctive features of the way they both discuss the patient's case.

(c) The way in which the consultant converses directly with the patient.

Compare your responses with the commentary on page 164.

Student Doctor (SD): This is Mr Herbert Nicholls (.) he's a 64-year-old retired chemical plumber (.) he was routinely admitted from outpatients on 4th May (.) he has a four-year history of an ulcer on his right leg which went red and slightly pussy two days before admission (.) it's not painful; he has no other ulcers and it's dressed by his district nurse every other day he also suffers from rheumatoid arthritis and fibrosing alvulitis (.) so in summary this is a well-looking, overweight pleasant 64-year-old man with an infected eschemic ulcer of his right leg unresolved after four skin grafts he's a chronic arteriopath with eschemia of both legs worse on the left he's had a right femora poplitcal bypass graft

Consultant (C): right very good what do you think might have happened since he left hospital to cause his ulcer to break down yet again

SD: he could have either occluded his graft

C yes

SD: or the area could have become infected

C: OK now is there any clinical evidence that he might have occluded his graft what sort of symptoms would he have had

SD: he would have had pain at rest or

C: right

SD: pain in his calf when walking

C: good (*turning to Mr N*) have you had any pain in your leg Mr Nicholls?

Mr N: no

C: no rest pain (.) leg hasn't gone cold or anything

Mr N: no (.) no

C: or painful (.) it's been perfectly

Mr N: a little bit of pain (.) little bit of pain

C: around where the ulcer is

Mr N: not a lot (.) yeah

C: no obvious change as far as you're concerned (.) OK (*turns back to SD*) so certainly from a clinical point of view his graft seems to be perfectly all right (.) so we need to look into other aspects (.) there's (.) how would we tell if he'd got an arteritis

SD: we could take a biopsy

C: yes has he had that done

SD: yes

C: and what did that show

SD: it was negative

C: right (.) so

SD: no vasculitis

C: no sign of vasculitis (.) so what's the plan for his treatment

SD: they're going to try and eliminate any infection

C: yep

SD: by continuing his (*inaudible*)

C: yes how's he taking that

SD: he's having it intravenously

C: yes why is that

SD: er (.) better delivery to the site

C: yeah but he also has a little problem with all antibiotics

SD: sensitive

C: yes he gets sick with them (.) so he doesn't like them they upset his stomach (.) what do you think we should do in the long term to stop this keep coming back (.) he can't spend the rest of his life in bed can he

Communications in a workplace may have to be handled with some tact. No-one enjoys having their work directly criticised, and few people actually enjoy drawing attention to others' faults. Sometimes, though, this has to happen – though often in coded and 'hedged' ways that minimise personal affront and protect feelings.

ACTIVITY 16

In the following transcript, two hospital administrators are discussing a problem that has arisen in their 'information flow'. As you study the extract, focus your analysis on two areas:

(a) **Lexical/semantic:** identify different types of occupationally-specific jargon in their language.

(b) **Pragmatic:** how does either of the speakers negotiate any possible 'issues'.

A: actually there are a couple of things that I think we need to discuss (.) first is this issue of quality on budgetary control information reports coming out of BRIBUD

B: right you mean the lower level reports from GLM and GTI

A: yes that's right (.) I think the source of the problem is our feeder systems where potentially we're in a GIGO situation

B: we are going to have to watch that especially when we have live contracting information coming down through centre link from PAS

A: right I think we need to look at the size of the problem first actually

B: actually I think Ewan's got the error reports now

A: has he (.) let's try him

Compare your responses with the commentary on pages 164–5.

Meanwhile, in the operating theatre a team of surgeons (S1, 2 , 3, & 4) are carrying out a routine procedure on an anaesthetised patient, observed by a student doctor. Transcribed below are some extracts from their conversation.

ACTIVITY 17

(a) Identify those aspects of these conversations that may be surprising to an outsider.

(b) Try to offer an explanation for these.

Compare your responses with the commentary on page 165.

Surgeon I (S): (*to assistant*) thank you (.) a big one (.) a big one or even a holey one would do fine (.) a big one or a holey one (.) don't matter which…

(*later*)

SI: it's a small lump under the skin called a lymphoma (.) it's a rather unusual place to get it (.) but that's what it is…

(*later*)

SI: do you always operate like this?

S2: I think a man who's had his football team so heavily defeated shouldn't have a chance to talk like this

SI: I don't see why you should bring this up again (.) I mean the real tragedy is getting beaten by Sunderland...

(*later*)

S3: for (.) five (.) now (2) one (.) two (.) three (.) four (.) five (.)

S4: do you want me to save all these bits

S2: no I don't think so thank you

SI: take them home for your tea George

S4: I'm vegetarian

S2: after this operation so am I

SI: it's all right (.) he's always like this on a Friday

Extension study

ACTIVITY 18

You might find it interesting to compare this primary data with the fictional representation of a similar workplace situation in a TV programme such as *Casualty.* Tape and transcribe examples of scenes corresponding to the one in Activity 17 and carry out a detailed comparison of the two sets of data.

Talking the talk: business jargon

In the world of management and business, it is not unusual for 'buzzwords' to develop and for a particular kind of business-speak to become widespread. This kind of jargon can have several purposes besides the obvious one of allowing precise and economical communication:

- being deliberately obscure or vague to avoid a difficult question or 'issue' ('*we have an ongoing tactical review situation at this moment in time*' = '*we don't know what to do about it*')
- disguising an unpleasant reality with **euphemistic** or **periphrastic** words ('*we're downsizing the firm and we're letting you go*' = '*you're sacked*')
- making a relatively unimportant job sound much grander than it is (*vertical personnel distributor = lift operator*)
- the opposite – bringing someone above you in the company hierarchy down to earth by belittling their role (*e.g. describing office staff as 'pen pushers'*).

ACTIVITY 19

Owing to the powerful influence of America in the international business world, much of the professional language in this area may originate across the Atlantic, as illustrated by the following data. Below is an extract from a glossary of 'business jargon' terms listed on an American website, along with examples of their use in the business world.

Carry out your own 'grouping and classifying' exercise (as in Unit 1) with this data, in which you create categories and note patterns within the data set.

To get started, you might consider:

- the sources of different **metaphors** used in these expressions
- the ways words and phrases have been constructed and made memorable:
  - **blends:** a combination of parts of two different words to create one new one
  - **compounds**: the combination of two whole words to create a new phrase
  - **alliteration**
- **acronyms**
- terms that imply disrespect or contempt.

A

above board

visible, honest

*'Wegerd president Leonard Greer insists everything is above board. The **SEC** and state regulators are investigating.'* Forbes, 10 Oct. 1994

a 180

an about-face, a complete reversal

'Assistant Attorney General Anne Bingaman will reveal an enforcement agenda that represents a 180-degree turn from the antitrust policy that has reigned for the past 15 years.' Business Week, 7 March 1994

acid test

final decisive test, proof

*'Seven 'acid tests' of whether personnel was making an effective business contribution were discussed at the conference on Restructuring business: The **HR** contribution.'* People Management, 4 May 1995, p.18

administrivia

all the trivial activities and reports required by administrators

'As a project manager, I thoroughly enjoy the responsibility of coaching, supporting and managing people and projects but then there is the administrivia.' Mary Grace Allenchey, AT&T, 1996

B

back-door

of questionable ethics, dishonest

'Despite conceding some back-door deals, Delta Air Lines – and 6 other U.S. airlines – have made their $50 cap on travel agent commissions for domestic flights stick.' Fortune, 15 May 1995

bait and switch

an unethical sales technique where low-priced goods are advertised but not available when customers come to the store

'Sellers sometimes practise a form of false advertising known as bait and switch. A low-priced good is advertised but replaced by a different good at the showroom.' Journal of Political Economy, Aug. 1995, p.813

bang for the buck

the most impact or results for your money

'Brown tries to get a lot of bang for the buck by not paying too much more than the market for a stock while finding companies with dramatically superior earnings growth and return on equity.' Fortune, 21 Aug. 1995, p.127

basket case

a hopeless situation/person

'By downsizing government, privatizing state-owned industry and pegging its currency to the dollar, Argentina has gone from economic basket case to miracle in just three years.' Financial World, 1 Feb. 1994, p.54

batting average

percentage of the time you are successful (baseball)

'The U.S.' largest pension funds have accumulated major-league batting averages in selecting top-performing domestic equity and fixed-income money managers during the last five years.' Pensions & Investments, 2 May 1994, p.1

beef up

expand, make stronger

'In a major strategic shift, Prudential Insurance Co. of America is beefing up its money-management business to play an equal role with its huge insurance operations.' Wall Street Journal, 16 Nov. 1995

bells and whistles

features, details

'However, everything in the BOX amounts to very little without the applications. Too much time and energy are spent on bells and whistles.' Journal of Systems Management, July/Aug. 1995, p.12

boot camp

training facility or program (military)

'Erlene Mikels ... attended the group's boot camp a year ago to ***rub elbows with*** *experts in the field and to polish up rusty marketing techniques.' Wall Street Journal,* 16 Jan. 1996, p. B1

bps

bits per second, the transmission speed of a modem or other electronic communications device

C

can of worms

a complex problem

'One area that was targeted for cuts was federal food insurance; the premiums charged are considered artificially low by some people. Congress is reluctant to open a can of worms with so many potential voters.' Barron's, 31 July 1995, p.41

Career Limiting Move (CLM)

an action that will adversely affect your future

'If at a party you commented that the ***CEO*** *'s spouse had put on a few pounds it would likely be a CLM.'* Brian Chilla, Rock-Tenn Company, 1995

catch-22 situation

an unresolvable contradiction or logic trap, The phrase comes from Joseph Heller's best-selling 1950s novel

'It's a Catch-22 for employers and employees alike: In theory, work-family programs, including flexible schedules, aim to ***level the playing field*** *for people with family duties,... But in practice, many women ... who need to use them resist for fear of being relegated to the* ***Mommy Track****.' Wall Street Journal*, 13 Dec. 1995

click throughs

number of people who see and then open a banner or link on a website, usually expressed as a percentage compared to the number of people who saw the banner or link.

comer

Someone or something with recognised potential.

'Last year's comer was clearly the ready-to-drink tea segment, which boosted its share of the New Age market to 22.6% from 15.3% in 1993' Supermarket Business, September 1995, p.91

cook the books (to)

falsify records

'In the same way a company can use ***'creative accounting'*** *to make its financials look the way it wants them to, the federal government can cook its books, too.' Secured Lender* , May/June 1995, p.44

cookie

a number code a website uses to identify visitors

core business

basic activities

'This term almost always includes an announcement by the straight-faced president, CEO or chairman of the board, "We are pleased to announce that the company is returning to its core business."..Actually, core business means that the company is bordering on insolvency as a result of ego-driven forays into a series of unrelated enterprises for which it had no knowledge or expertise – and then failed.' Supervision, Jan. 1994

D

dead wood

people who are part of an organisation but no longer contribute to the firm's output. Before **downsizing** in corporate America, people who were considered *dead wood* were often **pushed upstairs**.

'"Get rid of dead wood," advises Economic Notes, a monthly newsletter for unions, in a piece on how to revitalize union locals.' Wall Street Journal, 20 Feb. 1996, A1
devil's advocate (let me play)
ponder or predict criticism of a project as a means to improve the quality of the proposal
'In addition to being an effective role model, the new strategic leader needs at least one good alter ego, devil's advocate, or contrarian to avoid getting into a rut.' Planning Review, 10 Sept. 1994, p. 6
Dilbert/Dilbert Principle
popular 1990s cartoon by Scott Adams which finds humour in corporate absurdities
'The Dilbert Principle is adapted from the ***Peter Principle****, a popular management aphorism of a few years ago. Mr Adams observes that the most ineffective workers are systematically moved to the place where they can do the least damage: management.' Wall Street Journal,* 30 May 1996, p. A11

Further reading

S. Cockroft, *Investigating Talk.* Hodder Murray, 15 July 1999. ISBN 0340730862

N. Fairclough, *Language and Power.* Longman, 2001. ISBN 0582414830

See also:

the section on 'Occupational Varieties' in D. Crystal, *Cambridge Encyclopedia of the English Language.* CUP, 2003. ISBN 0521530334

www.universalteacher.org.uk

Language and gender

In recent years there has been a great deal of interest in the relationship between gender and language use. This reflects a more general concern with the changing roles of men and women in society, and the social trends of the past 30 years or so in which many traditional assumptions about gender roles have been challenged.

Two main issues are implied in an investigation of language and gender:

- Does vocabulary that is used to refer to men and women reflect a kind of institutionalised sexism in our language – and if so, what can be done about it? This is a question of language and representation.
- What differences are there in the ways men and women use language? This is an issue of language usage.

Language and representation

It is clear from the way we use English that we think gender is significant. When we refer to someone, we usually specify their gender, even when it is not particularly relevant. We talk about a 'boy' or a 'girl' more often than a 'child', a 'father' or 'mother' more often than a 'parent', and 'brother' or 'sister' rather than 'sibling'. There is no word in English for 'aunt' or 'uncle' that is not gender specific, and the overwhelming majority of first names immediately identify their bearer's gender. So, if we routinely represent people in terms of their gender, are there any differences in the ways males and females are referred to? We don't need to think very long before coming up with the answer.

Let's start by looking at the titles that we give or are given when identifying ourselves. Unless we have an inherited or other special title, there are two traditional alternatives for men and two for women. If you are male, you have the choice of either Mr or Master. If you are female, you might be Mrs or Miss. On the face of it, these two pairs of titles look as if they are equivalents of each other – Mr/Mrs and Miss/Master. In fact, their use and meanings are very different.

ACTIVITY 20

(a) Define the differences between the uses and meanings of 'Master' and 'Miss'.

(b) Explain the differences between the titles available to adult men and women, and suggest what these differences reveal about different attitudes towards men and women.

(c) What reasons do you think 1960s feminist groups may have given for popularising the term 'Ms'? Describe your attitude towards its use.

(d) Brainstorm a list of the terms of abuse most commonly used about people of either gender. Sum up the differences you find, and try to account for them.

(e) The following titles or jobs are listed in male/female pairs. For each pair, decide whether the terms are true equivalents, and describe any differences between them:

- manager/manageress
- father/mother
- author /authoress
- lord/lady
- master/mistress.

Now compare all your responses with the commentary on pages 165–6.

Gender and semantics: marked and unmarked categories

As we have just seen, one feature of our English vocabulary is a tendency for the female form of a title to be more obviously **marked** than the male form. This can often reflect a particular 'mindset', in which we assume that certain roles or occupations are inevitably assigned to a particular gender.

ACTIVITY 21

The following extract from a careers bulletin mentions a number of professional people.

(a) Supply the words that you think are most likely to fill the numbered gaps in the text.

(b) What do you think these choices reveal about language and gender?

Compare your answers with the commentary on page 166.

CAREERS BULLETIN

Next week as part of our Careers programme a number of specialist professionals will be visiting the college. An engineer will talk about careers in the mechanical and electrical engineering industries. (1) ___ will meet any interested students in Room 12. A nurse will also be available to discuss career routes into nursing, and (2) ___ will be in Room 20. Meanwhile Dr Hibbert from the Cambridge Road Medical Practice will speak to potential medical students in Room 14, where (3) ___ will also show a video entitled 'Careers in Medicine'.

One small step: generic man

One example of our gender-related use of language is the word 'man' itself. When Neil Armstrong stepped onto the moon in 1969 he delivered a carefully scripted epigram. In fact, he slightly misquoted his own lines. He intended to say: 'That's one small step for a man, one giant leap for mankind'. Armstrong omitted the 'a', saying instead: 'That's one small step for man . . .'.

The 'correct' version uses two different senses of the idea 'man'. Had he used this version, Armstrong would have referred to himself as 'a man'. This can mean both an adult male and a member of the human species (as in 'man evolved from apes'). We can call this second meaning of the term the **generic** use. But which meaning did Armstrong intend? In the event of the first person to land being female, would we have referred to her as the first 'woman' on the moon, and would she have said, 'That's one small step for a woman . . . .'? Of course, the epigram works by contrasting the first reference to 'man' with the unmistakably generic 'mankind'. However, in the version that Armstrong actually spoke, 'man' without the 'a' sounds as if it is generic too, thus reducing the effectiveness of the saying.

This illustrates a problem with 'man'. It is ambiguous, being used as both a generic and a gender-specific term. In practice, this can lead to problems: it is quite possible to say 'all men [generic] should live in peace' and intend to include women; but we can hardly say 'the man [generic] next door has just become a mother'! In the second example, where a specific person is identified, the word must refer to gender.

Some people object to the generic use of 'man' because it ignores or devalues the role of women. So should we change our use of English to reflect modern ideas about gender roles and equality of opportunity?

ACTIVITY 22

Below are several examples of commonly used expressions involving the generic 'man'. Add any more you can think of, then provide reasoned objections to the use of the term as it stands. Suggest an alternative that is free of any gender reference.

- The chairman is expected to address the shareholders this morning.
- Sam the fireman put on a shiny new jacket.
- Report to the site foreman at 9.00 am.
- There's a new postman on our route.
- We'll have to reduce manning levels in every department.

Compare your notes with the commentary on pages 166–7.

In recent years there has been considerable controversy over the issue of so-called 'political correctness' in language. Traditional uses of language embody inequalities and discriminatory attitudes that we no longer see as acceptable or desirable, so a number of questions arise:

- Does the 'sexist' use of language do active harm in reinforcing unhelpful stereotypes and attitudes?
- Should we consciously try to change the language – as in some of the examples discussed above – or will our language eventually change 'of its own accord' and catch up with the new social realities?
- This is all part of an even bigger debate – the question of how far the words of our language shape and construct the ways we think about the world. In its most extreme form, made famous by the linguists Sapir and Whorf in the 1930s, the concept of **linguistic relativism** suggests that our language imposes on us the mental categories with which we organise and make sense of our perceptions of the world. This would, of course, imply that speakers of different languages actually think differently too.

ACTIVITY 23 **C3.1a**

Imagine that your school or college has decided to devote one section of its equal-opportunities policy to the question of language. In groups, try to agree on the outline of a language policy for your school/ college in respect of gender.

Representations of gender

One important area for investigation is the question of how males and females are represented in different kinds of texts. This goes further than the problems of inherent semantic asymmetries, lexical gaps, gender-marked terms and semantic pejoration which we have already noted; it is a question of the ways in which whole texts – news articles, narratives, advertisements, and others – represent gender. How far, if at all, does the linguistic representation of gender reinforce stereotypes and prejudices?

ACTIVITY 24

(a) Read the extract below, which is the ending of *The Call of the Glen*, a story by Helen Stewart, published by *The People's Friend*. Some changes have been made to the original text. What do you think they are?

Tom said nothing, only looked up at Virginia as she stood beside him, dark against the sky. All the sounds he loved were caught up and held there in her voice; all the peace and strong, sweet steadfastness of the fields and hills and moorlands which he loved, were caught up and held in her.

She stood beside him, but her eyes were fixed on the hills across the valley, and they glittered darkly in the level sun rays. . . There was silence for a moment and then she said, 'There's something I have to say to you, Tom. I've been meaning to say it since that morning at Craigdhu, but – it's difficult. . . .'

He laid a hand on her arm to silence her.

'No,' he said, and his voice was a little unsteady. 'Oh, Virginia! You, too! You think I was – in love with her? Why?'

She shrugged. 'Because of the way you looked, the way you spoke, the tone of your voice and the light of your eyes. I know I'm not mistaken, Tom; you are in love.'

He said nothing to that, and she looked down and went on in a low voice, 'I know the signs, you see, for I'm in the same sad way myself. I didn't mean to tell you, but there it is. I've known for a long time that I love you, but there was Rosy, and though it's better this way, it's hard on you. I thought – Tom, you're crying!'

'Yes.' He looked up at her. 'I'm crying because I'm happier than I've ever been before. I've read about people crying because they were happy but I never believed it. But it's true!'

She put a hand on his shoulder, disbelief, hope, joy, struggling in her face. Then she shook him gently.

'You mean – you love me?'

'So much – so much!' he whispered.

And then he was in her arms.

For a long moment everything was forgotten. Earth, sky, the evening light about them and the night to come were lost, forgotten incidents in some far shadowy world. Only this was real in all eternity.

At last she let him go.

'Fools that we were!' she said softly. 'A pair of proud stiff-necked fools!'

They strolled down the hill side by side. At the gate of the cottage he stopped.

'Don't come any farther, Virginia. I want to go in alone.'

They faced each other, their eyes shining with the clear light of a love that was sure, complete and steadfast.

When she had gone he stood still until the sound of her footsteps died away, then turned to the cottage.

The moon was rising, a slim silver crescent behind the Roman's Hill. A late partridge was calling in the stubble. He could smell wet bracken and the clean scent of dewy grass.

Moon and hill, scent and silence took on a deeper beauty as he thought of her.

A deep, sweet contentment flowed over him, and kissing his hand to the hills and to the sky and to the road where she had been, he walked into the cottage and shut the door.

Compare your ideas with the commentary on page 167.

(b) In what ways did the version of the story printed above strike you as odd? If you can answer this question, you can begin to identify some of the gender stereotypes implicit in its representation of men and women. Use the table below to investigate some specific linguistic features of the text as it originally appeared. After listing more examples in the different categories, comment on the differences in the way the two characters are represented, and how this might be typical of gender stereotyping.

	Actions attributed (verbs, adverbs)	Qualities attributed (adjectives)	Speech attributed
Tom	Stood beside her Eyes were fixed on the hills (Eyes) glittered darkly	Dark against the sky Strong, sweet steadfastness	'There's something I have to say . . .'
Virginia	Said nothing Looked up at Tom		'No,' she said, and her voice was a little unsteady

(c) Study the text below, from a car advert. In what ways do you think it reflects gender stereotypes in targeting its intended audience/market?

Kinky Boots

Try on the special edition Seicento 2Tone and turn a few heads next time you're in town. Designed with exquisite details like electric front windows, Sony CD player, metallic paint, matching interior trim and body colour co-ordinated features such as bumpers and door mirrors.

In fact, there's a whole range of extras available on any Seicento including driver's airbag, electronic power steering and engine immobiliser. Look drop-dead-gorgeous for just £6,199. Go on, treat yourself. Call 0800 71 7000 or visit us at our website.

Listed below are some suggestions for text-based investigations which will allow you to research some of the gender-related issues raised so far. A framework of possible questions is suggested, which you could apply to whichever type of text you choose to investigate.

Key issues	Linguistic focus	Text types
How are males and females identified and referred to? How are they described? What actions are attributed to males and females? How far do your texts exhibit other forms of implicit sexism?	Collate the nouns and titles that are used to identify people referred to in your texts. How often are women described as the wife/partner/mistress/girlfriend of a male? Collate the words and phrases (mainly adjectives) used to provide additional information about males and females. How often are men/women described in terms of appearance as opposed to profession/skills? What kinds of positive and negative judgments are implied by the terms used? Collate the verbs and adverbs used to describe males and females. Are males represented as active, dynamic? Are females represented as passive, having things done to or for them rather than doing?	News reports in tabloid and broadsheet newspapers Advertisements Personal ads placed by men and women Children's books – past and present Romantic fiction (e.g. Mills and Boon novels)

Language usage

The second part of our investigation concerns the ways in which men and women use language themselves. The questions that researchers have been asking over the past 20 years or so include:

- Are there any significant differences in the vocabularies used by males and females?
- Are there any differences in the way males and females behave in conversational contexts?
- Are there any differences between the use of non-standard accents and dialects between men and women?
- What might be the explanations for, and implications of, these differences?

Gender and conversation

When we examined conversation earlier in this module, we found that the status, power and influence of speakers are reflected in the way people interact and converse. As women have traditionally been associated with less powerful positions in society, and are stereotypically associated with subordinate roles, could it be that men and women behave differently in conversation?

ACTIVITY 25

C3.1a

In investigating this area, most researchers have tended to focus on one or more of the following orthodox ideas. For each of these:

(a) Hold a discussion in your group and suggest whether you think your own experience and observation support the idea.

(b) Design a piece of research that would enable you test it. Identify the type of data you would need to collect, and how you would need to analyse it.

- In single-sex groups, women tend to be very supportive and co-operative whereas men tend to be more competitive.
- Women tend to listen more actively and supportively, giving plenty of supportive feedback with **minimal responses** ('mm', 'yes', 'did you') during another speaker's turn to indicate interest and agreement.
- Men may delay their minimal responses and thus convey impatience or lack of interest.
- Men are more likely to compete for the floor, interrupt, and use aggressive forms of language such as insults, raised voices, threats and swearing.
- In mixed-sex groups, men dominate women.
- Women tend to spend longer on phatic talk; men's talk is functional.
- Women tend to swear less than men.
- Some lexical items are used more by women than men.
- Women are better at articulating emotions.
- Women tend to be more tentative and use more **hedges** and **question tags**.
- In general, women tend towards co-operation, men towards competition.

One often-quoted study set out to test some of these suppositions. In 1975, two academics (Zimmerman and West) published an account of the research they had carried out at the University of California. They taped conversations between pairs of males and females and examined the way they took turns in same-sex and mixed conversations. They noted the frequency with which speakers of each gender overlapped (started speaking just before the previous one had finished) or interrupted (cut off the previous speaker, preventing him or her from finishing).

Their findings can be summarised as follows:

- Same sex: in 20 conversations, there were 22 overlaps and 7 interruptions.
- Mixed sex: in 11 conversations, there were 9 overlaps by men and 0 by women, and 46 interruptions by men and 2 by women.

Activity 26

(a) Write down any conclusions that you think can be drawn from Zimmerman and West's findings. Also note down your reactions: are you surprised or alarmed, for example? Offer some explanations for the differences in behaviour that these findings seem to reveal.

(b) Compare your notes with the analysis offered by Jennifer Coates in 'Women, Men and Language', as quoted in the commentary on page 167.

(c) Suggest any reasons you can think of to challenge the validity of Zimmerman and West's data. Consider the sample size, where the study was carried out, and any other aspects of the experiment which might limit its wider applicability.

More recently, some people have questioned the validity of some research in this area. Sometimes research (such as that of Zimmerman and West) based on a very small and not very representative sample of speakers has been used to support sweeping generalisations about men and women in a range of situations. Besides, times are changing; perhaps modern female speakers are tending to adopt more traditionally 'masculine' discourse features. It is time to try out some of these ideas by collecting and analysing data of your own.

Activity 27

C3.3

Design and carry out an investigation in your own school/college to test the ideas and findings of Zimmerman and West. Arrange to make a recording of either a mixed-sex conversation or two similar conversations involving only males or only females. These may be taken from the broadcast media but will preferably be a live conversation. (If you tape live speech, remember always to follow the guidelines given on page 16.) Transcribe a section of the tape, making sure you indicate where interruptions or overlapping occur. Examine the data closely to test the ideas discussed above.

- count and compare examples of interruptions/overlaps, questions, minimal responses, hedges and question tags.
- comment closely on these examples.
- apply the conversational analysis framework (see page 94).
- present your findings in a report.

Further reading: some key texts on language and gender

J. Coates, 'Women, Men and Language: A Sociolinguistic Account of Gender Differences in Language' (*Studies in Language and Linguistics*), Longman, 14 June 1993. ISBN 0582074924

C. Grey, Overview of Work on Language and Gender Variation (link to this web page through www.heinemann.co.uk/hotlinks)

D. Tannen, *You Just Don't Understand: Women and Men in Conversation*, Virago Press, 26 March 1992. ISBN: 1853814717

D. Tannen, *Talking from 9 to 5: Men and Women at Work*, Virago Press, 11 April 1996. ISBN 1860492002

A. Goddard, L. Meân Patterson, *Language and Gender*, Routledge, an imprint of Taylor & Francis Books Ltd, 17 February 2000. ISBN 0415201772

Accents and dialects of the British Isles

First, you would find it useful to review the work on this topic covered in Module 1. This included:

- examples of a literary **representation** (in D. H. Lawrence's *Sons and Lovers*) and an accurate transcription of regional speech (the Sunderland speaker)
- the terms **Received Pronunciation** and **Standard English**
- some ways in which the lexis and grammar of regional speech differ from Standard English
- a review of some attitudes towards Standard English and regional varieties
- the fact that the dialect we call Standard English (SE) has come to be regarded as the model of 'correct' English, and that the non-regional accent known as Received Pronunciation (RP) enjoys prestige as the 'proper' way to talk.

As the prestige form of English, SE dominates the printed word, the education system and our public and professional life – but there remain some colourful regional variations that continue to express the distinct local character of the towns, cities and counties of Britain. The study of these regional varieties is sometimes referred to as **dialectology**.

It would take a very thick book indeed to discuss all of these regional varieties in any detail; as with the other sections of this module, the activities and examples included here should be used to provide the basis for extended explorations and investigations of your own.

The scope of this examination topic
Although you will see that the terms 'accent' and 'dialect' have distinct meanings, the Examination Board has stated that the topic *Dialects of the British Isles* also includes consideration of issues relating to **accents**, as illustrated by the materials in this section.

To prepare for the examination, your studies should include some exploration of at least some of the many regional varieties in the UK (perhaps starting with your own region), and the development of appropriate terminology and ideas with which to discuss these.

The kinds of data you might meet in the exam include:

Data (Primary)	transcripts of spoken language including regional features
Attitudes	articles or other material exploring attitudes towards regional varieties
Texts	examples of written texts that attempt to represent regional speech
Academic studies	summaries of or extracts from research into accents and dialects (e.g. surveys)

Accents of English

As we have seen, people tend to have different attitudes towards RP and the regional accents of English. An accent can trigger a whole stereotype of a city or region, and can be the means by which we continue to reinforce unhelpful prejudices.

ACTIVITY 28

(a) Read the following article. It originally appeared in the early 1990s in the *Northern Echo*, a regional newspaper published in the north-east of England.

PUTTING THE ACCENT ON A NORTH MOUTH DIVIDE

The voice on the television advert persuading you to buy bread, beer or crisps probably sounds familiar.

For market researchers associate these products with the North-East accent and qualities of being friendly, down-to-earth – and undynamic.

But the man selling flash cars, holidays or pension schemes is likely to have a southern accent because advert makers say it denotes ambition, authority and intelligence.

Now speech coaches say many Northern businessmen are trying to change the way they speak because they feel they are not taken seriously enough.

As one (southern-based) national newspaper summed it up: 'Northerners are rushing to prove they are not as thick as the accent that marks them out.' It is just the latest example of an increasing North Mouth Divide which is threatening to stifle strong regional accents.

And language experts argued that the trend should be strongly resisted.

York University lecturer Dr John Local said: 'The media use accents all the time in subtle ways. But it is hard to say with this kind of thing whether the media lead or follow.'

(b) Carry out your own survey of accents in TV advertisements during an evening's viewing, and present your findings to the class. Your investigation should ask:

- What kinds of products are advertised by using different regional accents?
- What kinds of products are advertised using mainly RP accents? Is it true that these tend to be 'high prestige' products?
- How do some adverts use both regional and RP speech? Consider, for example, how often RP voices provide the voice-over or the last word in an advert that uses regional speakers on-screen.

(c) The article's closing sentence raises the question of how far the media are to blame for the perpetuation of these stereotypes. In the light of your findings, try to decide which of the following statements most accurately describes the role of the media in the use of regional accents:

- The media simply reflect stereotypes that already exist in society.
- The media help reinforce and strengthen social stereotypes.
- The media create and spread stereotypes.

In considering these issues, you may like refer to the following review of a book by Dr J. Honey, *Does Accent Matter?* In this extract, reviewer D. J. Enright summarises some of the research findings reported in Honey's book:

Experimental research shows that RP heads the prestige league (its speakers are even reckoned to be handsomer, taller, cleaner), followed by Scottish (Edinburgh), Welsh and Irish (kept within bounds), while cockney, Scouse, Glaswegian, West Midlands and Belfast come bottom. Yorkshire is relatively well thought of, as the language of farmers and cricketers, and so are rustic accents, a fact ascribed here to the nineteenth-century worship of the countryside. Unattributed theories put Scouse down to the prevalence of adenoids and Glaswegian to ill-fitting false teeth.

We can extend our study of accents in the media to include news broadcasts, so often seen as the benchmark for 'proper English'. National newsreaders almost invariably speak using an RP accent, and even readers of the local news tend to have only the gentlest hint of a regional accent in their speech. Why is this? The following may help you answer this question. It is an account of a much-quoted experiment carried out in the 1970s by the researcher Howard Giles:

In the 1970s a team of researchers led by Howard Giles carried out a number of research experiments called matched guise experiments, designed to test people's responses to different accents. In one of these, Giles delivered two identical presentations on a controversial topic to different groups of Midlands sixth-form students using RP with one group and the local regional accent with the other. Afterwards, he surveyed his audiences for their opinions of his intelligence and knowledge. The students who had heard the presentation in RP rated his intelligence and authoritativeness considerably higher than those he had addressed in the regional accent.

ACTIVITY 29

Bear in mind the results of Giles's experiment as you consider which of the following statements offers the most likely explanation for the universal use of RP among newsreaders. Place them in order of importance, then compare your findings with the commentary on page 168.

- All newsreaders went to similar kinds of schools and had a similar education, so they all have a similar accent.
- Not everyone would be able to understand the broadcasts if they used regional accents.
- People would find the news less believable and take it less seriously if it were spoken in a regional accent.

Accent and social class

The accent of English we seem to respect the most happens to be the one that is used principally by middle-class, usually university-educated people working in professional occupations. In other words, RP's unique status is largely due to its being the accent of the powerful. RP has what linguists sometimes describe as **overt prestige** – an 'official' status of which most speakers seem to be consciously aware.

ACTIVITY 30

(a) The relationship between our accent and our social background is complex. Some researchers (e.g. Peter Trudgill in *Sociolinguistics*, 1974) have carried out surveys to explore the complex relationship between our regional speech and our social class. Use your library to track down some of this research.

(b) Some recent research suggests that the association of RP speech with education, authority and power may be slipping. Other accents, such as the so-called Estuary English, may be gaining ground, as reported in the article below from *The Times Educational Supplement* in October 1984.

After reading the article, answer the following questions:

- What are some of the distinctive features of Estuary English?
- What social reasons are suggested for its growing popularity?

ESTUARY ENGLISH

It seems . . . that the pronunciation of British English is changing quite rapidly. What I have chosen to term Estuary English may now and for the foreseeable future be the strongest native influence upon RP. 'Estuary English' is a variety of modified regional speech. It is a mixture of non-regional and local south-eastern English pronunciation and intonation. If one imagines a continuum with RP and London speech at either end, 'Estuary English' speakers are to be found grouped in the middle ground.

The heartland of this variety lies by the banks of the Thames and its estuary, but it seems to be the most influential accent in the south-east of England. It is to be heard on the front and back benches of the House of Commons and is used by some members of the Lords, whether life or hereditary peers. It is well established in the City, business circles, the Civil Service, local government, the media, advertising as well as the medical and teaching professions in the south-east. 'Estuary English' is in a strong position to exert influence on the pronunciation of the future.

On the level of individual sounds, or phonemes, 'Estuary English' is a mixture of 'London' and General RP forms. Although there are individual differences resulting from the speech background and choices of pronunciation made by the speaker, there is a general pattern. An example of this is the use of 'w' where RP uses 'l' in the final position or in a final consonant cluster. An 'Estuary English' speaker might use an articulation like a 'w' instead of the RP 'l' as many as four times in the utterance: 'Bill will build the wall.'

Non-Londoners often comment on what they see as the jerkiness of the speech of the capital. This is because of the use of a glottal stop in the place of the 't' or 'd' found in RP, as in the stage Cockney phrase: 'A li'le bi' of breab wiv a bi' of bu'er on i'.' This process seems to be analogous to the loss of the 't' in such words as 'Sco'land', 'ga'eway', 'Ga'wick', 'sta'ement', 'sea'-belt', 'trea'ment', and 'ne'work'. Not all RP speakers would sound these 't's. As would be expected, an 'Estuary English' speaker uses fewer glottal stops for 't' or 'd' than a 'London' speaker, but more than an RP speaker.

.... Because it obscures sociolinguistic origins, 'Estuary English' is attractive to many. The motivation, often unconscious, of those who are rising and falling socio-economically is to fit into their new environments by compromising but not losing their original linguistic identity. Again, often unconsciously, those RP speakers who wish to hold on to what they have got are often aware that General RP is no longer perceived as a neutral accent in many circles. They are also aware that 'Conservative' and more so 'Advanced' RP can arouse hostility. What for many starts as an adaptation first to school and then working life, can lead to progressive adoption of 'Estuary English' into private life as well. Complicated as this may sound to a foreign user of English, these developments may be seen as a linguistic reflection of the changes in class barriers in Britain.

For many, RP has long served to disguise origins. 'Estuary English' may now be taking over this function. For large and influential sections of the young, the new model for general imitation may already be 'Estuary English', which may become the RP of the future.

Regional dialects and Standard English

In discussing accents we are concerned with variations in pronunciation (**phonology**); when we widen the enquiry to look at dialectal variation we consider differences in vocabulary and grammatical constructions. Some of the issues here become even more controversial, especially when they centre on the importance of Standard English, the notion of correctness and the relative status of regional dialects.

ACTIVITY 31

First we need to ask the question: why is it necessary for us to have a 'standard' vocabulary and grammar of English for all speakers? In groups, discuss this issue; try to suggest at least five reasons. List your responses and present them to the class, then compare your list with the commentary on page 168.

For most of us, **Standard English** means the vocabulary laid down in good dictionaries, and the grammar of 'correct' English as taught in schools, used in books and broadcast by news media. However, only a relatively small number of us use Standard English exclusively; many of us also include in our speech words, expressions and grammatical constructions that are part of our regional dialects, as the *Guardian* article from April 1998 (see below) makes clear.

CHILDREN USING GEATT WORDS INSTEAD OF STANDARD ENGLISH 'IS DEAD WRONG'

Children may choose not to speak properly even when they have a clear knowledge of standard English, a report for the Government's main curriculum quango said yesterday.

Tape recordings made of 11- and 15-year-olds in four regions of England revealed that many speakers used phrases such as 'They have fell out of the picture' or 'It could have came in the window' at the same time as Standard English.

The most common wrong usage was of 'there is' followed by a plural. In the south-west, children used 'them books' or 'they books', when they meant 'those books'.

On Merseyside, 'dead' meant 'very' as in 'dead good', on Tyneside 'geatt' was a versatile alternative to 'really', as in 'do it up geatt tight' or 'it's a geatt 20 miles'.

Richard Hudson, of University College, London, who analysed the speech of more than 350 children taped in class eight years ago, found that a third used no non-standard English at all, and that girls used fewer non-standard forms.

'Our evidence may indicate that mere exposure is not sufficient, and that some kind of direct teaching or encouragement is needed', Professor Hudson said.

ACTIVITY 32

Discuss and consider the following issues raised by the article, writing down your findings before comparing your ideas with the commentary on page 168:

- What reasons might children have for deliberately avoiding Standard English forms?
- What reasons are there to be either concerned or unconcerned that children are not using Standard English?

On the other hand, some people have expressed concern that some traditional dialectal forms are in the process of disappearing.

Activity 33

Read the following *Guardian* article carefully. Make a note of the evidence and explanations it offers for the claim that dialect lexis is disappearing. What appears to be the writer's attitude to this development? What do you think will be lost if our dialectal vocabulary disappears?

OUR DISAPPEARING DIALECTS

Britain's rich fund of slang is fast dwindling. Terms such as 'cow-pawed' or 'thwart-eyed' – insults meaning left-handed or cross-eyed which were once commonplace in their native communities – are not thought likely to make it far into the next century.

Many regional forms of invective are already extinct, and the trend is set to continue.

The English spoken in Britain appears to be shedding its quirks comparatively faster than languages spoken in surrounding Western countries.

'The power of standard English seems to be a stronger force here than elsewhere', explained Leeds University lecturer Dr Clive Upton.

The decrease in the use of words such as 'urchin' for a hedgehog and 'lop' for a flea is the result of increased mobility in the population. In the past 50 years people's need to deal with others over a wider geographical area has put a premium on clear communication.

Dialects: lexical variation

To varying extents, each region or major town/city in the UK has its own dialectal vocabulary which differs from Standard English. Many of these dialect words have a very long history, and survive as relics of different dialects first brought to Britain by various Anglo-Saxon and Viking invaders. Dr Clive Upton, the researcher mentioned in the *Observer* article, helped to compile a linguistic atlas of Britain and has produced maps that show the geographical distribution of hundreds of dialect terms (*Word Maps: A Dialect Atlas of England*). For example, if we return to our Sunderland speaker's use of 'bairn' and 'clarts' (see Module 1), the maps indicate that 'bairn' is retreating northwards as the Standard English form 'child' becomes increasingly universal, and that 'clarts' is only one of many alternatives to the Standard English 'mud' spread throughout the country.

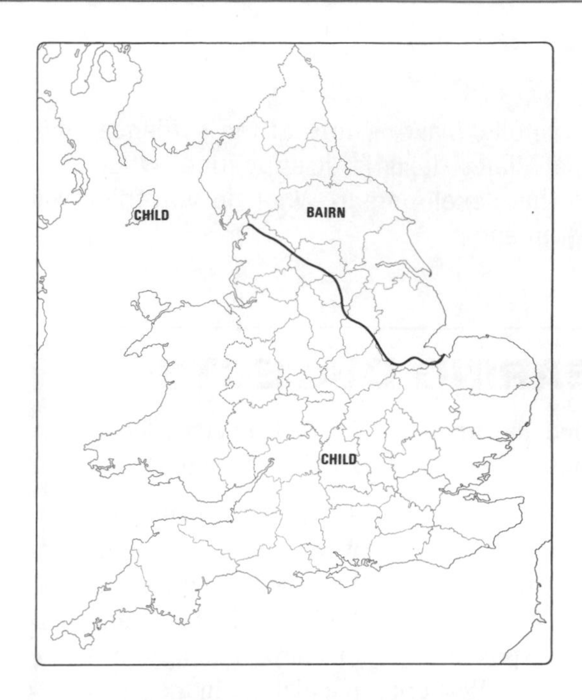

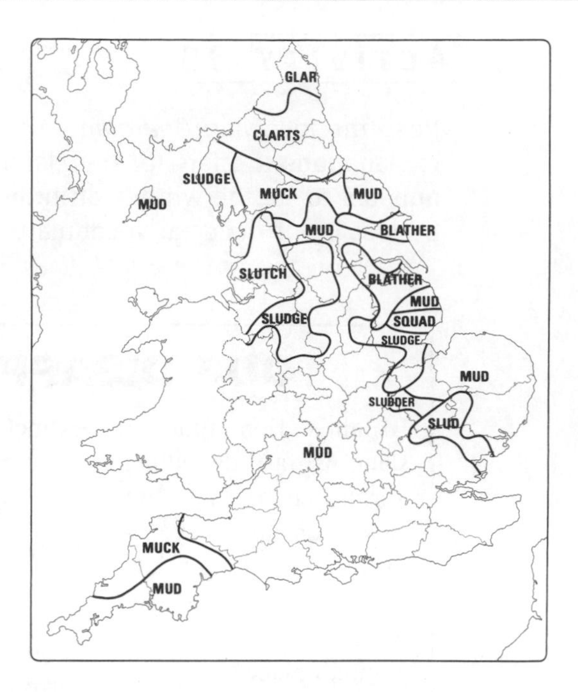

Activity 34

Find examples of your region's dialect. Carry out interviews with members of your family or neighbours, especially more elderly ones – it would be interesting to interview older people who were brought up in different parts of the country. One useful approach is to ask your interviewees to suggest alternative words for terms that often show marked regional variations. Some suggestions are:

- cold (adjective)
- a narrow alleyway running between houses
- a blister or blemish on the skin
- a gooseberry
- a silly or stupid person
- a splinter (of wood)
- a small bread bun
- a scarecrow.

Dialects: grammatical variation

Although people are often interested in and sympathetic to regional lexis, attitudes towards the distinctive grammar of regional dialects are often more hostile. Dialectal grammar tends to differ from Standard English in one or more of the following ways.

Subject–verb agreement: verbs 'to be', 'to do'	Past tense forms may vary: 'we was', 'you was', 'I were' Present tense variations may include 'it do'
Other verb tense formations become 'I done' or 'I seen'	The past tense of verbs 'do' and 'see' may
Negative verb constructions	Forms such as 'ain't' Multiple negation as in 'I ain't done nothing' is common in many non-standard dialects
Reflexive pronouns ('myself', 'yourself') Other pronouns	Many variations include 'hissel', 'hissen', 'theirselves' The plural 'youse' is found in several dialects

ACTIVITY 35

(a) Identify any examples of your own regional dialect grammar which correspond to the categories in the table above.

(b) Consider the following examples of dialect grammar, which are quoted from Peter Trudgill's *The Dialects of England* (1990). For each of these examples, decide whether or not you consider it to be 'good' grammar, and suggest a Standard English equivalent.

- Them books there.
- She sings nice.
- I don't want no trouble.
- Are any of youse coming?
- I never seed he.
- I sees the dentist tomorrow.
- He ain't coming.
- Give us a kiss.

Now compare your responses with the commentary on page 169.

(c) How did we come to have a number of non-standard and generally low-prestige dialectal varieties alongside the standard version of English? In groups, try to agree which of these statements you think offers the best explanation of how such varieties have arisen:

- Dialect speakers are simply making mistakes as a result of their faulty education, laziness or lack of intelligence.
- Dialects are derived from, and therefore corrupted versions of, the standard, correct version of English that we started off with.
- Other dialects of English have always existed alongside Standard English, but gradually lost respectability as Standard English became more important.

Compare your findings with the commentary on page 169.

Dialects, Standard English and correctness

It is all too easy to see the grammar of regional dialects as a simplified or corrupted form of the language. This way of looking at non-standard varieties of the language is sometimes called a **deficit model**, and is based on a view that there is a preferred variety of English (Standard English) the rules of which can be laid down, or prescribed. For this reason, such a view of language is described as **prescriptive**.

Accent, dialect and gender

Some researchers have asked the question: 'Do men and women differ in their use of regional speech features?' They have reported some significant findings.

ACTIVITY 36

From your own experience and observation, what difference, if any, would you expect to find between men and women of a similar social class in their use of regional speech? Think in terms of the 'strength' of accents and the use of non-standard dialectal grammar. Compare your findings with the commentary on pages 169–70.

In 1982, the researcher Jenny Cheshire set out to find some answers by investigating the speech of some young speakers in Reading. Her findings are shown in the table below.

Use of non-standard grammar by adolescent boys and girls in Reading

Example of non-standard form used	Boys	Girls
'I don't want nothing' (double negative)	100	75
'That ain't working' (non-standard negative 'to be')	74	42
'That's what I does' (non-standard first person 'do')	71	50

ACTIVITY 37

C3.3

(a) Examine Cheshire's data carefully. Note down any conclusions that can reasonably be drawn from her findings, and suggest possible explanations for the apparent trend that they reveal. Compare your notes with the commentary on page 170.

(b) Design an investigation that will allow you to survey use of non-standard lexis and grammar among students of similar backgrounds in your own school/college.

The origins of Standard English and regional dialects

Earlier, we considered the social and technological factors that made a 'standard' version of the language necessary (see page 127). However, if we retrace our steps to a time before electronic communications (the Internet, TV, telephones, radio), fast and convenient transport (aircraft, cars, railways), and widespread literacy with the availability of written texts, we arrive at a time when a standard was not really necessary. Such a time was the fifteenth century – at least until a single technological invention signalled the beginning of the process that would eventually lead to the Standard English we take for granted today. That invention was, of course, the printing press, developed and introduced to England by William Caxton in the 1470s.

Until then, manuscripts were all handwritten and literacy was the preserve of a small, privileged minority. In the two or three centuries after the invention of the press, books began to appear in large numbers, and we were on our way to becoming a print-based literate culture. However, for Caxton and the authors and printers who came after him, there was a problem: which dialect should they use?

ACTIVITY 38

Study the map below, which shows the approximate linguistic geography of fifteenth-century England, together with its principal dialect divisions. In the centuries after Caxton, the development of a print industry accelerated the pressures for a version of the language that could be recognised as 'standard'. In groups, try to agree on which of the dialects indicated on the map you would back as the most likely candidate. As you make your judgement, consider the following factors:

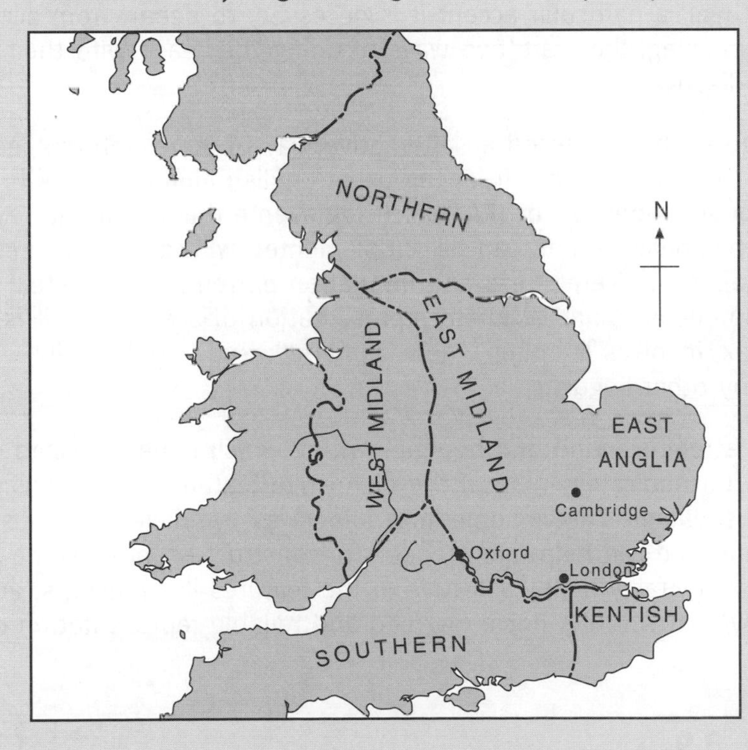

- the centre of political power in England was London, where the monarch and the court were based
- the church – a very powerful institution during this period – was also based in London, though the universities of Oxford and Cambridge were

important seats of learning and centres for the training of priests, who would come from different parts of the kingdom to study there

- commercial printing was based in London
- there seems to have been considerable migration of people from the east and central Midlands to London during the fourteenth century.

Now compare your suggestion with the commentary on page 170.

The outcome of this process of standardisation might have been very different if the distribution of power and influence had been otherwise. If, say, Newcastle upon Tyne had been the seat of government and the cathedral city of Durham exercised greater power than Oxford and Cambridge, this book might well have been written in the variety of English we now know as 'Geordie'.

Representations of accents and dialects

As you have already seen, transcribing regional speech presents some problems (see texts B and I in Module 1, pages 10 and 13). It is unusual to see regional lexis or grammar in texts, unless it is being quoted. We also tend to associate the conventional spelling of Standard English with RP pronunciation, so if we wish readers to 'hear' a particular accent it is necessary to depart from accepted usage. Broadly speaking, there are two ways of doing this, each with their advantages and disadvantages.

(1) Academic linguists have devised an alternative way of representing speech sounds: a set of symbols different from the usual English alphabet. This is the International Phonetic Alphabet, or IPA, which represents the individual phonemes used by speakers, and can be supplemented with a complex set of marks and symbols to indicate stress and intonation patterns. This system allows for a comprehensive and accurate representation of accent, but it is extremely complex, involves learning a new 'alphabet', and is only really comprehensible by other linguists.

(2) Writers often attempt a kind of 'phonetic' writing which remains based on Standard English but indicates some of the distinctive features of an accent by using alternative spellings. This is sometimes known as **eye-dialect**. It is usually easy to understand and can help most readers re-construct or 'hear' some accent features, but it is inevitably highly selective in the features it represents, and it uses a spelling system which is not an agreed and reliable representation of sounds.

ACTIVITY 39 **C3.3**

(a) An example of Method (2) above is reproduced below. It is part of a poem designed to represent the accent of a speaker from Wigan in Lancashire, alongside a 'translation' in Standard English. When you have studied both versions of the poem, work through the following tasks:

- Identify the distinctive lexis and grammar of the Wigan dialect represented in the poem.
- Identify the distinctive phonological (accent) features represented by the eye-dialect of the poem.
- Identify the specific devices used (the non-standard orthography) to represent these accent features.

(b) Try to write a short text – perhaps a short account of your day, or a meeting you have had – to reflect your own regional speech, and accompany it with a commentary in which you explain how you have used non-standard lexis, grammar and orthography to convey selected features of your local speech.

Faythers Day Eawt	**Father's Day Out (Translation)**
Eeh, owd cock, tha looks smart in yon jackit.	Old man, you look smart in that jacket.
Them britches thi fit thi reet weel.	Those trousers, they fit you very well.
Just wait till tha's geet thi new cap on.	Just wait till you've got your new hat on.
That collar, eaw does it feel?	That collar, how does it feel?
Come here, al tuck thi shart lap in.	Come here, I'll tuck your shirt tail in.
Un them draws tha's geet on, are they clen?	Those underpants you've got on, are they clean?
Un dust know that thi flies on thi pants are undone?	And do you know that the flies on your trousers are undone?
But tha'l at butt'n them up thi sen.	But you'll have to button those up yourself.

Further reading

Take your studies further by making use of your school/college library. Here are some useful titles:

J. K. Chambers & P. Trudgill, *Dialectology*. CUP, 10 December 1998. ISBN 0521596467 (an established introductory undergraduate text)

A. Hughes, P. Trudgill, & D. Watt, *English Accents and Dialects*. Hodder Arnold, 2005. ISBN 0340887184 (a CD accompanies the book)

M. Sebba, *London Jamaican*. Longman, 27 September 1993. ISBN 0582080959

C. Upton & J. D. A. Widdowson, *An Atlas of English Dialects*. OUP, 1996. ISBN 0198692749

BBC voices website: www.bbc.co.uk/voices

British Library 'Texts in Contexts' @: bllearning.co.uk

Language and technology

Although from the invention of printing onwards, technology has affected the way we communicate, at the start of the twenty-first century, some people would claim that a new era has dawned – that of the electronic media – and that the forms of communication it has thrown up are likely to have as great an impact on our lives – and our language – as print itself.

The focus of this topic is on the specific characteristics of some of these new modes of language, and the nature of their impact on their users.

In particular, the examination paper may present you with examples of the following:

Technology/Medium	Genres
Telephone	Conversations SMS texts
Radio and television	Sports commentaries Phone-ins
Computers	E-mails Web pages

As we consider each of these forms and genres, the **three** key questions we will be asking are:

- What are the distinctive forms of language associated with them?
- In what ways has the nature of technology itself shaped and constrained these?
- In what ways has technology had a wider impact on the way we communicate?

The language of telephone calls

Faced with a communications technology which in some respects resembles face-to-face conversation but in others is very different from it, we have gradually developed a distinctive set of conventions and procedures relating to the use of the telephone. As we try to establish what these are, we need to start by considering the ways in which a phone call differs from 'normal' conversation, and how these differences have shaped the nature of 'telephone talk'.

ACTIVITY 40

The table below lists some of the distinctive features of phone talk alongside some of the technological and contextual characteristics of the medium.

Your task is to match the features suggested with the characteristics that you think may have given rise to them.

Some observed features of telephone conversations	e.g.	Technological and contextual characteristics
Some speakers may make an extra effort at vocal clarity, even modifying their local accent		Identity of caller and respondent not immediately obvious to either
Some speakers prefer not to discuss sensitive or confidential issues on the phone		Lack of visual contact between speakers
Turn-taking tends to be more carefully observed than in some face-to-face conversations		Sound quality degraded; some high-frequency sounds (e.g. consonants) may be ambiguous or unclear
When giving important information on the phone, specific strategies are used to ensure clarity e.g. when spelling words or quoting postcodes, letters may be referred to as 'F' for Freddie (as opposed to 'S' for Susan)		Possibility that call may be interrupted
Conversations always begin with 'identification routines' in which both caller and respondent identify themselves		Possibility that call may be overheard
When listening to a caller, back-channel behaviour (i.e. all those reassuring 'yeah's, 'really?'s and 'mm's) is even more important than in 'normal' speech		Call may be a 'cold' one from stranger to stranger, or may catch the respondent at an inconvenient moment
After an initial identification routine, there may be some attempt by the caller to give a good reason for the call and apologise for the disturbance		
Phone calls may include more requests for clarification (sorry…I didn't quite catch that…) or so-called 'repair sequences' (putting right misunderstandings or misheard items) than face-to-face conversations		

The discourse structure of phone calls

ACTIVITY 41

It would appear that many telephone conversations – ranging from informal, personal calls right through to commercial, professional and business transactions – tend to follow similar patterns. Consider, for example, the structure suggested below.

Telephone calls: a common discourse structure?	
Identification routines	Usually the receiver speaks first, though it is the caller who has initiated the call If the speakers are known to each other, a brief 'Hi, it's Brian' or even 'It's me' may be enough; otherwise, a fuller identification exchange may be needed: 'My name is xxxx – you may remember we spoke last week about. . .'
Call validation routines	As the caller, we will usually feel obliged to give a reason for our call – 'I'm just calling to. . .' Or 'The reason I'm calling is. . .'. This may even be accompanied by an apology (' Sorry to disturb you. . .') or a permissive enquiry (' have I caught you at a bad time? Can you spare a minute?. . . etc.)
Phatic elements	As with face-to-face talk, there may either a token phatic exchange ('How are you today?') or a more extended sequence before getting to the main 'business' of the call
Main issue	Eventually the caller will move towards the main point of the call
Closing sequences	When the main business has been dealt with, there is likely to be some kind of 'wind down' involving a repetition or summary of what has been discussed or agreed
Call termination routines	As with face-to-face talk, it is considered rude and abrupt simply to terminate a conversation without due preamble. This is likely to include politeness markers ('Thanks for your time. . .' 'Thanks for your call. . .' etc.) and a restatement of any action or arrangement arising out for the call ('So I'll look forward to hearing from you. . . .' Before at least one exchange of 'bye's' and 'see you later's' finally terminates the call

Now look at the following two extracts from transcripts of calls, (recorded and transcribed with the prior permission of the participants, and with real names replaced by letters). Transcript 1 is the opening of a conversation, Transcript 2 the latter part of a different call.

For each of them, identify and comment on the way language is used to fulfil these various 'phases' of the conversation.

Transcript 1: A = female employee of building firm calling B, customer & friend C = wife of B	**Transcript 2**: Internal call between members of staff at a college A & B are teachers: they have been discussing the progress of C, a student whom they both teach
B: Hello A: Hiya B B: Oh hi A (.) how are you A: Oh fine (.) I bet you're thinking there's nothing happens for weeks and then it it there's everything happening at once (laughs) B: (laughs) well (.) I suppose so A: I thought I'd better give you a call just to see where we're up to 'cos I know er B: Yeah A: we'd come and look at was it the damp proofing and (.) well you'll have seen that we've been up today to finish the windows B: yeah we've seen that (.) but I've just this minute got in so (.) er A: well I won't keep you 'cos I expect you'll be wanting to get on with your tea B: oh it's OK (.) C's not in yet A: oh right (.) cos we really could do with seeing you really (.) we were wondering if you had any time we could perhaps come over	A: Yeah (.) that's just it (.) I mean we've already had that conversation and we're still waiting for C to come up with the goods B: Well I should see him later today er I I think it's this afternoon actually A: Right B: So I'll make sure he gets the message(.) will you let me know if he doesn't see you as arranged A: Of course (.) thanks for that B B: OK (.) see you later A: Yeah (.) bye

Mini-investigations

Activity 42

Whilst making tape recordings of telephone conversations for investigative purposes is fraught with legal and ethical difficulties, one area of telephone talk certainly *does* lend itself to data gathering and analysis – automated reply systems.

Many people report an uneasiness about leaving such messages, perhaps due to the lack of any feedback from a machine and the sense that one's unrehearsed words are being recorded for possibly repeated scrutiny.

One interesting 'norms and variations' investigation in as follows: over a period of several days, save as many messages on your own answer service as its memory will allow, and investigate the similarities and differences between them, trying to account for these in terms of the contextual factors shown below:

Variations to investigate	Possible contextual factors
• Is there a common structure to the message, e.g. self-identification, recipient identification, call validation, main message, closing sequence? • Does it include repetition of key information? • How much variation is there in the lengths of the messages? • How much evidence is there of nervousness and/or uncertainty (non-fluency features?)	• Relationship of caller to receiver • Awareness of caller that message may be accessed by people other than the intended recipient • Time and place the caller makes the call • Perceived urgency or importance of call • Potential/probable purpose of the call

The mobile phone

On the face of it, it might seem as though calls on mobiles and land-line calls differ little. However, the very mobility of the phone and the possibilities of (a) calling someone at an extremely inconvenient moment, (b) in a very public place and (c) with the possibility of signal break-up all present new problems to users.

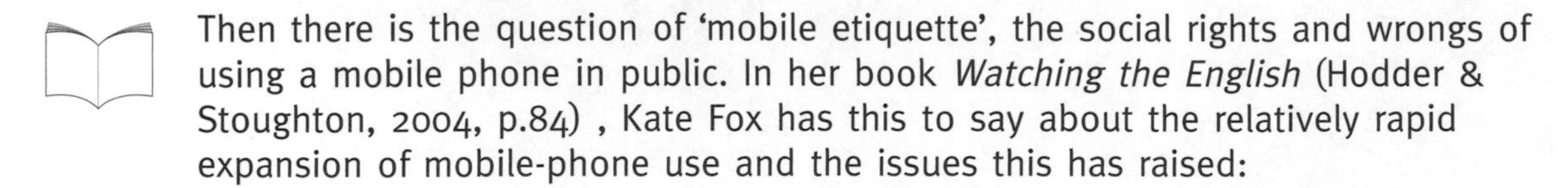

Then there is the question of 'mobile etiquette', the social rights and wrongs of using a mobile phone in public. In her book *Watching the English* (Hodder & Stoughton, 2004, p.84) , Kate Fox has this to say about the relatively rapid expansion of mobile-phone use and the issues this has raised:

Suddenly almost everyone in England has a mobile phone, but because this is new, unfamiliar technology, there are no set rules of etiquette governing when, how and in what manner these phones should be used. We are having to make up and negotiate these rules as we go along.

There are some early signs of emerging rules regarding mobile-phone use in public places, and it looks as though loud 'I'm on a train' conversations – or mobiles ringing in cinemas and theatres – may eventually become as unacceptable as queue jumping, but we cannot yet be certain, particularly given English inhibitions about confronting offenders. Inappropriate mobile-phone use on trains and in other public places is at least a social issue of which everyone is now aware. But there are other aspects of emerging mobile-phone etiquette that are even more blurred and controversial.

ACTIVITY 43

In the light of Kate Fox's ideas, study the following quotations from a discussion about the impact of mobile phones on modern behaviour.

(a) Suggest what they tell us about the impact of mobile-phone technologies on social communication – think in terms of (i) benefits of mobile-phone technology and (ii) its shortcomings compared to more traditional forms of communication.

(b) To what extent do you agree with the ideas quoted below?

Compare your ideas with the commentary on pages 170–1.

I don't know how people ever survived without mobile phones! It's great to be able to keep in touch with friends and family wherever you are. I suppose they make you feel less lonely, in a way – you know – wherever you are there's always someone just a moment away. So you do feel kind of secure, I suppose. I guess I'd feel a bit strange without one! And of course they're great if you're a bit disorganised, forget things, or have to sort things out on the move. To be honest, I'm normally quite shy, but on the phone I can talk to people more easily.

If you ask me, mobile phones can be a curse. Some people seem to be surgically attached to their phones and are forever playing with them, texting someone or other and disturbing people with their mindless jabbering and their stupid ringtones. Why can't people just pay others the basic courtesy of giving their full attention to the people they're actually with at the time? Try switching it off and let people see – hey, *you're* the one I'm with right now, and you're important enough for me not to be interested in what some sad caller or texter may want to say to me at this precise moment. Maybe *I* want to decide whether or not I'm available, and whether the situation I'm in is sufficiently unimportant to me to warrant being disturbed by anyone who wants to pester me. Anyway, all this phoning and texting – does anyone actually *talk* to anyone properly any more?

Two technologies meet: the language of phone-ins

One genre of programme that has become a common staple of radio broadcasting (also found to a much more limited extent on some television channels like Sky Sports) is the 'phone-in', where a presenter hosts a discussion and invites members of the public to participate by phoning the station and putting their point 'on air'. These may be general 'topical issue' programmes, or even more personal confessional shows (such as are often found on local stations in the late evening hours) or more specifically focused (as in sports phone-in programmes). They appear to offer the illusion of a democratic, public-participation discussion, though always with the presenter in control.

Before a caller goes on air, they may have followed these steps:

1. Presenter or host invites potential callers to ring a given number.
2. If the caller succeeds in getting through, a 'researcher' will usually take their details, establish roughly what they wish to discuss, and either put them on hold or promise to ring them back when the host is ready.
3. A sequence of callers is thus lined up, with the host/presenter having the basic details gathered by the researcher displayed when they are connected.
4. Some stations employ an 'instant delay' device that enables them to cut off any callers whose contributions may be obscene or otherwise unsuitable before they reach the air-waves.

What happens next will usually follow a predictable pattern, though with variations depending on the nature of the programme and the 'character' of the host presenter. In some cases, the host is generally courteous and friendly with callers, reassuring them and helping them to feel at ease. In others, the presenter may adopt a more deliberately confrontational and opinionated style, appearing to flout basic 'politeness principles' in order to provoke callers and create a more shocking impact on listeners.

We'll start to explore these 'norms and variations' by looking at an example of two different types of phone-in; the first, a popular sports phone-in on BBC national radio, usually broadcast immediately after the 6 o'clock news on Saturdays in the football season (hence its name), the second an example of a personal issue–orientated phone-in broadcast on local radio in the late evening (after 11 pm).

ACTIVITY 44

Study these transcripts carefully, and answer as many of the questions below that apply to the data, filing your responses under the headings 'norms' (things they have in common that are probably common to the genre of phone-ins) and 'variations' (ways in which they differ as a result of various contextual factors).

(Note: transcript 2 only covers the middle part of the call.)

Framework for investigating phone-ins

- How does the host initiate the conversation?
- What phatic features, if any, are present?
- What degrees of politeness and courtesy are extended to the caller?
- How does the caller convey their opinions and feelings?
- In what ways is the professionalism of the presenter/host apparent by contrast with a caller unused to public broadcasting?
- To what extent doers the host express agreement or disagreement with the caller, and how does s/he do so?
- What closure routine (if any) does the host use before terminating each call?
- In what ways does the host/presenter achieve control of the discourse?
- Is there any evidence that the host is imposing a specific time constraint on each caller?
- In what ways do you think the host's awareness of the listening audience is influencing their conduct of the conversation?

Compare your analysis with the commentary on page 171.

Transcript 1: 6.06

AG: It's half time there now and the score is Sunderland I West Ham nil (.) but let's quickly get to your calls er Tommy in Cumbria (.) you're first

Caller: good evening Alan

AG: Hi Tommy (.) what's on your mind

Caller: first of all what a terrible score what's just come in there

AG: (laughs) I take it you're a Newcastle fan then

Caller: a very disappointed Newcastle fan

AG: well OK OK well what hap what went on today

Caller: well I've just been reading the internet there and I've got the match report and (.) I'll say it's (.) I've been a season ticket holder for fifteen year mate and I've missed this is the first game I've missed in eight year (.) er there's no heart in that team at all (.) they had I they'll (.) I've stood up for them for the last three years but it the manager's got to go now Alan

AG: Tommy (.) I'm sorry (.) I'm not with this at all (.) I mean I thought (.) you know A you've got a lot of injury concerns and the latest of them Michael Owen today and B you've had some decent results of late

Caller:	Alan I've said this (.) I've we've we've we've talked about this before Alan (.) when (.) Alan Shearer at the moment should not be playing for lNewcastle United
AG:	and why do you say that
Caller:	because he struts about (.) he wait he he even last season(.) he used to fight back for the ball (.) that's gone (.) now if Lee Clarke plays for the toon there's a heart in that team along with Scott Parker (.) Souness does not (.) you're just talking about Neil Warnock there (.) he gets a bit excited of a game right (.) Souness he stands there like a statue all the way through the game Alan
AG:	Well Tommy that is not the Graham Souness I know I've got I've got to say er I know very few more passionate figures in football than Graham Souness (.) er I'm really surprised to hear you say that (.) and also think if the players if you're correct if the players show a lack of passion then that's down to the players themselves
Caller:	well as I was saying er I was I just said to your researcher there before came on I'd love to see a Geordie manager I'd love to see Steve Bruce at the toon
AG:	Might happen at some point in the future thanks for your call Tommy (.) Daniel
Caller:	cheers pal

Transcript 2: late-night phone-in

DJ:	why's your life a mess
Caller:	em I don't know (.) I'm a single parent
DJ:	Yeah
Caller:	I've got one daughter
DJ:	right
Caller:	and and that's it
DJ:	Yeah
Caller:	eh
DJ:	and why are you a mess
Caller:	because her da (.) his her my daughter's father (.) takes the xxx all the time
DJ:	what (.) out of you
Caller:	yeah he takes the xxxx out of me
DJ:	well why do you allow it

Caller:	I don't know (.) I really don't know
DJ:	Mandy can't you speak without swearing
C:	sorry
DJ:	is that a problem for you
Caller:	no I ju I don't know I'm terrible aren't I
DJ:	no you're a mess (.) certainly
Caller:	no I'm not a mess

Radio and television

Radio and TV are self-evidently different media; exactly how different, and how this difference affects the way language is used, we will explore as we look at a specific genre of broadcasting that has become a staple of both: the sporting commentary.

ACTIVITY 45

First, let's explore some of the differences between these two media. Use the table below to focus your exploration of the differences – and similarities – between them.

	Radio	TV	Implications?
Where, and when, are you most likely to tune in?			How will these situational contexts impact on the way we listen? . . .
When watching/listening, how likely are you to be doing something else at the same time?			. . . and thus on the way broadcasters use language?
How likely is it, for each medium, that you will watch/listen to a programme in its entirety from start to finish?			How do broadcasters make allowance for 'late arrivals' and people channel-hopping?
Comment on the quality of the speech-sound received, and what might affect this			What limitations might degraded sound place on the quality of spoken communication?
How does each of the two media establish location and identity of speakers, and show action?			How does the presence/absence of images influence the uses of language?

The language of sports commentary

Activity 46

We now take it for granted that any sports coverage on TV or radio will be accompanied by an 'expert' commentary. In the early days of radio, the primary function of this commentary was to convey a clear description of the action in the absence of live pictures. If this were the only function, however, the sports commentary would have been made redundant by the coming of TV.

For each of the following suggested functions of commentaries, arrange them in rank order of importance – 1 as the most important, 5 as the least – for each of the two media. Then discuss the significance of the differences between your two lists.

	Radio	TV
Description of what is happening **(narrative)**		
Creating an accurate 'picture' of the action **(spatial orientation)**		
Identification of players/teams		
Explanation and interpretation of the action **(analysis)**		
Conveying **atmosphere** and emotional impact of event/venue **(stimulus)**		
Simulating a sense of companionship: commentator as fellow-fan **(empathy)**		

Compare your discussion with the commentary on pages 171–2.

Activity 47

The following commentaries were recorded simultaneously five minutes into a football match between Liverpool and Chelsea which was being covered by radio and TV. The 'Action' column has been added to describe what was happening on the pitch at the time.

(a) Carry out a detailed analysis of these commentaries, in which you:

- identify the ways each one fulfils the functions listed in Activity 46
- identify precisely the ways the commentators use language to do so – you might find it helpful to refer to the table below
- try to note aspects of language use related to several different frameworks – **lexical, semantic, phonological** and **grammatical** are obviously key areas.

The language of sports commentaries: some common features and conventions

- frequent player identification using surname only
- alternation between **narrative** commentator and **analysis** expert
- variation in prosodic features (pace, dynamics, intonation) to convey drama of action
- **minor sentences** and **ellipsis**/elliptical expressions
- **semi-technical lexis** associated with sport in question
- **sport-specific usages** of common words e.g. 'heading'
- switches in verb tense: predominantly simple present tense
- frequent metaphorical/ figurative/ idiomatic uses of language.

Compare your analysis with the commentary on page 172.

Action	Radio Five Live C1: Main commentator C2: Expert analyst ('pundit')	TV Sky Sports Live – Live Football Special (Channel 401) C1: Main commentator C2: Expert analyst ('pundit')
Ball is collected by the Chelsea goalkeeper and cleared	**C2:** I think it is difficult at times (.) I think the some of the er sort of statistics show that er I think Peter's probably given away more fouls than (.) anyone else in the premiership (.) and to a degree that's understandable but I do think he gets unfairly treated on occasions simply because of (.) er his size his height	**C1:** and we'll keep an eye on (.) Peter Crouch (.) you can (.) use the playercam facility if you're a Sky digital viewer (.) Crouch being followed (.) under that particular (.) deal at the moment
Ball collected on the right by Joe Cole (Chelsea) who runs with the ball pursued by defenders and is tackled – but a corner is awarded Cole embraces linesman!	**C1:** Cole turning well against Sissoko but he's got Rise and Warnock around him over on that right-hand side and that's a (.) well looked like a dive that by Joe Cole (.) he hasn't got the free kick but he's got the corner (.) Joe Cole scored in the last three premiership meetings between Chelsea (.) and Liverpool (.) we've	(2) but Chelsea have got a corner (4)

Action	Radio Five Live C1: Main commentator C2: Expert analyst ('pundit')	TV Sky Sports Live – Live Football Special (Channel 401) C1: Main commentator C2: Expert analyst ('pundit')
Lampard prepares to take corner	three of England's likely world cup midfield of course out there today Joe Cole Gerrard and (.) Lampard and here comes Lampard his two-hundred and fiftieth appearance today for Chelsea preparing to take a corner for them (.) over on the right-hand side of the field	**C2**: (laughs) **C1**: at last (.) a decision to the home club's liking (3) **C2**: well here you see Liverpool that zonal marking **C1**: mm **C2**: you see the six-yard box the four of them (.) stretched across it
Corner taken Ball headed towards goal by one Chelsea player William Gallas (Chelsea) scores from close range Celebration of goal	(.) in goes the corner (.) from Lampard (.) HEADER DOWN AND TURNED IN BY GALLAS (2)) WILLIAM GALLAS WAS THERE NO MORE THAN THREE YARDS OUT (.) Initially Chelsea won the corner (.) in the air following Lampard's (.) delivery from the right (.) and William Gallas no more than two or three yards out against the run of play gives Chelsea a 1-0 lead (.) thirty-four and a half minutes gone	**C1**: it cost them against Manchester United (4) and it might cost them here (.) IT HAS DONE (.) William Gallas (.) with the second touch (.) the scoring touch (.) for 30 minutes or so it was Liverpool's game (.) in the thirty-fifth minute it's Chelsea's lead

(b) Carrying out your own mini-investigations

There are many different kinds of further investigations you could carry out in this area. Here are just a few suggestions:

- SKY TV football coverage includes a feature which allows 'amateur' commentators who are fans of the opposing teams to do their own commentaries on the action. Compare their efforts with those of the 'professionals' covering the same match.
- Compare the commentaries on the same event in the same medium but on different channels e.g. BBC and Sky commentary on the same premiership match. You might also be able to include a local radio commentary in your comparison.
- Study the differences between the commentaries on different sports (in the same medium and channel). For example, you could compare the commentary on a golf tournament with one on a horse-race.

The language of SMS: texting

SMS technology offers users both opportunities and restrictions, and the rapid development of conventions for its use illustrates how people respond to these parameters.

Some observers have suggested that this new form of language (and its close relatives, the language used in e-mails and chat-rooms) is a hybrid form of communication that shares some of the characteristics of writing, and some of speech.

So, before we start to look at some specific examples of texts, we'll consider in general terms the nature of this mongrel mode.

ACTIVITY 48

(a) In Unit 1 we considered at some length some of the differences between spoken and written language, and how they relate to each other – it's worth revisiting some of these ideas at this point (see pages 20–25 above).

Bearing all of those ideas in mind, where on the 'speech . . . writing' spectrum do we put text messages? Are they more like one than the other? Use the following checklist to decide:

Texting characteristic	More like speech?	More like writing?
Uses written symbols & characters		
Can be saved but more usually deleted once read		
Often uses non-standard spellings to represent pronunciation (e.g. 'u' for you)		
Exchanges can take place more or less instantly		
Ideas/feelings may be expressed graphically (e.g. via 'emoticons', punctuation marks)		
Once familiar with the technology, messages can be composed and sent easily and quickly		

(b) What are the potential pros and cons of texting as a means of communication? And what are the advantages and disadvantages of texting compared with making a call?

Draw up your own list under the headings below before comparing your suggestions with those in the commentary on page 173.

Opportunities	Restrictions	Better than a phone call	Not as good as a phone call

As with many styles and genres of language use, our investigation of the language of texts can focus on two key questions:

1. **'Norms':** what common features do most texts seem to adopt – and in what ways do these arise from the nature and 'restrictions' of the technology we have just explored?
2. **'Variations':** to what extent do these 'norms' vary between texters, and what might account for these variations? Individuals may differ in the ways they respond to the limitations of the SMS – and as with any other form of communication, may also vary their texting style according to the audience and purpose of the message.

   There is no shortage of books and Internet sites claiming to provide a 'guide to texting', complete with lists of 'commonly used abbreviations'. But as with the earliest attempts to write a dictionary of English – as we will see in the 'Language Change' part of the A2 course (Unit 6) – the language often moves far more quickly than those who attempt to pin it down long enough to photograph it.

The 'grammar' of text

ACTIVITY 49

(a) Drawing on your own experience as a producer and receiver of texts, compile your own list of 'rules' and guidelines to help someone new to texting – in other words, come up with your own 'grammar' of texts.

As you do this, try to distinguish between 'rules' that seem to be almost universally observed, and those which are more flexible and varied.

(b) Now compare your suggestions with the list of 'common features' listed below. For the features listed here and in your list, try to suggest how they may have arisen in response to the 'restrictions' or constraints of the medium noted earlier:

Some suggested 'common features' of text language

Txt feature	Example	Link to constraints of technology
Deletion of vowels from words, as far as possible without affecting intelligibility	e.g. dltn of vwls frm wrds.....	
Reduction of double consonant spellings to single	e.g. realy	
Use of abbreviated forms of commonly accepted polysyllabic lexis	e.g. tomoz = tomorrow	

Use of acronyms and initialisms – combinations of letters that stand for whole phrases	e.g. – tmb = text me back	
Avoidance of most punctuation marks, especially apostrophes		
Avoidance of 'standard' lower/upper case switching for grammatical purposes, especially in the case of 1st person 'i'		
Use of punctuation marks and upper/ lower case switching for rhetorical purposes, and to mimic the use of prosodic features in speech		
Use of numeric homophones to replace words or parts of words	e.g. m8 = mate, u = you 4get = forget 2 = to	
Use of letter-names to replace equivalent sounds in words or parts of words	e.g. r = are, bab = baby	
Preference for more 'phonetic' spellings where this 'saves' characters	e.g. deletion of final 'g' in verbs like goin(g), seein(g)	
Preference for phonetic spellings even if no net 'saving' is achieved		
Creative use of characters to create emoticons, conveying feelings	e.g. :-(	

(c) Group investigation

Now examine and survey the collection of texts below compiled by a student carrying out an investigation into the language of texting. He wanted to find out:

- how much variation there is in the text language of different users
- whether these variations reflected any differences in the way males and females used text.

To answer these questions, we will need to allocate one of the following tasks to different members of the group:

Groups 1–4 : For each of the **four** sets of messages, carry out a statistical analysis of some the frequency of key txt features (as listed above) throughout the data:

- how often is 'you' spelt as 'u', how often as 'ya', how often as 'you'.
- how often is first person spelt with lower case?
- how often are apostrophes missed from contractions and possessives?
- how often are numeric homophones used?

. . . and so on.

Other groups may be allocated to additional tasks looking at all four sets of data as follows:

Group 5: What proportion of the texts are given over to (a) phatic talk, (b) making arrangements, (c) expressing emotions, (d) other purposes – and does this seem to vary according to gender?

Group 6: How are different people addressed and referred to in the texts?

Text messages between female students:

1. Hi im realy sorry but I 4got the hearsay concert is this Sun so im goin 2 b stayin but do u fancy sleepin sat getting a take away? A real girls nite in! tmb luv a
2. happy birthday 2 u.kissed wiffo not stu.oh wot a drunken state but its not 2 late!...happy b'day bex! Soz its late! At least I didn't 4get! Luv u loads, XxX
3. Hi XXX! I have got loads of goss 4 u! cant wait til thurs 2 tell u bout it!!! Hope u're havin fun at college! C u soon, luv Vx
4. luv u bec, hope the hol is gr8
5. He left voicemail & text sayin why fone not wrkn, but IO textd him after fonecall; askin him then, he hasn't replied! We talked bout coll,2nt,wwud, u&chris,tesco,now intr.

Male to male:

1. Gav cancel the taxi as paul is not coming and im not going down on my own
2. Are wor going to the pub tonight you loser?
3. Gav u comin out 2nite mate?
4. Im watching the game in a place down town so u can meet me after work if u want. Txt back as soon as u can.
5. Wot r u doin 2nite dick?

Male to female:

1. Hiya sweet, hope ur home ok! Ill see you 2moz luv dan

2. elo u soz I didn't cya! We didn't hide! We had a top time! But we neva saw u o wel! Wot u up 2 then im bak at wk now I evn gt a bit ofa tan! Wot u doin?
3. I just want u2 no I love you with ALL my HEART and I wouldn't no wat 2do if I ever lost u I just want u2 no I love u and I miss u like crazy
4. Popcorn? Huh? Word. What? Friday:im sorry. Work:dammit. Money:im poor. 2 nitcs:work. Futurama:missin it. Solution: tape it. Reason: its*1.Popcorn what? Word
5. Congratulations sexy ill get u a drink 2nite. If u need 2 practice stuff like massages I am more than willing 2 volunteer myself – it is a good cause obviously.

Female to male:

1. I'm beginning to fink u av 4got about me! Id luv 2 cu again, just 2 chat n dat. I got de job @m&s by the way.im well chuffed! Got a letter 4u! luv 4eva. L xxxx
2. Hi there big g! im fine. I haven't seen u at col in ages but ill chat to u 2mz.im doin nowt 2nite, what bout u? wahts big g got planned? Txtb. g.
3. 2nd. Zo isn't answern 2my txts so she's no nice gal. My day has been ok.best part sat in gardn readn with my cat,orr! But I wanted to go out 2ntr, ur the lucky I, bein out.
4. no what? Rnt u gonna write a song 4 m3? Ah well its not that big a deal neway. It pobs wud b crap
5. GOD!ur so impatient pot noodle guy! I had remembered 2 send u I!wat was up with her? Wat u do 2 her! UR SO SNIDE!

The language of e-mail

At first sight, the ability to send e-mails via the Internet might seem simply to allow people to exchange more or less instantly the kinds of information that would have taken two days to exchange by letter.

However, it has rapidly become clear that e-mail and 'snail mail' are actually quite different beasts – and that far from bringing about the extinction of traditional forms of written communication, the two forms now sit alongside each other with their distinctive features.

ACTIVITY 50

First let's remind ourselves of some of the similarities and differences between e-mail and conventional mail as forms of communication. Make and complete your own table similar to the one below.

Features of conventional mail	Similar to e-mail?	Different from e-mail?
Provides a permanent record		
Can be either personal, or more 'public', according to context		
May be deemed 'private'		
Can be re-drafted and edited		
Has a standard layout including address, openings and closings		
Register varies according to context – especially relationship of author/ receiver and purpose		
High standard of accuracy in spelling and grammar expected		
Writer and receiver do not share the same location, and expect a delay of at least a few days before replying		

Some problems with e-mails

As with texts, e-mail may appear to be a 'hybrid' form that combines some aspects of writing (protection from face-to-face contact, re-draftability) with those of speech (immediacy and spontaneity). However, this can lead us into unseen dangers; we may react to messages with an impulsive retort even though once sent, our message becomes a permanent record of our momentary indiscretion. The e-mail can also seem to be a confidential, personal form of communication, but it is, of course, nothing of the sort, as our more sensitive and embarrassing messages can easily be forwarded to a huge audience and may come back to haunt us.

Investigating the variety of e-mails

ACTIVITY 51

E-mails can take many forms: brief personal exchanges similar to text messages, 'round robin' jokes, official communication, unsolicited advertising, and internal memos within organisations, to name just a few.

(a) Collect examples of as many different types of e-mail communication as you can over a set period, and for each one, try to answer these questions:

- What are the purpose and function of the communication?

- How wide is the intended audience, and what is the relationship between sender and receiver?
- How does the language of the message reflect any of these factors?

(b) Select from your collection of messages some examples for more detailed study. You may find it useful to focus on the following issues:

- The **graphology** and **format** of messages will usually be dictated by the software and includes **address** and **subject** boxes. But how do the senders of your e-mails try to catch your attention?
- Discourse structure: **greetings, openings, closure** and **valedictions.**

As with letters, the convention seems to require at least some kind of greeting at the start of the text, though the level of formality will obviously vary. Do even professional/business e-mails include some phatic elements? And do we feel obliged to 'sign off' as in a letter, with phrases like 'best wishes', 'bye for now', or 'see ya'? Has anyone ever found 'yours sincerely' in an e-mail?

The language of web pages

The Internet is now so vast and so varied, that to talk about 'the language of web pages' is almost as meaningless as talking about 'the language of books'. Almost, but not quite – as in a very short time, we have all learned to 'navigate' our way around web sites using metaphorical 'gateways', 'portals' and 'signposts', taking our directions from 'home pages' and 'navigation menus', and clicking on hypertext links.

As with text messages and e-mails, the study of the language of web pages lends itself to a 'norms and variations' investigation – that is:

- **Norms:** what features do web pages generally seem to have in common, and how far are these the product of the technology itself?
- What kinds of **variations** do we find in these features, and what differences in purpose, audience and content account for them?

Investigating web pages: a framework for analysis

ACTIVITY 52

Web sites, like any texts, seek out target audiences/readers; once found, they will hope that they will be attracted to linger on the site, and be able to navigate their way to the information they require/find interesting. They may direct visitors to related pages via hypertext, but aim to return them to the home page. The blend of information/ entertainment may vary, but the desire to attract 'hits' is constant. So, we'll look first at how a web site attracts, speaks to and guides its target audience via its home page.

(a) Select your own web site home page for investigation; you could start with your own school or college. Apply the framework and carry out your own analysis.

- **Graphology/Design:** how does the layout/appearance of the home page appeal to its audience? (How much text? Font? Size? Colour? Images/graphics?)
- **Tone/Relationship to reader:** how is the reader addressed? How is s/he 'welcomed' to the site? How does the lexical content of the page 'match' the assumed interests and personality of the target 'visitor'?
- **Identity of site:** how does the site claim for itself any authority or authenticity?
- **Navigation aids:** how does the home page direct the 'visitor' to the rest of the site?
- **Style/Register:** focus on the level of formality and technicality, any references that assume a common knowledge with its 'visitors', and any evidence of the tendency for sites to use more colloquial styles of language than is usual in printed texts (= **conversationalisation)**.

Mini-investigation: home pages

ACTIVITY 53

- The extract below, 'How do people read web pages?' sets out to demonstrate the 'do's' and 'don't's of 'good' web-page writing, at least according to its author, Jakob Nielsen. Study it carefully.
- Select a range of home pages from different kinds of web sites – educational, recreational, informative, etc. For each of them, investigate how far, and in what ways, they live up to Jakob Nielsen's guidelines (concise, scannable, objective), focusing closely on key language frameworks (e.g. graphology, lexis, semantics, pragmatics, discourse structure and grammar).

How do people read web pages?

They **don't**.

People rarely read Web pages word by word; instead, **they** scan **the page**, picking out individual words and sentences. In a recent study John Morkes and I found that 79 percent of our test users always scanned any new page they came across; only 16 percent read word-by-word.

As a result, Web pages have to employ **scannable text**, using

- highlighted **keywords** (hypertext links serve as one form of highlighting; typeface variations and color are others)
- meaningful **sub-headings** (not 'clever' ones)
- bulleted **lists**
- **one idea** per paragraph (users will skip over any additional ideas if they are not caught by the first few words in the paragraph)
- the inverted pyramid style, starting with the conclusion
- **half the word count** (or less) than conventional writing

We found that **credibility is important** for Web users, since it is unclear who is behind information on the Web and whether a page can be trusted. Credibility can be increased by high-quality graphics, good writing, and use of **outbound hypertext links**. Links to other sites show that the authors have done their homework and are not afraid to let readers visit other sites.

Users **detested 'marketese'**; the promotional writing style with boastful subjective claims ('hottest ever') that currently is prevalent on the Web. Web users are busy: they want to get the straight facts. Also, credibility suffers when users clearly see that the site exaggerates.

Further reading

A. Beard, *The Language of Sport*. Routledge, 26 February 1998. ISBN 0415169119

M. Boardman, *The Language of Websites*. Routledge, 14 October 2004. ISBN 0415328543

D. Crystal, *The Language of the Internet*. CUP, 20 September 2001. ISBN 0521802121

T. Shortis, *The Language of ICT*. Routledge, August 2000. ISBN 0415222753

Preparing for the examination

The unit examination for this module lasts 1½ hours. In that time you have to:

- study a selection of short spoken and written extracts illustrating aspects of the three topics set this year (from 'Language and power', 'Language and occupational groups', 'Language and gender', 'Accents and dialects of the British Isles' and 'Language and technology')
- answer two questions based on these extracts, dividing your time equally between them.

Whatever the topic or question, you will be presented with an appropriate text or set of 'data' relating to the topic and ideas you have studied (see page 83 above).

Your task is to discuss these data/texts in as much detail and depth as you can, using whichever analytical frameworks and ideas about language are appropriate.

Caution!!!
It *may* be useful to make some reference to related ideas and material you have encountered in your studies – such as examples of your own short research investigations, as suggested on page 82, and the work of published academics.

BUT – it is vital that you work with the material you have been given on the exam paper. Many disastrous answers have resulted from students determined to 'name drop' knowledge of published research in an irrelevant, unhelpful and unthinking way.

In order to satisfy the Assessment Objectives in your answers you will need to:

(AO1) Write accurate, coherent analysis using appropriate terminology	Revise and learn the linguistic terminology you will need. Remember to revise the ideas and terms in both modules 1 and 2 – use your personal glossary, and the one at the back of this book, to help
(AO3) Demonstrate your skills of linguistic analysis by applying the relevant frameworks	The exam involves analysis of samples of data. Your analysis should always be the primary aspect of your answer. **Don't try to make it fit into the 'theories' or conclusions of the research you have studied**; be open-minded, and always start from the data, which may often appear to go against what you'd expect
(AO4) Show you know, understand and can apply relevant ideas from language study to your analysis of data	You will be asked to analyse individual texts, but also to show that you can bring to your analysis a wider knowledge and experience of linguistic matters. You will need to be able to refer to the findings of different kinds of investigation and research. This can include your own, those carried out in class and by other students, and those published in academic textbooks. Revise for the exam by summarising some of these. ***Remember: start with the analysis of the data in front of you***
(AO5) Show that you understand how different aspects of social context influence specific features of language use	For each linguistic detail you discuss – graphological, lexical, grammatical, etc. – try to identify a specific social factor which has directly influenced it. Avoid simply 'feature spotting'; straightforward identification of linguistic features is not sufficient for this unit

Commentaries

Activity 1

(a) Charlotte is fairly typical of many people these days, in that she has moved both geographically (from Manchester to Birmingham and now London) and socially (her parents had occupations that might traditionally be regarded as working class, but she is now in a professional, middle-class occupation). She also plays many different roles in the course of her week, so her correspondingly wide language repertoire makes her a particularly interesting linguistic subject.

The issues that you discussed may have included several relating to the five key topics in this module:

- How much of a Manchester accent or dialect did she grow up with, and does she still have it? Will she have lost it at university or afterwards? What might have caused her to do so – or not? ('Accents and dialects of the British Isles')
- In formal management meetings at work, would she adopt rather formal language styles and an accent closer to RP? As a manager, what sort of language does she use to give instructions to staff and exert her authority? Does she use terminology or jargon that is specific to the technology with which her company deals? ('Language and power'; 'Language and occupational groups')
- What happens when she meets her parents or friends from the North? Perhaps her original accent resurfaces as she re-establishes her bonds with her school friends. Does the same thing happen when she visits her parents? How would they react if she spoke to them in the same way as she speaks to her colleagues at work? ('Dialects')
- You may have also have identified **gender** as a factor in Charlotte's use of language; perhaps the way she talks with her female friends is different from the way she talks to men, or it may be that as a woman she uses language differently from men. ('Language and gender')
- Both in her job, and as a regular user of both mobile phone and laptop, Charlotte is likely to be taking advantage of the new forms of communication (such as e-mails, text messages,) arising from modern information technology. ('Language and technology')

(b) Telephones have been around since the early twentieth century but the nature of this technology makes for conversations somewhat different from those conducted face to face. As illustrated in this example, we have developed specific **routines** for initiating, greeting and identification, and the absence of visual contexts and paralinguistic cues (or even the degraded audio quality) may affect the degree of explicitness, the way turn-taking is managed, and the need for greater-than-usual clarity.

Of course, in the context of this conversation, the way the interaction develops is determined by the fact that the customer expects a response to his concerns, whereas the role of the adviser is to represent the company and do what he can to satisfy the customer. In terms of status, the relationship is clearly an unequal one –

the adviser addresses the caller politely, as 'Mr Brown' and 'sir', while identifying himself as Adam. The adviser speaks only when it is clearly his turn, whereas at the end of the extract the customer cuts in and interrupts him. Advisers are trained to handle calls like this in a particular way – whatever they might personally feel about the caller, they have to enact a particular role and use language in the ways required by their employers. Underpinning the dialogue there are two distinct pragmatic meanings – (1) the customer wishes to express his annoyance with the company, and (2) the employee wishes to retain his business and goodwill. Therefore the adviser uses polite phrases such as 'How may I help you?', whereas the customer is blunt and casual ('I'm getting a bit fed up') and even resorts to sarcasm ('name, number and shoe size'). The adviser skilfully combines his requests for information with expressions of concern ('I'm very sorry') and reassurance ('I'm sure I'll be able to sort things out') to calm the customer's irritation. He also makes sympathetic noises as the customer starts to explain the problem ('mm', 'oh').

Whether the conversation would be any different if it was a male/female, female/male, or female/female interaction is highly debatable, though some evidence and intuition suggest that this might be the case. Our reaction to different accents does seem to be significant; call centres are often staffed by speakers with accents which surveys have suggested are perceived as 'friendly', whereas an RP accent is often seen as carrying authority.

Activity 2

(a) Text A is an example of an institutional switchboard message, its characteristic features largely dictated by the **occupational context** and the nature of the **technology** (telephone). The need for clarity, and absence of visual clues, impose obvious phonological requirements on the speaker, and the importance of greeting callers with an appropriate blend of friendliness and professionalism influences the choice of **accent** (RP for professional authority, with a hint of local accent for approachability) and lexis (formal in so far as it prefers 'require' to 'want', but very polite in its use of 'please' and 'thank you'). The pragmatic intent is presumably to create a favourable impression of friendly, polite efficiency. The choice of a female voice raises the question of **gender**; do callers perceive a female voice as more 'friendly' than a male voice? Might male and female callers respond differently?

In the conversation in text B, the symmetrical terms of address (first names) suggests an approximate equality of status and **power** although the relationship is complex; caller A, as a teacher, is notionally of a higher status than the technician B, but B's superior knowledge in this **occupational** area almost reverses this, and in seeking assistance A is careful to use a range of politeness features ('sorry to bother you ....') more usually associated with lower-status speakers. The influence of **technology** here is significant; not only does it follow many conventions of a telephone conversation but the subject matter refers to the ICT system, and the speakers share – to some extent – a knowledge of the technical lexis associated with it.

In text C the teacher's comments typify the way superior **power** or status is expressed in the right to evaluate the language of others. The text is a genre which is specific to a given **occupational context** – a teacher's evaluation of an academic assignment – and the writer's intention is to help the student improve without harming her self-confidence. This is directly reflected in the typical text structure: (1) positive point (2) things to improve (3) reassuring summary. The text is personalised by the use of the student's first name, but it is unlikely that the student would be able to reciprocate. The shared educational context enables the teacher to use several abbreviated references ('AOs').

Activity 4

(a) *Powerful individuals*: It would be surprising if you hadn't at least considered the Prime Minister and perhaps the Chancellor of the Exchequer as powerful individuals. You may have thought about the Queen, and then thought again – how much power does she really have these days? On the other hand, media giants such as Rupert Murdoch (owner of Sky and News International, which controls *The Times*, the *Sun* and the *News of the World*) clearly have tremendous influence, as does someone like Bill Gates, the owner of Microsoft, or leaders of big business and industry. You may also have decided that individual scientists, artists or even sporting figures exercise considerable power, although the influence of some of these – especially in the realms of popular culture – may be rather short-lived.

Powerful groups: The answers to these questions may at first seem obvious. People from non-white backgrounds are generally under-represented in professions where power and influence are to be found (politics, the law, business management, the media), as are women, despite some advances in their position in the past 30 years. On the face of it, the people who control large businesses (managers, directors) would seem to have more power than those who work in them, and people who work in key positions in the media may have more influence than those who merely consume their products. In the north/south debate, northerners often complain that people closest to the southern centres of political and economic power enjoy greater wealth and influence.

However, in all of these cases, you may have thought of some contexts where these 'official' power structures are reversed. In some contexts, women may have more power, or at least more influence; well-organised groups of workers may, in some circumstances, appear to have more power than their bosses; and it might be argued that consumers exert ultimate power over big business by being able to decide whether or not to buy their products. Some figures may have huge influence even though they are 'only' pop stars or footballers, and within a group of apparently 'equal' friends and peers, there may be one individual who enjoys more status and respect because he or she is more witty, attractive, confident, rebellious, or whatever. In other words, some kinds of power are 'official' or obvious (overt) and others more 'unofficial' or less obvious (covert).

Activity 6

Research suggests that we recognise a number of signs that a speaker is coming to the end of what she or he wants to say:

- *Paralinguistic cues*: the speaker's gestures, posture and eye contact may help us. For example, he or she may start to lean back in the seat, or sustain prolonged eye contact. Where this happens, it is likely that the person who receives the gaze will be the next speaker.

- *Phonetic and prosodic cues:* the speaker may pause, or intonation may indicate that he or she is approaching the end of an utterance. Undue hesitancy or non-fluency can therefore act as a turn-taking opportunity.
- *Syntactic cues*: we may recognise the approach of the end of a speaker's sentence.
- Nomination and direction: a speaker may explicitly identify the next speaker, as in 'Don't you think, Brian?'

Activity 7

(b) A's invitation includes some built-in protection in case of rejection. A suggests it is not a thing of huge importance – 'I was just wondering ....' – so can save face if the answer is 'no'. A also creates a trivial social pretext (having a drink) for the proposed date. The pause before B's reply is awkward. Long pauses are not easily tolerated in English speech – we experience tension and embarrassment when they occur. Here the pause has the effect of suggesting that B is desperately trying to come up with an excuse. Why not just say 'No', or even 'Look, I just don't fancy you'? Because we negotiate many situations involving proposal and acceptance/rejection in such a way as to protect the feelings of those involved. This is one aspect of what is sometimes called the 'politeness principle'.

Activity 8

(e) A starts by leading this part of the conversation, and at first B doesn't make a serious attempt to seize the floor or attempt to change the topic. B's first comments – 'oh', 'mm' and 'yeah' – are typical minimal responses, brief utterances that signal sympathetic encouragement and assure A that B is listening. However, A's speech shows some signs of non-fluency with two 2-second pauses and the breakdown of grammatical sense ('and (2) being (2) prejudging this bloke'), which prompts B to 'help out' by providing the supportive 'well that's all we can do'. However, by ending this turn with 'did he', a question tag, B in effect yields the floor back to A. A similar pattern can be seen in the next pair of turns. A pauses twice, but B refrains from interrupting, waiting instead until A seems to stumble over a phrase ('deputy's job'), which B helpfully suggests before giving way again. A is allowed to finish, and B adds the supportive agreement 'absolutely'. So B is certainly behaving in a very co-operative and helpful way, granting the floor and topic control to A, providing supportive minimal responses and even completing A's utterances when A seems to be stumbling.

Activity 11

At the start, Mandela uses the pronoun 'us' (a use of the first-person plural that he sustains) to unite himself with his audience, creating the sense of unity that is one of the key themes of the speech. It is a tremendously emotional and optimistically forward-looking speech, as it anticipates 'liberty' which he personifies as a newly born infant. He also uses a pair of words that are often found together – 'hope' and 'glory' – and repeats this idea later. In the third sentence he lists three aims to try to inspire his listeners – 'ordinary South

Africans' – to share the responsibilities for the future: to reinforce humanity's belief in justice, to strengthen its confidence in nobility etc., and to sustain all our hopes for a glorious life. Groups of three are oddly powerful in language, and are often to be found in persuasive texts.

As the speech moves on, his use of language becomes increasingly figurative, referring to South Africa as a body whose wounds are now to be healed, marred by chasms that need to be bridged and the bondage of poverty, deprivation, etc. As usual, the metaphors provide concrete images that express abstract ideas more vividly than the abstractions on their own, and when he talks of leading the country out of the 'valley of darkness', many of his listeners will be aware of the religious register of his language (and a reference to the Psalms of the Old Testament, in particular). The 'road' metaphor is frequently used, and compares the developments of an individual or country to a journey.

The speech builds to a climax with a series of repetitions that become very rhythmical. There are several 'let there be' statements (another echo from the Old Testament, here reminding listeners of another account of the creation of a 'new world' – in the story of Genesis, God says 'Let there be light'). This repetition of phrase or sentence structures is known as **parallelism**. Then there is the repeated 'never' – three times, once again – and the startling contrast between the image of the 'beautiful land' and the 'skunk' to which he compares a South Africa that was for many years shunned by the international community (skunks are shunned because of the vile smell they emit). The climax of the speech works through its simplicity and the shortness of its phrases, as well as the religious reference ('God bless Africa') and the final note of humility with which Mandela thanks his audience.

Activity 13

The specialist terms you have learned to use are likely to include 'technical' terms for specific objects and processes involved in the job. These may take the form of abbreviated words and phrases, or even acronyms – abbreviations consisting of the initial letters of the phrase they stand for. These terms are important for two obvious reasons: to enable fellow 'experts' to refer precisely and unambiguously to this item, and to save time and breath by reducing a complex phrase or expression to one or two words.

Forms of address will vary according to the 'management culture' of an organisation. In strictly **hierarchical cultures** (such as the armed forces), there may be strictly observed codes which define how members of the organisation address their immediate superiors and juniors – elsewhere, these practices (such as the use of first names and titles) may be more flexible, depending on the degree of informality in the workplace.

Any job that involves interaction with customers and clients is likely to involve some kind of adjustment to your 'normal' language style; some may engage you in very specific training for this (e.g. in telephone call centres), especially in regard to 'tricky' situations such as dealing with customer complaints. The unofficial **slang** you may share with colleagues may have an additional function, of course – it helps to bind you all together as a team, and may also humorously mock or undermine the 'official' culture. For example, catering staff may share a private 'code' to describe different types of customer according to their appearance, behaviour or likelihood (or otherwise) to tip generously.

Activity 15

(a) The consultant's conversational behaviour with the student is similar to many teacher/student interactions. He leads the **turn-taking** with a series of questions designed to test the student's knowledge rather than elicit information he lacks himself. His responses may seem a little brusque, as he almost cuts her off on a couple of occasions, and they include some evaluative comments (good...right...).as well as a hint of sarcasm at the end. For her part, the student seems a little hesitant at times after her initial, presumably well-rehearsed case-diagnosis, and one or two non-fluency features appear later in the transcript.

(b) Perhaps most notable is the way in which the medical professionals discuss the patient's condition in the third person even though he is present. This even extends to a description of his personal characteristics (pleasant, overweight) admissible here as they may have some bearing on his condition and treatment. Only after a lengthy preamble does the consultant actually turn to the patient and address him directly. In most contexts this would be considered inappropriate and rude – clearly, the usual politeness principles are suspended here.

Then there is the nature of the medical jargon itself; there is the use of specific terms for his condition – fibrosing alvulitis, eschemic. They permit economical and precise communication between professionals, though they probably have the inadvertent effect of excluding the patient himself from the discussion of his own complaint.

A note about ***etymology****: many specialist scientific terms have Latin or Greek origins – for example, vasculitis = inflammation of a blood vessel; derived from* vas*, Latin for a fluid-carrying duct +* cul *= a diminutive suffix +* itis *= inflammation*

(d) By contrast, when addressing the patient directly, the consultant reverts to a non-specialist register such as 'pain hasn't gone cold or anything' and allows himself at one point to be cut off by the patient.

Activity 16

(a) There are a couple of things to note here. Most obvious is the use of **initialised acronyms** (like BRIBUD, GLM, GTI and GIGO) standing for much longer phrases. As with the medical jargon of the doctors, this clearly allows for very economical reference to complex systems, and at the same time appears to create a kind of code which is impenetrable to outsiders. The 'GIGO situation' is interesting as a reference to the computer-related saying, 'Garbage in Garbage out' – in other words, what you get out of any IT system is only as good as the data that you put in (or input). The other notable feature here is the tendency to use extended **noun phrases** like *budgetary control information reports* and *live contracting information* which consist of a string of qualifying terms before the main noun – a feature known as **multiple pre-modification.**

(b) Pragmatically, it is far from clear who is the senior partner here, or whether one person is in any sense 'blaming' another. A seems to **control the agenda** by announcing *there are a couple of things that I think we need to discuss*, but **hedges** this apparently dominating remark with *I think*. The **empty discourse marker** *actually* may be a warning that these 'things' represent 'issues'. A continues to control the agenda by itemising these – *first is this issue....* Indeed, 'Issue' has become widely used to refer euphemistically to all sorts of problems/ errors/ conflicts in the workplace. After confirming B's request for clarification, A continues to hedge *(I think)* and offers a diagnosis – '*our feeder systems'*. However, B's response of '*we're going to have to watch that*' itself begins to sound almost like a reprimand, and A again resorts to the hedges of *I think* and a*ctually* to disagree somewhat with their colleague. B echoes these hedges whilst implicitly suggesting that a third party (Ewan) may have relevant information.

Activity 17

(a) At first the language of the surgeons seems to be remarkably vague, compared to the extreme precision of the medical language we saw earlier. *A big one* or *a holey one* do not appear to be very technical terms for items of surgical equipment! Then, we may be surprised to hear that the latest football scores would be a suitable topic of conversation as we are being subjected to the surgeon's knife! Finally, more imprecision (precisely which body parts are *those bits*?!) and worse, the grisly cannibalistic humour of *taking them home for tea*!

(b) If we assume that this operation is a relatively straightforward one, perhaps we should not be too surprised that the surgeons are capable of carrying out the procedure whilst discussing other things – it is possible, after all, to chew gum and walk down the street at the same time. Besides, the phatic nature of the banter between the surgeons no doubt helps to develop a relaxed working relationship between colleagues. Neither should we be too shocked by the 'black' humour; professionals who deal with life-and-death issues on a daily basis inevitably develop a humorous 'safety valve'.

Activity 20

(a) As a title, 'Master' is relatively rare, being confined to rather formal use when applied to young boys. It has a rather old-fashioned upper-class connotation too, as it might have been used by a domestic servant when addressing the young man of a wealthy household. It may have struck you that in its other forms – to 'master an art', or to 'achieve mastery', or to 'be masterful', it implies command and authority. 'Miss', on the other hand, applies not just to young girls but to women who are unmarried. Even mature women may be described as 'Miss', but not always with positive connotations. So although we have a pair of words that appear to be symmetrical, in fact their usage and connotations are quite different. We call such a difference **semantic asymmetry**.

(b) and **(c)** The title taken by adult women ('Miss' or 'Mrs') reveals their marital status, something that men do not reveal when entitling themselves 'Mr'. Women are thus defined in terms of their relationship to a man, reflecting their lack of social, economic or personal independence in former times. For this reason, the term 'Ms' was coined as an optional equivalent to the male 'Mr'. However, it is by no means universally used or accepted, and is derided by some as the choice of adult women with feminist inclinations.

(d) No doubt you know that English offers a rich source of unpleasant insults to be applied to women – many of which attack them for suggestions of sexual impropriety ('slag', 'slut', 'slapper' etc). Few such terms are available for abusing promiscuous men, though some, such as 'tart', are beginning to be applied to males in an ironic way. The absence of words to insult promiscuous men is an example of what is called a **lexical gap** – an area of experience or meaning for which the language does not seem to supply a suitable word.

(e) While 'manager' and 'manageress' appear to describe the same job, in practice there are differences. Would we expect the female boss of a major international company to be called the manageress? Probably not. Actually, the term 'manageress' seems to be reserved for lower-status managerial positions, reflecting an expectation that women would not occupy the very top jobs. The morpheme '-ess' also draws our attention to the gender of the person in an explicit way, which the term 'manager' does not, as is the case with 'author' and 'authoress'. Another way of putting this is to say that the female is the **marked** form.

'Father' and 'mother' seem unproblematic enough as nouns, but when we think about their use as verbs ('he fathered three children' and 'she mothered him somewhat'), we discover very different connotations. Fathering is a rather proud act of reproduction which ends with conception. Mothering begins after the birth, and can have connotations of unhealthy protectiveness and smothering.

'Lord' and 'Lady' also reveal an asymmetry in their wider use. 'To lord it' over someone implies authority, status and assertiveness, reflecting the original social and economic power that a 'lord' enjoyed; however, we cannot say 'to lady it' over someone – 'ladies' don't assert or enforce power; to be 'ladylike' implies a quiet gentility that is in keeping with traditional stereotypes of gracious feminine behaviour. 'Master' we have already touched on; the apparently opposite term 'mistress' has very different connotations, of course. A married man involved in an extra-marital affair may have a mistress, but a married woman in a similar situation is not said to have 'taken a master'.

Activity 21

When this test was given to a group of Year 11 school students, the most common choices were 'he' for numbers 1 and 3 and 'she' for 2. Some students spotted the trick, of course, and suggested 'he or she' or 's/he', but the majority assumption was clear. The term 'engineer' is apparently a gender-free term – there is no single word meaning 'female engineer' – but it seems to contain an invisible male marking. 'Nurse' works in the opposite way, so much so that the term 'male nurse' is often used in the same way as people can sometimes be heard referring to a 'lady doctor'; the term 'doctor' is felt to imply maleness. In fact the term 'doctoress' was in use until the nineteenth century. So it seems that our language often encodes historical assumptions about gender roles and the occupations that men and women follow.

Activity 22

The 'chairman' issue is still unresolved. Although its use is generic, as with the other examples in the list the word nevertheless encodes an assumption that the person in question – here, the most powerful person on a committee – must be male. Nowadays, if the chairman is a woman, we may feel this to be a contradiction. Nevertheless, 'chairwoman' is not widely used as it uses a female-marked gender form and thus seems to draw attention to the gender of the person in a way that 'chairman' does not. 'Chairperson' is unwieldy, and as with other cases where 'person' has been substituted for 'man', has been the butt of jokes about 'political correctness'. 'Chair' may be the best alternative as it already exists as a verb ('to chair a meeting'), but its use is by no means universal.

Similar objections apply to many of the other examples. 'Fireman' has now been replaced by the generic 'firefighter' as a job title, 'foreman' is just as likely to be 'supervisor', and 'manning' is just as easily referred to as 'staffing'.

Activity 24

(a) Throughout the text, the genders have been reversed; that is, all of Tom's actions, speech and thoughts have been attributed to Virginia, and vice versa. To restore the original text, simply substitute 'Tom' for 'Virginia' (and vice versa) and reverse all the he/him she/her references. ('Rosy' was originally 'Ross'.)

Activity 26

(b) Jennifer Coates writes in her book *Women, Men and Language*:

> What effects do such violations of normal turn-taking in conversation have? It seems that after overlaps and especially after interruptions, speakers tend to fall silent. Since most interruptions are produced by men in mixed-sex conversations, the speaker who falls silent is usually a woman. Silence is often a sign of malfunction in conversation. These silences resulted not just from interruptions and overlaps, but also from delayed minimal responses. In mixed-sex conversations male speakers often delayed their minimal responses, signalling a lack of interest in the speaker's topic.
>
> When talking with women, men seem to use interruptions and delayed minimal responses to deny women the right to control the topic of conversation. Men disobey the normal turn-taking rules in order to control topics.

However, many researchers would now take issue both with the methods used in this experiment and Coates's rather simplistic conclusions – see part **(c)** of the Activity.

Activity 29

While it may be true that most newsreaders are university-educated, it is unlikely that they all grew up speaking RP, so the 'schools' explanation is likely to be the least significant one. The 'understanding' explanation seems more attractive: after all, RP is widely used and understood, and is associated with clarity of delivery. However, programmes such as *EastEnders* and *Coronation Street* regularly top the popularity ratings, and even the weather reports that precede or follow news bulletins are often delivered by speakers with regional accents. Does this mean that we spend our time watching soap operas and weather forecasts that we can barely understand? No; rather, as Giles's study suggests, it is because RP is associated in our culture with intelligence, authority and education. We are more likely to believe that the news is truthful and to be taken seriously if it is delivered in RP than if it were spoken in, say, a Liverpudlian accent. Ultimately, this is linked to the stereotypes commonly associated with people from different regions and different social backgrounds. The weather is a different matter, as it is less 'serious' than the news, and soap operas are, of course, fictional.

Activity 31

Among the many possible reasons, perhaps you included these:

- the mass media (TV, press) are produced for national and international consumption
- printed texts have to be written for universal understanding and consumption – it would be impractical to produce different versions of the same books in different dialects
- electronic communications reach not just across the UK but (via the Internet) the world
- we now belong to a very mobile community of English speakers – many of us travel frequently for business and pleasure
- English is a world language and foreign learners need to have one version to learn.

Activity 32

Perhaps you suggested that it was important to the children to use the language of their friends and fit in with them, rather than use the standard forms – an example of the **covert prestige** of non-standard forms in action. Turning to the second question, children need to be able to use Standard English to gain qualifications and function effectively in a print-orientated society. Even in speech, non-standard English is often seen as 'poor' or 'incorrect' and may present an unfavourable impression if used in formal or professional contexts. The counter-argument is that children can understand the need to use Standard English when necessary, but should not be discouraged from using regional speech in informal contexts where it is perfectly acceptable. Besides, it is impossible for schools to tell children how to speak in the playground or among friends.

Activity 35

(b) It would not be surprising if you decided that none of these expressions was 'good' grammar; by definition, none of them belongs to the grammatical structures of Standard English and therefore, in many people's eyes, they are not correct or proper English. Whereas people seem happy to accept that dialects preserve an interesting lexical diversity, the view has taken root that dialect grammar is a corruption of 'proper' English grammar, and that thousands of people in a particular region must somehow be making grammatical 'mistakes' whenever they speak.

However, this is a misguided view. No less than its lexis, a dialect's grammatical system is rooted in that dialect's history – and far from being incorrect or corrupt versions of what we now know as Standard English, dialects have enjoyed a parallel development to the prestige variety of the language. As you will learn in your A2 course, the notion of Standard English that emerged gradually from the fifteenth to the eighteenth centuries was based largely on the speech of those who happened to enjoy some education, influence and power in the south-east of England. By the eighteenth century a clear notion of 'correctness' established itself, with the effect that other dialects were increasingly castigated as inferior or uneducated.

(c) All speakers sometimes make mistakes in their language use – slips of the tongue, minor grammatical errors, sentences getting muddled up, and so on – but it would be remarkable if thousands of speakers were simultaneously and consistently making the same mistakes, which is what statement (1) seems to imply. The examples given are themselves part of the grammatical system of the local dialect, rather than 'mistakes'. Neither is it true to say that non-standard varieties are all derived from a superior, standard version of the language. Many of the dialects we now speak can be traced back to the centuries before the Norman conquest, when Anglo Saxon and Norse tribes first arrived in Britain from different parts of Germany and Scandinavia. Many distinctive Yorkshire and north-eastern dialect expressions, for example, owe their origins to the presence of the Vikings. So statement (3) offers the most accurate description here.

Activity 36

There seems to be a marked difference between male and female speakers, especially within the lower middle class. Researchers have reported that more than a quarter of males use a particular accent feature, whereas only a tiny minority of females do so. Of course, what you expected to find would depend on your individual observations and speculation. Many people do report, however, an anecdotal perception that boys and men are more likely to talk with a stronger, more pronounced regional accent than their female counterparts. There is considerable speculation and disagreement about the reasons for this. One argument is that local accents tend to be associated with working-class life, which is also identified with 'tough' masculine qualities. Female speakers are therefore less likely to identify with such values; a male speaker with a strong accent may be described as 'tough', whereas men may describe a woman with a similar accent as 'rough' or unfeminine. Another theory is that traditional working-class social networks based on the workplace serve to 'bond' men more closely than women, and that regional speech becomes one of the ways in which men signal the fact that they belong to this group. Other explanations focus on women's alleged sensitivity to the importance of social mobility and a greater anxiety to make a favourable social impression. Needless to say, many of these speculations have proved highly controversial.

Activity 37

(a) The figures from Cheshire's study seem to confirm that males are more likely to prefer the non-standard, lower-prestige form than females within the same social class. Interestingly, the researcher tried to relate individuals' use of these dialect forms to their perceived toughness in the eyes of their peers. Sure enough, the boys who used most of the dialectal forms also emerged as those with a high 'toughness' rating. We might conclude that the covert prestige of the dialect seems to be strongest among male speakers because of its association with desirable masculine attributes such as toughness, aggression and even rebelliousness.

Activity 38

You were probably correct in your deduction – it was indeed the East Midlands dialect, spoken in the area including Oxford and Cambridge as well as London, that became the model. After all, this was the dialect used by anyone with power and influence – the court, the church and the printing industry. The dialect we now respectfully see as 'correct' English became so not because it was in any sense a 'purer' or 'better' version of English, but simply because it was the language of power.

Activity 43

The main benefits of mobile-phone technology suggested in the quotations are:

- the ability to make spontaneous arrangements 'on the move'
- they allow people who might be 'shy' in face-to-face contexts to communicate freely
- they have actually **increased** the amount of **phatic** communication that goes on – thus extending and intensifying our social relationships.

On the other hand:

- mobile phones have created the need for a new set of 'good manners'. The act of visibly switching off a phone can send strong signals to the person you are with that they have your undivided attention! On the other hand, if the person you are with seems more concerned to continue a conversation with someone else (via texting or otherwise) this can appear insulting and disrespectful

- because it is so easy to make a call or send a text, these communications may be valued less by the recipients than more traditional methods that require a little more effort
- there is no substitute for face-to-face interaction.

Activity 44

The host of *6.06* mainly conforms to the presenter-as-friendly-host model. After a brisk caller identification (using first names and regional origin) and phatic exchange, he cues the caller to make his point, allowing him to do so without interruption. It is clear AG disagrees with the caller, but he expresses this with due observance of politeness, hedging his disagreement with 'I'm sorry...' and 'I mean I thought ... you know'. The easy familiarity of first-name address contributes to the sense of friendly disagreement. Again, the host allows the caller to 'hold the floor' at length when making his point about Alan Shearer – it is notable that the caller's speech includes some non-fluency and dialectal features. Again, the host hedges his diagreement with 'Well Tommy ... I've got to say' and 'I'm really surprised to hear you say that'. The call is skilfully brought to an end by the host; he turns what could have been the caller's attempt to open up a new conversational topic ('I'd love to see Steve Bruce at the toon') into the first part of a closing sequence ('might happen at some point in the future') and without pausing at the sentence boundary (which might have been seen by the caller as a cue to come back) moves on directly to 'thanks for your call' and the swift closing exchange.

The 'shock jock' of the second transcript, by contrast, does not hedge what looks like his contempt for the caller at all. His minimal responses ('yeah') offer only the barest encouragement to the caller to continue, though she is obviously not very confident about doing so, and his repeated questions of 'why are you a mess' are blunt to the point of rudeness. For her part, the caller seems to disregard the usual protocol regarding swearing on air – she seems to accept the fiction that she is participating in a confidential 1-2-1 as opposed to be being overheard by thousands of listeners. Eventually the host draws attention to her bad language, but in the form of an implied insult – 'can't you speak without swearing' – shortly followed by the kind of direct attack that would be rare in a face-to-face conversations with a complete stranger – 'you're a mess certainly'. This seems to have the desired effect of provoking a conflict with the caller – presumably one source of 'entertainment' the programme's producers are aiming to provide.

Activity 46

The **narrative** and **spatial orientation** functions are clearly paramount for radio, and – you might think – largely redundant for television. Player **identification**, however, may still be necessary for some sports on TV; less so for 'close-up' 1-2-1 sports like snooker where the proximity of the players to the camera enables viewers to see for themselves, more so in football or rugby where more players are involved in distance shots. For both media, the additional functions of **empathy**, **stimulus** and **analysis** are desirable, though we might guess that there is more room for these on TV, freed as it is from the need to maintain a moment-by-moment narrative of the action.

Activity 47

The radio commentary is virtually continuous, with only the briefest of micropauses between utterances; the pauses in the action (such as the goalkeeper's clearance and the corner kick here) are filled with analysis and/or contextual information; any significant break in the commentary may cause listeners to wonder if there has been a loss of signal/transmission. So, as the Chelsea goalkeeper prepares to clear the ball, Commentator 2 (the analysis specialist) seizes the opportunity of a break in play for a brief evaluative comment. The presence of some non-fluency features distinguishes his contribution from that of the principal match commentator.

The TV commentator also exploits the lull in play to remind viewers about the 'playercam' option, but it is clear from what follows that longer pauses can be sustained on TV and the commentators clearly don't feel the need to describe every action – indeed the TV commentator describes none of the action involving Joe Cole's run during the phase of play that produces Chelsea's corner. There's a certain amount of player identification in both cases, though more so on the radio commentary, which notes the names of four players involved in the build-up to the corner. This is part of the ongoing narrative on radio – conducted largely present-tense verb forms (*Cole's turning well . . . he's got Rise and Warnock around him)* and with a high degree of spatial orientation (*on the right-hand side . . . over on the right-hand side of the field* etc.). On TV, the interaction between commentator and pundit more closely resembles 'normal' conversational patterns, with more closely connected turn-taking (as with the way C1 immediately picks up C2's comment about zonal marking) and even spontaneous back-channel feedback such as C1's 'mm'.

Lexically and semantically, the commentaries have some things in common: a significant proportion of proper nouns, of course, arising from the identification function, and a variety of semi-specialist terms from the semantic field of football – 'turning', 'corner', 'midfield', 'zonal marking' etc.

Grammatically and phonologically, the very sudden burst of action that produces the goal makes great demands on the radio commentator – producing both an explosive increase in the dynamics and tempo of his speech and considerable economy of expression, as with the ellipsis in *Header down and turned in by Gallas*. The fast-moving action means he has to provide spatial/orientation information after the event, using past-tense forms (*William Gallas was there no more than three yards out*). The TV commentary, by contrast, under less pressure to provide a full visual description, is able to reflect the sudden threat in a rhetorically skilful pair of **parallel sentences** (*it cost them against Manchester Utd . . . and it might cost them here . . .*), even followed up by a balanced antithesis (*for 30 minutes . . . it was Liverpool's game . . . in the thirty-fifth minute it's Chelsea's lead*).

Activity 48

Opportunities	Restrictions	Better than a call	Not as good as a call
• enables people throughout the world to stay in contact round the clock • allows for almost instantaneous conversations to take place in real time • communications can be discreet and conducted wherever there is a signal • multi-function key-pads allow access to alphabet, numbers, punctuation and icons • much cheaper than phone calls • much quicker than a letter • unlike e-mail, does not require 'logging on' to a computer	• messages are limited to a finite number of characters • multi-function key-pads can be awkward to use – switching between upper/lower case and selection of punctuation marks can be time-consuming and 'fiddly' • speed of use only comes with practice and experience • some forms of short-hand developed by individual users may not be universally intelligible	• cheaper • as with writing, can be planned, corrected & edited before sending • less exposure to possible embarrassment in the case of tricky, sensitive – or even flirtatious messages?	• response may be instant or deferred • severe limitation on how much can be said in one message • absence of 'live' feedback from recipient

This module counts for **30%** of the AS qualification, or **15%** of the total A level marks.

ASSESSMENT OBJECTIVES

The skills and knowledge that you develop in this module, and which you will be required to demonstrate in your coursework folder, are defined by the examination board's Assessment Objectives. These require that you:

- **AO1**: communicate clearly the knowledge, understanding and insight appropriate to the study of language, using appropriate terminology and accurate and coherent written expression
(5 out of the 30 marks for the Unit; 5% of the final AS mark; $2^1/_2$% of the final A Level mark)

- **AO2**: demonstrate expertise and accuracy in writing for a variety of specific purposes and audiences, drawing on knowledge of linguistic features to explain and comment on choices made
(20 out of the 30 marks for the Unit; 20% of the final AS mark; 10% of the final A Level mark)

- **AO4**: understand, discuss and explore concepts and issues relating to language in use
(5 out of the 30 marks for the Unit; 5% of the final AS mark; $2^1/_2$% of the final A Level mark)

What this module is all about

In this module, you have the opportunity to apply your growing knowledge about and understanding of texts to some writing of your own. As this is a coursework module, it also allows you to develop pieces of writing over a period of time, redrafting and refining them until they are as good as you can make them.

The **basic requirements** for your coursework folder are as follows:

- Two pieces of your own writing totalling between 1500 and 3000 words. The choice of subject matter of the pieces is entirely open.

- The two pieces should be for distinctly **different** primary purposes.

- The pieces should also achieve a variety in their intended audiences and **genres**.

- The two pieces need to be accompanied by **commentaries** of up to 1500 words in which you explain, justify and evaluate your own writing.

Some aspects of this work may appear familiar from the kinds of writing you did as part of your GCSE coursework; in some important respects, however, Original

Writing presents you with a different kind of challenge from GCSE. It is designed to lay the foundations for Module 5, Editorial Writing, which is part of the A2 English Language course.

In addition, this module provides opportunities to meet several of the requirements for Key Skills Communication Level 3, as it involves reading and synthesising (C3.2) and the production of two documents, at least one of which will be 'extended' (C3.3). If you decide to produce the script for a talk or presentation, you can also satisfy the requirement for C3.1b.

ACTIVITY 1

Some of the key features of Original Writing are summed up in the following table. Answer the questions in the third column, either through discussion or in writing.

Key concept	Explanation	Discussion issue
Produce **real** texts for **real** purposes	You are aiming to produce texts that could fulfil a purpose and find a market in the world beyond the classroom. This means writing material that 'real' people – not just your teacher – would either need or want to read or hear. The texts you write must be much more than mere writing exercises.	How far was this true of the writing assignments in your GCSE English course? Suggest examples of assignments which either met, or did not meet, this condition.
Aim for **professional and publishable** standards	Your aim should be to produce texts which would be worthy of serious consideration for publication. This means that the control of expression, tone, style and technical accuracy should be of a significantly higher standard than at GCSE. 'Publication' may, of course, include local outlets such as student magazines, local newspapers, fanzines and websites, as well as more ambitious media like national newspapers and magazines.	Find out if anyone you know has had writing published in any form. How did they go about it? What was involved in the process?
Writing should be underpinned by **key language concepts** from Modules 1 and 2	You should consciously make links between your writing and the knowledge about language you have gained in Modules 1 and 2. This is your chance to apply theories about language in use to your own practical writing. There may even be opportunities to turn a piece work carried out as part of your work on Modules 1 and 2 into an Original Writing submission.	Brainstorm any 10 ways in which the work you have done so far on Modules 1 and 2 might relate to your own work as a producer of texts.

<table>
<tr><th>Key concept</th><th>Explanation</th><th>Discussion issue</th></tr>
<tr><td>Writing should be a developmental process</td><td>You should expect to draft and re-draft your work several times, taking on board the editorial advice of your teacher and fellow students and testing the piece on 'guinea pig' readers typical of your target audience.</td><td>Suggest 5 reasons why this process is going to be necessary.</td></tr>
<tr><td>Commentaries should be self-critical and reflective</td><td>The process of writing involves making choices of structure and style, and as you work on your writing and apply your growing understanding of language, you should become increasingly reflective, and analytical about your own work. This is where the commentaries come in; in fact, these count for one-third of the total marks for this module. Watch out for the 'Commentary tips' throughout this module; they will flag up many of the writing issues you should discuss.</td><td>Start by defining for yourself your strengths and weaknesses as a writer.</td></tr>
<tr><td>Research and study model texts</td><td>Nobody produces texts in a vacuum. If you are aiming to write a particular type of text, it makes sense first of all to carry out a study of texts of a similar type to understand the usual conventions and expectations of the genre. You can then try to make your text use these creatively. Such examples are known as style models.</td><td rowspan="2">Consider these two points together. How far do they contradict one other?</td></tr>
<tr><td>Writing should be original</td><td>The pieces you submit are not likely to be the same as that of other students in your class – the best work usually arises not from class exercises set by the teacher but from individual writing projects which reflect your own interests. To some extent, your own work should have a distinctive style and voice.

Important note: It is essential that the work you submit is your own; material which is reproduced from other sources (such as the Internet) could cause you to be disqualified.</td></tr>
<tr><td>Not all writing is 'literary'</td><td>You may like to include some 'literary' writing – a genre of fiction, drama, or even poetry – as part of your submission, but the emphasis on the course as a whole is not on the kinds of writing you would study as part of an English Literature course.</td><td>List some genres of writing which might be described as non-literary.</td></tr>
</table>

Producing your texts

Much of your work in Module 1 focused on the various influences which help determine what texts are like, and how these contextual factors – especially **audience, purpose, genre** and **medium** – shape the way language is used in a given situation. In particular the **structure, register, tone** and **style** of the text are influenced by these factors.

As you create your own pieces of writing, you need to ask the same questions, and eventually answer these questions in the accompanying commentaries.

'Primary purposes' of texts

A cautionary note: in this module we will organise our investigation of Original Writing according to the four primary purposes introduced in Module 1 (see page 15):

- to inform
- to instruct
- to entertain
- to persuade.

However, as you have already discovered in Module 1, it is important to remember many texts have multiple purposes and that it is not always easy to define which one is primary. The important issue when you eventually choose your two pieces to submit is that they are significantly different in purpose from each other – but any one piece may have two or more purposes, as the following examples illustrate.

ACTIVITY 2

Listed below are several types of text which may be attractive options for individual Original Writing tasks. Use a table like this one to note how far they fulfil the different purposes indicated, and decide which of the purposes is *primary*.

Text	Purposes	Comment
A review of a concert or film	Inform, entertain or persuade?	
A guide to a particular town or holiday resort	Inform or persuade?	
An article about a musician or a footballer in a lifestyle magazine	Entertain or inform?	

Text	Purposes	Comment
A story written for children	Entertain or persuade?	
A website devoted to a musician or celebrity	Entertain, inform, persuade or instruct?	
The script for a TV 'food and drink' programme, including recipes	Instruct or entertain?	
An audio guide given to visitors to an exhibition or historic site	Instruct, inform or entertain?	
The script of a satirical TV/radio show, such as Alistair McGowan's *Big Impression*	Entertain or persuade?	

Commentary tip

When reflecting on your writing, acknowledge and explain that it may have primary and secondary purposes. Go on to discuss how these are reflected in the language you have used.

As you work through this module, you will have the opportunity of attempting several different pieces of writing before finally choosing two pieces which you will develop fully as your own individual writing submission. Whatever kinds of writing you attempt, here are some hints which may help you to become a better writer.

Good writing practice

- To be a good writer you need to be a **reader** – so make sure you read plenty of different kinds of writing in newspapers, magazines and the media generally.
- Good writing is anything that communicates effectively with its intended audience – so as you read, consider the different ways in which writers of different texts communicate (e.g. *The Guardian*, *NME*, *Just 17*, Radio 1, Radio 4).
- As you browse and read, you may come across items of particular interest which may be the seed of a writing idea. Keep a **scrapbook** for such items.
- You might want to keep a separate notebook or **writer's log** – paper-based or electronic – or use the back of your scrapbook for scribbling down ideas for pieces of writing. These may strike you at any time, so keep your log handy!

- Writing is a skill you can improve only through regular practice – so try to **write frequently**. Use your notebook to scribble down reflections, observations or accounts of experiences. Use it as a diary if you like – and don't discard or delete anything! It may come in useful one day – especially for writing your commentaries (see pages 226–7 below).

Writing to inform

There are many different kinds of texts in different media whose primary purpose is to inform, even though there may well also be elements of entertainment, instruction and persuasion involved.

In every case, for the informative writing to be successful, there needs to be:

- something a group of people need or want to know
- a writer able to fill this gap by providing the relevant information
- an appropriate form or medium which enables the writer to reach his or her audience
- a shared language which the writer can use so as to make the information accessible to the audience.

Activity 3

(a) For each of the contexts given here, complete the missing details by considering either **who** needs to know (target audience), **what** they need to know (subject/information) or via which **media** they can best be reached.

(b) Collect or make a note of texts similar in kind to those listed.

Context *Where/when?*	**Target audience** *Who needs to know?*	**Subject/information** *What do they need to know?*	**Media/genres** *How can the audience best be reached?*
Your school or college	Students in the institution	How to choose and apply to a university	Tutorial presentation Pamphlet/handouts Intranet site
School	Year 11s thinking of studying A levels	What studying A level English Language is like	
Teenage girls' magazine	Girls aged 12–16		Magazine article
Tourist information	Visitors to your area		
Current affairs magazine	Adult non-scientists with a general interest	How cloning works	

Context *Where/when?*	**Target audience** *Who needs to know?*	**Subject/information** *What do they need to know?*	**Media/genres** *How can the audience best be reached?*
Local museum/ exhibition	Visitors to the museum	The subject of the exhibition; background information to explain the items displayed	
Local Health Authority campaign		How to be protected against flu this winter	

(c) Collect and add to the table your own list of informative texts, both spoken and written. These may include:

- news/sports reports and articles in various kinds of newspapers and magazines and on radio
- pamphlets, leaflets and hand-outs
- text books
- CD ROMs
- radio/tape reports
- different kinds of talks and presentations
- websites
- popular encyclopaedias (e.g. David Crystal's *Cambridge Encyclopaedia of the English Language*, CUP)
- 'part works' (weekly or monthly instalment-based reference magazines on a variety of subjects; those launched in 2003 included one series devoted entirely to miniature teapots!)
- posters and wall charts
- factual books aimed at younger readers (e.g. *Horrible Histories*, published by Eaglemoss Publications).

As you begin to look closely at your examples of informative writing, the most important question to ask is: How does each text bridge the **'information gap'** in a way that suits the intended audience?

Activity 4

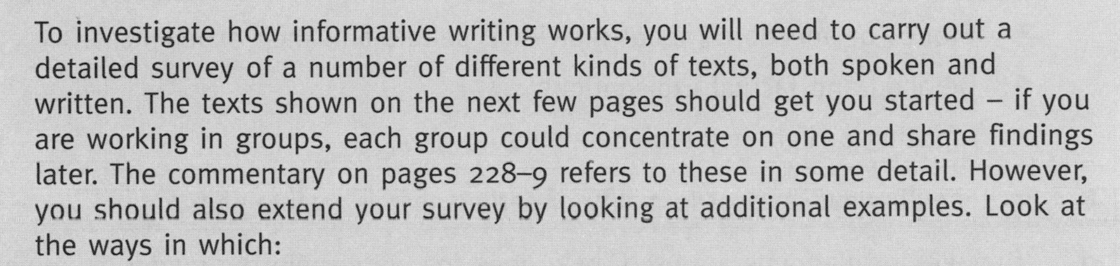

To investigate how informative writing works, you will need to carry out a detailed survey of a number of different kinds of texts, both spoken and written. The texts shown on the next few pages should get you started – if you are working in groups, each group could concentrate on one and share findings later. The commentary on pages 228–9 refers to these in some detail. However, you should also extend your survey by looking at additional examples. Look at the ways in which:

- factual material is presented to younger readers in the *Horrible Histories* series
- travel writers/journalists describe their experiences of holiday destinations in the travel sections of newspapers
- technical or scientific material is presented to a non-specialist audience in newspaper supplements such as *Guardian Education.*

For each of the texts you survey, try to answer the following questions:

	Key question
1	How does the writer 'hook' the audience and convince them that they need or ought to be interested in what follows?
2	How is the information organised and structured, and how easy is it for the reader/listener to follow? Look out for the use of section headings, panels, boxes, bullet points and sub-headings in written texts.
3	For audio texts, what use is made of different voices, music and sound effects (SFX), and how are the listeners made aware of the structure of the text (the equivalent of headings and sub-headings)?
4	What does the writer of the text seem to assume about the audience and their interest in or knowledge of the topic? How can you tell?
5	How does the writer refer to people, places, films, TV programmes, etc, and what does this say about the assumptions made about the audience? For example, if an article refers to 'Paris', does it simply say 'Paris', or 'Paris, the capital of France', or 'a city in France called Paris', or even 'a big city in a country called France'?
6	Identify any specialist or technical terms introduced. How, if at all, are they explained?
7	Consider the following types of information that might appear in an informative text. What are the proportions of each in the texts you are examining? • Facts and figures. • Diagrams, images and charts.

Key question	
	• Stories or anecdotes about individual people and their experiences. • Detailed and factual explanations. • Amusing or light-hearted comments.
8	In general, what level of formality or seriousness is maintained?
9	If images or diagrams are used, how does the writer help the reader make sense of them?
10	Does the text directly address the reader or listener using the second-person pronoun ('you'), and if so with what effect?
11	Does the text use either the first-person singular 'I', or the plural 'we'? This is rare in information texts. What might be the reasons for these choices?
12	How far does the text also fulfil an instructive, entertaining or persuasive function?

TEXT A

TEN WAYS TO FILL THE GAP

CREATIVE OPTIONS FOR TAKING A YEAR OUT

1 CASH IN HAND

First things first - let's earn some money! Your year could start at home, working round the clock, saving like mad to finance any travel planned for later on. Alternatively, you can combine job & adventure by working abroad. Follow the French *vendange* as the grapes ripen, work the winter season as a waiter in a Swiss ski resort; spend the summer as a courier on the Spanish coast . . . Elizabeth worked in hotels in Germany, Switzerland and France, interspersed with travel around Europe and Canada: *My year out financed itself completely, with money to do some travelling I couldn't otherwise have done.*

Iain worked in Curry's in order to finance a trip to Australia; Jacci stacked shelves for 7 months at Tesco to pay for an expedition to Indonesia. Both feel that it was more than worth it. Rachel was doing hotel work when her luck was in one Saturday; her £10,000 share of a lottery win went to fund voluntary work and some travel.

If you see the gap as a chance to gain work experience, perhaps leading to sponsorship or a future career, then you could apply for an industrial or commercial placement, where you'll do real work for a real salary. Henry spent most of his year on a feasibility study for Shell: *It was meaningful and relevant work, and valuable experience for someone about to start a degree in engineering.*

○ **Where to find out more** (see ***Resources***)
- *Working Holidays*: short-term/seasonal work
- *A Year Between*: work placements and more
- *Workplace*: work experience options

Gain new skills, develop existing ones, broaden horizons. The gap year is a rare chance to stand back, assess where life has brought you so far, and seize the freedom to take on a different challenge.

4 VOLUNTEER!

Maybe you would like to contribute something to society by working as a volunteer, though this demands commitment, not just an urge to see the world with a bit of work thrown in. There are thousands of projects to choose from; most gap year placements are in Europe or America, rather than the Third World. Development projects need those with specialist skills and experience, though there are openings helping less privileged members of your own society. Overseas placements are an educational experience as well as a period of service; you may have to pay a fee and cover your own travel expenses to offset any costs to the host community.

Jo worked on a project building village health centres in Tanzania: *Definitely a beneficial experience, working in a team, getting first-hand experience of life in a developing country. I learned Swahili, saw the way of life in rural Africa and came back with greater awareness and self-confidence.*

Jayne volunteered for 6 months at a hostel for homeless people: *I found myself in an environment that was often challenging, frequently confronted with new situations. I'd recommend voluntary service as a way of discovering your expectations and uncovering problems that exist in society.*

○ **Where to find out more** (see ***Resources***)
- *Working Holidays*: short-term projects
- *A Year Between*: volunteering in a year out
- *Volunteer Work*: for those with experience

(continued)

GLOBE TROTTING 2

Travel to far flung corners on a Round-The-World (RTW) ticket, stop off for an overland trek, a spot of river-rafting or lazy days on the beach. Take a tour round Europe: sample sunlit Italy or explore Scandinavia. RTW air tickets can be tailor-made; route combinations are endless, restricted only by the time and money you have available. Keep going in the same direction; backtracking puts up the price. Pick your final destination, say Sydney, then places to visit en route: New York on the way out, Bangkok and Vienna on your way home. An open ticket means you can enter and leave a country or continent by different airports - ideal for overland trekkers.

Planning a grand tour? Inter-Rail passes allow up to a month's rail travel through Europe and around the Med. Eurotrain tickets, valid for 2 months, allow you to plan your route and stop off along the way. Obtainable at student travel agencies; Inter-Rail and other passes from major railway stations. On a tight budget? The cheapest way round Europe is by coach; stow your luggage in the boot and forget about it till you get there. Eurolines offers coach services to over 400 destinations. Bookings can be made through student travel agencies.

Where to find out more

- Campus Travel: offices on student campuses nationwide (in London ✆ 0171-730 8111)
- STA Travel: offices in London (✆ 0171-361 6166) and throughout the UK
- USIT: office in Belfast (✆ 01232 324073)

ADVENTURE & DISCOVERY 3

A variety of operators specialise in adventure packages: overland tours/treks across Asia, Africa or Latin America; student travel agencies can make bookings. Expedition and exploration programmes are great for developing self-confidence, teamwork, maturity and leadership skills.

They'll teach you survival in an Arctic climate or jungle terrain and will involve an aspect of community service, conservation or environmental research to challenge decision-making and problem-solving abilities. You'll need to raise money to take part - all part of the challenge, testing your resourcefulness and imagination. Sponsored events can be good ways to raise funds - the wackier the better. Try bungee jumping, racing rubber ducks down the river, or cleaning someone's car with a toothbrush!

Clare took part in an expedition to Indonesia working on a turtle project: *Definitely the most brilliant and valuable experience of my life so far. I learnt a great deal about the Indonesian way of life, the jungle, how to cope with people 24 hours a day, how to help each other through thick and thin, and how to cope with hardship. I made friends for life.*

Where to find out more (see ***Resources***)

- *A Year Between:* expeditions offering the opportunity to increase understanding of the environment, people and cultures
- Expedition Advisory Centre can advise on planning expeditions

LEARN A NEW LINGO 5

A year out offers a brilliant chance to learn or brush up on another language, perhaps by spending time studying abroad. In today's workplace, most employers expect an international outlook with foreign language fluency. Your future university course may involve work or study abroad. Get a head start by getting to grips with the language. Options range from 2 week intensive courses, through 1-2 month summer schools, right up to an academic year.

Miranda took an intensive Spanish course in Barcelona: *I was almost a complete beginner, but 3 weeks saw a real improvement. I'm now doing beginner's Spanish at university, where a high level has to be reached after one year. The course in Barcelona has definitely been an advantage in all aspects. As well as teaching me something about Spanish life, it has given me the confidence to participate in class. Overall my gap year improved my confidence, gave me independence and helped me organise things for myself. It's been the best year of my life and has contributed to having a fantastic time at university.*

Where to find out more (see ***Resources***)

- *A Year Between:* gap year courses
- *Home From Home:* language learning through homestays and exchanges

Over the page Exchange Cultures; At the Chalkface; Eco-Logic; Expand your Mind; Stay at Home! *and* Resources.

TEN WAYS TO FILL THE GAP is one of a series of leaflets published by the Central Bureau for Educational Visits & Exchanges, 10 Spring Gardens, London SW1A 2BN. For further information ✆ 0171-389 4886 Fax 0171-389 4426

TEXT B

N IS FOR NO MORE ALBUMS (OR SINGLES)

Thanks to internet piracy and CD burning, the way bands release their material is set to change forever

TEXT: PETER ROBINSON

Since the invention of the CD player and its marvellous skip facility, our listening habits have changed. We're now much less likely to wade through duff tracks by listening to albums end to end. Still, it's (kind of) nice to know that they're there. But if the events threatening to unfold during 2003 reach their logical conclusion, those few tracks we listen to most will actually be the only ones we ever hear. During the next 12 months, the music industry will make its first, lumbering steps towards a business model that will spell the end not just of the album – but of album tracks, too. Oh, and it's all our own fault.

2002 was the year the global music industry lost control, of its product and of its consumers. Sales were down – seven per cent year on year, according to one report from the Recording Industry Association of America (RIAA). Blame was laid squarely (and unfairly) at the door of internet piracy and CD burning. As the RIAA shut down file-sharing networks like Audiogalaxy and Muchmusic, so others sprang up with services more sophisticated but just as illegal, providing more than enough material to fill the 2.2 billion blank CDs sold last year . . .

The music industry should have seen the internet as its friend more than half a decade ago but, finally, it's decided to harness the evil and offer tracks for legitimate download. Microsoft's MSN network have already introduced such a service, and HMV are minimising the future damage to their high street sales by offering another. At a price, naturally, with different payment tiers depending on whether you want to stream a song, download it for a limited period, or download it and burn to disc . . .

Time for a comparison test, then: MSN's legal service vs WinMX's illegal peer-to-peer network. On MSN's service, only one in every seven of our searches found us an artist whose label had given permission for their artists to be included. (It's likely most indie labels haven't even been approached.) So: no Ladytron on MSN, though WinMX returns over 100 different files. No Streets (WinMX gave us the album, all the B-sides and mixes, and a couple of live recordings we hadn't come across), no Radiohead (we stopped counting when WinMX got to 3,000 files). No White Stripes, no Libertines. No Oasis, even though MSN's co-branded BT Broadband promotion uses a picture of Liam Gallagher. Oh, and MSN's nearest offering for The Smiths is 'String Quartet Op.11, Molto Adagio pt3' by the Smithsonian Chamber Players.

TEXT C

IF YOU'RE THINKING HOW EASY IT WOULD BE TO MAKE LIKE LIGHT-FINGERED STAR WINONA, THINK AGAIN. A GROWING NUMBER OF SHOPLIFTING TEENS ARE PAYING A HUGE PRICE FOR THEIR CRIME. ERIN KELLY REPORTS

THE *REAL* PRICE OF SHOPLIFTING

It's Saturday afternoon. You're checking out the make-up in a store, when you realise just how easy it would be to slip the lip balm into your bag. So you do. Your heart is pounding as you walk out on to the street. And then you feel it – a firm hand on your shoulder, asking if you can just step back inside and show them what's in your bag.

Scary stuff – but that's the kind of stupid thing you'd never do, right? Don't be so sure. Britain is currently in the grip of a shoplifting epidemic – 31% of people accused of the crime in 2000 in the UK were under 18. And girls overtook boys – 7,528 girls aged 13-15 were caught, compared with 6,370 boys.

JUST FOR KICKS

As more and more girls from middle-class backgrounds turn to the crime, it looks like peer pressure, bullying and seeking a 'buzz', are the real reasons behind the current shoplifting craze.

According to Harry Kauffer, chairman of Crisis Counselling for Alleged Shoplifters, 50% of the shoplifters his charity sees come from affluent families. "Girls often start with cosmetics but they graduate to trainers, CDs and radios. Many see it as a safe and 'victimless' crime because they're stealing from a big shop, not an individual," says Harry Kauffer. But when stock is stolen, shops have to make their money back – and they do this by putting up prices. So in the end, all of us pay.

46 CosmoGIRL! JANUARY 2003

shock report

IT HAPPENED TO ME

Two CG! readers share their shoplifting confessions

"I WISH I'D NEVER DONE IT NOW"

Lucy Metcalfe*, 16, from Sheffield, has lived to regret her shoplifting past – she now has a criminal record.

"There was a lot going on in my life when I started shoplifting. I was having a rough time at home, which meant I was getting into trouble at school and I was eventually expelled when I was 13. I got into all sorts of trouble in the year after that. Looking back, I was trying to kick out, rebel and get some attention from all the people who didn't understand me – teachers, parents and social workers. It was a cry for help.

LOCKED AWAY

I was 13, out of school, and too young to get a job, so the only way I could get things I wanted was to steal them. And I had loads of time to practise. I used to go on my own: I think you're less suspicious that way. I'd go into Sheffield town centre because it's so busy. I thought, 'Who's gonna notice me?' I'd go into clothes shops and stuff things in my bag or inside my jacket. I never got caught because I wasn't nervous, I guess because I didn't care. I was best at taking alcohol from supermarkets. I used to get away with huge bottles of Bacardi, which I would sell on or drink on my own. It seemed so easy.

Then, one day, a security guard from the supermarket followed me down the street. He waited until I took the bottle out of my jacket and that's when he nicked me. I went to the police station and was put in a cell. They took my phone off me, which they do so you've got no sense of time – I could have been inside three minutes or three hours. There were prostitutes and crackheads in there and I thought, 'If I don't stop this, this could be me in four years' time'.

Eventually, I was taken to an interview room and interviewed by a WPC, with a social worker present. They weren't horrible to me, which in a way was worse. It left me thinking about what I'd done, and I realised I didn't want my life to turn out like that of the other women in the cell. I've enrolled in SCAPE, a youth programme, and I tell other teens my story so they don't make the same mistake. I'm studying music and I'm going on a business studies course next year. I'm finally getting my education. I just wish I hadn't wasted it all in the first place. I'd tell anyone who's thinking of shoplifting – it's not worth it! You might think it's a solution to your problems but it's only going to make things worse."

> "I was taken to the police station and put in a cell with prostitutes and crackheads"

"WHAT STARTED AS FUN TURNED INTO MY WORST NIGHTMARE"

Janine Dobby*, 16, from Oldham, hasn't stolen anything since the day she was caught by a store detective.

"I started shoplifting as a laugh with my mates. It was just because we were bored. We started off with little things, make-up, sweets, anything you can fit up a sleeve. There were usually four of us, and three would stand around giggling to take the attention away from the one stealing.

But the more you get away with it, the more confident you get and before long we were going to Manchester for the day and nicking from clothes shops. You just found a top without a tag on it and then wore it under your clothes to walk out of the shop. I got loads of compliments on my new clothes – although I had to hide them from my mum! I always made sure I never stole anything from a little corner shop or anything like that. It was always a big chain store where they could afford to lose it."

SCARED AND CRYING

"The day I got caught was the only day I went shoplifting on my own. I put some shampoo in my bag, but then I lost my nerve and walked around the shop for about 15 minutes trying to pluck up the courage to leave. When I did it was just like your worst nightmare. They wait until you're outside and then they place their hands on your shoulder just as you think you've got away with it.

They took me to a little back room in the shop and I was crying so much they couldn't get any sense out of me. They said I could either go to the police or ring my mum. I didn't want to call home but I did because I thought getting a caution might have stopped me getting a Saturday job. My mum went mental. She found all my 'secret' clothes in the bottom of my wardrobe and made me give them to charity. I'll never do it again." CG!

> "You get outside and think you've got away with it – then they grab you"

* NAMES AND IDENTIFYING DETAILS IN THIS STORY HAVE BEEN CHANGED. THANKS TO RPS RAINER, A NATIONAL VOLUNTARY ORGANISATION WORKING WITH YOUNG PEOPLE AGED 10-25 YEARS. VISIT RPSRAINER.ORG.UK. SOURCES: CCAS, THE PORTIA CAMPAIGN, THE BRITISH RETAIL CONSORTIUM, SCAPE, RPS RAINER, THAMES VALLEY POLICE

Caught in the act!

If you are caught shoplifting, Inspector Gordon Sinclair of the Thames Valley Police can tell you what to expect

1 A police car will pick you up from the shop where you were caught and you'll be arrested.
2 The police will take you back to the station, where they'll remove all your personal belongings.
3 Most people are out within a couple of hours, but the police can hold you for up to 24 hours.
4 Mates won't cover for you and they'll usually squeal if they think it'll get them off the hook.
5 If you're under 17, the police have to let your parents know you're being held for questionning.
6 If it's your first offence, you'll get a caution. It stays on your record for five years and if you go for a job that requires a police check, it shows up.
7 If you're a repeat offender and you go to court, you'll have a criminal record for life.
8 Most shops ban teens who are caught shoplifing. If you're caught in your local mall, you can be banned from the entire shopping centre.

snip out and slip in your purse

Who to ask for help & advice

- **For information** on shoplifting, the law and you, go online to thamesvalley police.uk/tvp4kids.
- **If you're worried** about shoplifting you can contact Harry Kauffer at Crisis Counselling for Alleged Shoplifters on 020 8954 8987 between 9am-5pm, Monday-Friday and 9.30am-5.30pm, Saturday-Sunday.

JANUARY 2003 CosmoGIRL!

TEXT D

Transcript of a Radio 5 Live sports report:

Commentator: And at the Rec an important win for Bath as they try and pull away from the bottom of the table. They beat Harlequins 23 points to 9. Alistair Hignell.

Hignell: No happy return to big match action for Harlequins wing Dan Luger. The England and Lions pace man playing his first game for eight months was always eager for work but was restricted to a watching role as Bath took early control and thanks to a Kevin Maggs try and three penalties from Ollie Barclay established a comfortable 16-3 lead at half time. And the ball didn't run Luger's way even when Bath went off the boil at the beginning of the second half, allowing Paul Burke to kick his second and third penalties. Ian Bolshaw, another on the comeback trail, was far more involved in both attack and defence for Bath, but he was only a decoy runner as Mike Tyndall scored the try that sank Quins, their late onslaught failing to yield a desperately needed bonus point.

Commentary tip

When you write your informative text, you will have to think about the questions given in Activity 4 from a writer's point of view. Your comments about some of them should be included in your final commentary.

Choosing an assignment

Once you have studied a good range of informative texts, it is time to choose an assignment for yourself. The following activity should help you do so.

ACTIVITY 5

First, remind yourself of the basic guidelines on Original Writing on pages 175–6 above. Remember: the task needs to be **realistic**, **practical** and **original**.

When you write your informative piece, you will need to feel confident that you are something of an 'expert' in the area you are writing about. So it makes sense to choose a subject which you already know quite a lot about, or on which you can easily carry out the required research. This will usually mean starting from something close to home.

Working in pairs, your task is to suggest some possible writing tasks for a partner with this in mind. Interview your partner to find out what kinds of knowledge or information he or she already has. Use the prompts and suggestions below – but of course, there are many other questions you could ask!

Prompt question	Who might like/need to learn about this?	In what medium/genre?
What school/college subjects are you studying?	Year 11 students contemplating taking any of these subjects, and their parents, might welcome information on what the course is like from a student's perspective. If you have carried out some research as part of your work for Module 2, Language and Social Contexts, other language students may want to read about it.	A **short pamphlet**, or an **illustrated presentation** to be given 'live' at an Open Evening. An in-house **English Language magazine** for articles of linguistic interest.
What kinds of part-time work have you done?	Anyone taking on a part-time job might like to know the best way of getting a job in the first place, how to get the application right, how to survive the interview, and then how to cope with the demands of the job.	An **article** in a local or student news-sheet, or a **leaflet** for the Careers Area.
How well do you know the area where you live?	Visitors – perhaps students moving to the area to go to college/university – might welcome a guide to the region, its shops, sporting facilities, restaurants, pubs and clubs.	An **article** in a students magazine, or local paper, a **pamphlet** for the local Tourist Information office, an item for your **local radio** station, or a contribution to your town's official **website**.
Where else have you travelled to?	If you know a holiday destination very well, it may be that you can provide a more realistic and up-to-date guide than the ones commercially available.	Look at **travel guides** like *The Rough Guides*, or the *Time Out* series, for possible formats. Also, travel sections can be found in weekend newspapers.
What do you do with your spare time? Do you: • enjoy going out? • play sports? • take part in music/drama/ arts? • spend time on computing/ games/ICT?	People less familiar with your area may well need to know about its cinemas, and sporting and leisure facilities. If you follow your local team(s), there is always a market for well-written information about them and their players, and some people might like to know about how to get started in a particular sport that you enjoy. Similarly, the inside story of a music or drama production might be of interest to many readers. Perhaps your reviews of new CDs, gigs or films would be of interest.	Many **local radio** stations, **newspapers and magazines** have *What's On* programmes/sections and may also include reviews. Some **websites** also invite contributions. A **radio documentary** or feature article could describe your school team's cup run, your

Prompt question	Who might like/need to learn about this?	In what medium/genre?
• have other special interests/ hobbies/ expertise?	Games enthusiasts may be able to share tips and hints about how to climb up the higher levels of the latest game, and there is always a market for well-informed coverage of the latest technological developments. Perhaps you have a special interest, expertise or experience – from work experience to learning to ski, from stamp-collecting to bereavement – which someone, somewhere would like to hear about.	drama production or concert. Your local sports team may have a **fanzine** – or start one of your own. A general interest or specialist **magazine** could be an outlet for articles on hobbies and interests.

As you make your choice of writing assignment, you may find it helpful to submit to your supervising teacher a 'Proposal/Pre-commentary' form like the one below. Be prepared to take on board the advice of your teacher.

Proposal/Pre-commentary: Writing to inform

Key point	Explanation	Your ideas	Teacher comments
Content/subject matter	What is the information content you are going to include?		
Your research	How much do you already know about the subject, and how will you go about becoming an 'expert'?		
Target audience	Which group(s) of people are you hoping to reach?		
Why do they need/want to know the information? How much or how little do they already know?	Identify the 'information gap' and be clear about what you think you can assume about your audience's prior knowledge.		
Which aspects of the information will they be least/most interested in?	Think carefully about the kinds of information to include and omit.		
Which medium/genre do you intend to use to reach your audience?	Define as precisely as you can your intended medium. Don't just say 'a magazine', but decide which specific title.		
What style models do you intend to study?	Note the titles of similar texts, aimed at a similar audience but *not* on the same topic.		

Commentary tip

Write these key details of your assignment on a separate sheet of paper called a 'Pre-commentary'.

You can briefly discuss your reasons for choosing your assignment in the first part of your final commentary.

Preparing to produce a text

Once you decide on a writing assignment, the next step is to collect the **information** you need for your text. The principal sources are likely to be:

- yourself – choose a subject you already know something about and brainstorm the topic thoroughly
- reference sources – text books, encyclopaedias, reference books, etc.
- printed media – newspapers, magazines, etc.
- the Internet
- personal interviews with relevant people.

Remember:

- Always keep a record and copy of the resources you use; you will need to submit these and refer to them in your commentary and bibliography.
- You must not simply reproduce the words or methods of presentation used in your sources without acknowledgement – this is plagiarism and will be penalised.

When you feel you have as much information as you – or your readers or listeners – need, organise it by dividing it into sub-sections, and then start to make some decisions about what to include, and in what order.

Activity 6

C3.1a

Imagine that you have decided to write a piece about the health risks involved in smoking, and that you have already gathered a fair amount of possible source material. You have sorted this material into a number of categories, as listed below:

A A picture of a diseased lung.

B Statistics comparing the numbers of deaths each year from heart disease and lung cancer among smokers and non-smokers.

C The personal story of someone who is dying of lung cancer, having smoked for many years.

D Technical and scientific data about the nicotine, carbon monoxide and tar emissions produced by different kinds of cigarettes.

E Biological/scientific explanations of how tobacco by-products are associated with cancer development, heart disease and other circulatory problems.

F Taped interviews with two teenagers about why they started smoking.

G Advice on how to give up smoking.

H The legal position regarding sales of tobacco products to young people.

(a) The first major choice you face is how much of these different types of material you should include or leave out. The answer to this question will, as always, depend on your purpose, medium and audience.

Listed below are six different possible texts on this topic. For each of them, your first task is to order the material **A–H** above, according to the amount of each type you would use in each assignment; use 1 to represent the most, and 8 little or nothing. If possible, discuss this in small groups before deciding on your order, and then compare your solution with those of other students.

- A health education pamphlet for teenagers.
- A health education leaflet for general use in a GP's surgery.
- An article in a medical journal, read mainly by health professionals.
- An article in a Sunday newspaper supplement with a family audience.
- A student's presentation on an AVCE Health & Social Care course.
- A Radio 1 news item about trends in teenage smoking.

(b) As well as deciding how much of each type of ingredient to put into the mix for your particular text, you also need to choose the best sequence and structure in which to arrange it. Where should you start? What path should you follow?

For the same set of six possible 'smoking' texts, your task is now to decide the best arrangement and sequence of the material, numbering the material from 1 (use at the start) to 8 (use at the end).

There is, of course, no single 'correct' solution to this problem. However, your discussions should raise the kinds of questions about selection and structure which apply to all kinds of informative writing.

Commentary tip

In your final commentary you should refer to the different sources of information you used and the different types of information you decided to include in your text. Explain why you decided to include more of some, and less of another type of material.

You should explain the choices you made about structure and sequence, and your reasons for them.

Using facts and statistical information

It is likely that at some stage in your text you will present your readers or listeners with some factual or statistical information. As your survey of different informative texts will have revealed, there are many ways of doing this. How will you achieve maximum impact and the desired effect?

ACTIVITY 7

Imagine you have decided to write a piece about food and drink, and in particular, about the growing popularity of pasta in the UK. Here are some alternative ways of conveying in words the basic facts of spaghetti consumption:

A Every year in the UK we consume 100,000 tons of spaghetti.

B Each UK household consumes an average of 4 kilos of spaghetti a year.

C If all the spaghetti consumed in the UK this year were tied end to end it would circle the earth three times.

D More than 60% of us eat spaghetti at least once a month.

E Nearly two in three people eat spaghetti once a month.

F Over a third of us eat spaghetti only rarely.

(a) Explain which version of the above information you would use, and why, if you were:

- writing for a non-specialist audience and wanted to emphasise the importance of spaghetti
- writing a more formal, specialised piece for people in the food industry
- trying to minimise the importance of spaghetti.

(b) In what non-verbal ways might you convey this information? Try expressing these facts using:

- a pie chart
- a cartoon or diagram.

Commentary tip

In your final commentary, you should discuss the ways you have decided to convey factual or statistical information, including any diagrams, pie charts, etc. you decide to use.

Writing for audio

At some point in your Original Writing course, it is a good idea to try writing for a listening audience; although it is not a requirement of the AS specification, the A2 Unit 5 examination (Editorial Writing) frequently includes writing for audio, so it makes sense to gain some experience of this skill on your AS course. This genre includes:

- 'live' talks and presentations
- speech radio broadcasts (either local or national radio, especially Radio 4)
- audio tapes
- audio guides, often available at museums, exhibitions and historic sites.

There may be a real opportunity to produce a script for a substantial presentation, either as part of your English Language studies (perhaps as a means of sharing the results of some research into gender, power or technology) or as part of your study of other subjects. If you deliver the talk to a real audience, this will allow you to generate relevant evidence for your Key Skills Communication portfolio.

ACTIVITY 8

C3.1b

Practise the skills involved in writing for audio by producing the script for short talks, tapes or programmes on one or more of the following subjects:

- choosing your AS subjects
- leisure facilities in your area
- student facilities in your school/college.

Writing for audio

Set out your script in three columns as shown: use the left column to specify speaker/voice, the centre column for the dialogue, and the right column to specify SFX (sound effects), visual aids (if part of a presentation) and music.

Voice/speaker	Dialogue	SFX/VA
M, 30s, unmarked RP	Good morning. Welcome to 'On the line' with Jenny Smith	

- Specify gender, age and accent for any speaker.
- Consider using more than one speaker.
- Identify speakers by name regularly.
- Use SFX or music to establish a mood or theme, e.g. short snatches of popular songs which refer to the topic of the text.
- Announce *regularly* what is coming next. Listeners can't look ahead or see headings or lists of contents.
- Speak the text aloud as you write.
- Make a recording of your text to see if it works.
- Don't try to script 'spontaneous' interviews.

Commentary tip

When writing your commentary, explain your choice of speakers and voices, perhaps by referring to relevant Unit 2 issues connected with gender, dialect or power.

Writing to instruct

There is a very grey area where 'informative' and 'instructive' types of writing overlap; instructions will, by definition, always include some information, and many of the informative texts you considered may well have contained elements of instruction, or at least advice. Here we will look briefly at some texts that are primarily instructive and/or advisory.

Remember:

If you decide to submit both an informative and an instructive text for your coursework, you should ensure that the two texts are significantly different in purpose, genre, audience and approach, and that they allow you to demonstrate a genuine variety of writing skills.

Many instructive texts – such as recipes, or 'how to do it' pamphlets associated with practical skills and activities, may appear relatively straightforward to write. But as with all your Original Writing choices, it is important that you attempt a task that is sufficiently challenging. Some 'instructions' may take the form of feature articles ('How to cope with leaving home/bereavement/divorce/multiple sclerosis . . .') which offer advice and tackle difficult or sensitive issues, and these may provide a greater challenge. Beware, however, of writing *impractical* instructions for practical activities, for which a set of written instructions is not very useful (e.g. 'How to salsa').

As with informative writing, you will need to study a range of suitable style models. Sometimes it is tempting to limit the notion of 'instruction' to the predictable kinds of pamphlets and leaflets we associate with this purpose, but it is important to include more imaginative ways in which writers convey instructions.

ACTIVITY 9

Below are two examples of instructional/advisory texts; the first is a conventional set of instructions, whereas the second is an example of a more imaginative approach which uses techniques more associated with other kinds of writing, such as writing to entertain.

For each of the texts you study, produce a short report on the methods they use to present their instructions/advice to their intended audience. Use the following prompt questions to structure your analysis:

- How does the introduction contribute to the effectiveness of the leaflet in text A?
- How do these texts address and establish a relationship with their target audience(s)?
- What use is made of bullets, headings and other graphological devices?
- What seem to be the 'rules' for using bullets effectively? (Look at the kinds of sentences/phrases that follow each bullet.)
- Are instructions/advice given with direct imperatives, or are they softened, for example by using modal verbs such as 'should', 'ought', 'could'?
- How do the texts give reassurance and confidence to their readers?

- How and when is the first person used, if at all?
- In what ways is the language tailored to its target audience?
- In what ways – if any – do the texts depart from the conventions of instructional texts?

Compare the findings of your investigation with the commentary on page 231.

TEXT A

You can beat bullying!

A Guide for Young People – Kidscape

Introduction
. . . It is surprising that all sorts of people who are now very successful adults were bullied when they were young. It is encouraging to know that it is possible to succeed in spite of being tormented at school. All of these well-known people were bullied at school: Phil Collins (singer), Harrison Ford (actor), Mel Gibson (actor), Daryl Hannah (actor), Tom Cruise (actor), Michelle Pfeiffer (actor), Dudley Moore (actor) . . .

CONTENTS
This booklet has three main sections: Bullies, Victims and Self-assertiveness Techniques. Bullies and victims sometimes have similar problems so you might find helpful suggestions in all the sections.

WHAT CAN I DO IF I AM BEING BULLIED?
Your school may already have a way of dealing with bullying.

For example, some schools:

- have anti-bullying guidelines and procedures for dealing with incidents
- encourage anyone who is being bullied or who witnesses bullying to tell about it
- have 'bully boxes' where students put in a note about what is happening
- have student meetings, circle time or 'courts' where problems like bullying are discussed and dealt with
- have specially trained students to help each other or teachers who are assigned to help.

If your school has an anti-bullying system, use it to get help. If you're not sure how it works, talk to your teacher or Year Head.

If your school ignores bullying, *don't become resigned to being a victim.* You can still help yourself and you can ask others to help you.

- **Tell a friend what is happening.** Ask him/her to help you. It will be harder for the bully to pick on you if you have a friend with you for support.
- **Try to ignore the bullying or say 'No' really firmly, then turn and walk away.** Don't worry if people think you're running away. Remember, it is very hard for the bully to go on bullying someone who won't stand still to listen.
- **Try not to show that you are upset or angry.** Bullies love to get a reaction – it's 'fun'. If you can keep calm and hide your emotions, they might get bored and leave you alone. As one teenager said, 'They can't bully you if you don't care'.
- **Don't fight back, if you can help it.** Most bullies are stronger or bigger than their victims. If you fight back, you could make the situation worse, get hurt or be blamed for starting the trouble.

TEXT B

The Easiest Sexiest Salad (from Jamie Oliver, *Happy Days with the Naked Chef*)

I love this salad. Apart from being a great combination, it always seems unbelievably effortless, which is the kind of recipe I like. The constant success of this is due to the common-sense marriage of salty Parma ham, milky buffalo mozzarella and sweet figs, which obviously need to be of good quality. The best figs to use are Italian and the best time to buy them is June to August when they are in season. Greek figs are a good second best and are in season from September to November. The best figs always seem to be those that are about to split their skins. Use green or black figs – it doesn't really matter.

One thing I do is to criss-cross the figs but not quite to the bottom – 1 fig per person is always a good start. Then, using your thumbs and forefingers, squeeze the base of the fig to expose the inside. At this point you'll think, 'Oooh, that looks nice, I'm quite clever . . .' or at least I do. More importantly, it allows your dressing to go right into the middle of the fig. All these little things really help to make a salad special. Simply place the figs in a dish, weave around 1 slice of Parma ham or prosciutto per fig, throw in some slices of buffalo mozzarella, rip over some green or purple basil and drizzle everything with the honey and lemon juice dressing. As far as salads go it's pretty damn sexy.

PS: it's a good idea to have some spare bread on the table to mop up the juices – always a treat.

Commentary tip

When reflecting on your own instructional writing, apply the questions given in Activity 9 to your text and write your answers in some detail.

ACTIVITY 10

For this activity you will need to collect a wide variety of instructional/advisory leaflets. They are not hard to find; you can start by collecting them from your own school or college (perhaps your English department has handouts instructing you how to go about your coursework!), local library, health centre, Social Services department, GP's surgery/clinic, and other public information outlets.

Study the range of leaflets carefully. Then design and draft your own leaflet, aimed at other A Level English Language students, on the subject of 'The Art of Writing Effective Leaflets'. This will be useful not only as part of your preparations for Original Writing, but also for A2 Module 5, Editorial Writing.

As you make your choice of writing assignment, you may find it helpful to submit to your supervising teacher a 'Proposal/Pre-commentary' form like the one used for informative writing above (page 189). The key points are somewhat different – use the ones given below. Add to them your own specific ideas for your writing task, and leave room for your teacher to comment.

Proposal/Pre-commentary: Writing to instruct

Key point	Explanation
Content/subject matter	What are the instructions/advice you aim to give?
Target audience	Which group(s) of people are you hoping to reach?
Why do they need/want the instructions/advice you are going to give? How much or how little do they already know?	Identify your audience's needs precisely, and be clear about the assumptions you are making about their prior knowledge and experience.
Which aspects of the information will they be least/most interested in?	Think carefully about the kinds of information to include or omit.
Which medium/genre do you intend to use to reach your audience?	Define as precisely as you can your intended medium. Don't just say 'a magazine', but decide which specific title
Which style models do you intend to study?	Note the titles of similar texts, aimed at a similar audience but *not* on the same topic.

Writing to entertain

This primary purpose is extremely broad and includes a multitude of possibilities. Sometimes the term 'entertainment' is used lightly to describe material which is trivial and undemanding. However, we can be 'entertained' in many ways; we can have our feelings and emotions engaged, we can be made to laugh or cry, and we can have our minds stimulated to think and reflect on different aspects of experience.

You need to keep in mind the full range of possibilities when planning a piece of coursework; while some kinds of light, undemanding material may be relatively easy to imitate, you may be more likely to achieve the highest standards of work – and marks – by tackling something a little more challenging.

ACTIVITY 11

Some possible interpretations of the term 'entertainment' are given below. Suggest two or three examples of specific texts you have encountered (spoken and/or written) which might fall into these categories:

- passes the time pleasantly
- causes amusement
- makes us think and reflect
- frightens us
- moves or touches us emotionally
- allows us to escape from the reality of our lives
- confronts us with the reality of our own or other people's lives.

In general, the range of possible texts for study and writing tasks might include:

- narrative fiction for different audiences (such as teenage, or younger) in various genres (romance, crime, sci-fi, fantasy, etc.)
- scripts for stage, radio, TV or film
- feature articles for magazines and newspapers
- autobiographical and biographical writing (including 'ghost' writing)
- humorous writing such as comic books, satirical sketches and observational comedy (either journalism or for 'stand-up' performances)
- verse or song lyrics.

In this book, we can consider briefly only a few examples of these; however, if you decide to attempt a form of writing not covered here, your approach is likely to be similar to that for other primary purposes:

1 Decide on a form and a topic for your writing.

2 Decide who you are going to entertain.

3 Study some varied examples (style models) of the genre you are attempting.

4 Attempt a first draft. Try not to just imitate the obvious features and conventions of the form you have chosen, but inject a little of your own voice and style.

Autobiographical writing

For many writers, the easiest place to start writing is from their personal experience. However, although it may be easy enough for you to write your life story, it does not necessarily follow that someone else will be interested in reading about it! Unless you have already achieved a degree of fame (or infamy) for your accomplishments, it is unlikely that there will be a market for a straightforward autobiography.

However, several newspapers and magazines *do* run columns in which relatively 'ordinary' people create a snapshot of their lives within a specified format. For example, the *Sunday Times* used to run a feature called 'A Day in the Life', in which subjects wrote about a typical day, but also used this as a vehicle for expressing their views on life generally and revealing their likes, dislikes, hopes and fears. For the purposes of your Original Writing submission, it is better to shape your writing to fit a format such as this than to launch into a full-scale story of your life, which would not find a realistic market.

Good autobiographical writing which might be published is not just a narrative of events and reminiscences; it will also include:

- some reflection on the importance and impact of your experiences
- some revelation of your values and preferences
- lively portraits of friends and families
- a glimpse of your whole approach to life.

ACTIVITY 12

(a) The *Times Educational Supplement*, a weekly journal aimed at education professionals, runs a feature entitled 'My Best Teacher' in which well-known personalities talk about their school experiences. As the title suggests, each piece focuses on a single teacher who has been a particularly strong influence on the person concerned, but the piece also allows interviewees to reflect more broadly on their educational experience and the ways in which it helped shape the person they became.

Read the example that follows, which is based on the experiences of Jennie Bond, the BBC TV journalist; then try to draft your own article of approximately 800 words. Be sure to include some of the features listed above.

MY BEST TEACHER

JENNIE BOND

I spent all my school life at St Francis' college, Letchworth, where I was a day girl. I remember my schooldays as happy, but my 12-year-old daughter was recently reading my old diaries and tells me I had written how much I hated school. I remember that the workload was great and I was very conscientious, working fantastically hard. I didn't like being told off, so was hideously well behaved. It is a matter of embarrassment to me that I never got a detention or a conduct mark.

Most of the teachers were nuns so it was very refreshing when I got to O-levels to have a lay English teacher who dressed rather sexily. Mrs Cherry had hennaed hair and a gravely, smoky voice, and we could see her legs under her gown. She was of the school of thought that I came across later at university: that books are fine, but are a means of making you think. But the most illuminating thing I remember her saying was that we'd know when we were really in love with a man because we wouldn't mind sharing his toothbrush . . .

Miss Wilson, the maths mistress, was a tiny lady who shouted a lot. I never enjoyed maths. I found the subject difficult and I don't think her method of teaching was helpful.

But Mrs English, who taught French, was delightful. She was gentle and interested in us and in our lives, and had a relaxed way of teaching. She inspired me and made me enjoy speaking the language. I liked working on pronunciation and enunciation. I thought I'd probably become a French teacher myself. English and French were my best subjects.

I went to Warwick University to read French and European literature, planning to teach, and as a part of the course was sent to France to work as an *assistante* for a year. My placement was at a lycée in Juan-les-Pins in the south of France, where I taught senior children conversational English. I only had to work eight or nine hours a week, but I was hopeless and soon learned that I could never be a teacher . . .

When a couple of my friends went into journalism, I thought it seemed like fun, and I got a job as a cub reporter on the *Richmond Herald*. I had no idea I would end up as the BBC's royal correspondent. I wasn't particularly interested in the royal family as a girl. My family had a middle-class respect for the monarchy, but life didn't stop for the Queen's Christmas message.

BBC royal correspondent Jennie Bond was talking to **Pamela Coleman**

(b) Another autobiographical format which has been used in the media is the **video diary**, where relatively 'ordinary' and unknown people make recordings over a period of time in which they talk about their lives in much the same ways as was once common with written diaries. Try drafting the script for your own video diary, aiming to write one minute of air time for each of four or five entries over a period of a couple of weeks.

(c) Perhaps there has been a particular aspect of your life that sets you apart from many other people of your age – a particular achievement, a disability or illness or some sort, or the need to care for a friend or relative. An example of such a piece of writing is the text which follows ('Shaken not stirred'), which is an extract from a student's account of coming to terms with epilepsy. It was published in *OM* Magazine, a supplement of the *Observer* newspaper.

After reading the article, consider whether you might be able to write a similar piece about yourself.

SHAKEN NOT STIRRED

BLACK EYES, BRUISED RIBS, A BROKEN NOSE . . . EPILEPSY LEAVES YOU WITH MUCH TO LEARN AT THE SCHOOL OF HARD KNOCKS. BY **FRANZISKA THOMAS**

I've have a bad month. I've had 13 seizures in four weeks, five of them over one weekend. Two weeks ago during the fourth week of my *Observer* internship, I had a fit (seizure) and woke up under the Sports desk. The next day I was asked if I might write an article about what it is like to live life as a 'practising epileptic' (as I tend to refer to it). I've got used to fits landing me in unusual positions over the years, both literally and figuratively speaking, but getting a job because of one has to be the most unusual to date.

I developed epilepsy four months and three days shy of my 16th birthday. Doctors have concluded that my case was most likely brought on by a febrile convulsion I experienced at 18 months, and while many who develop epilepsy in childhood grow out of it in later life, I apparently grew into mine.

Epilepsy is the tendency to have recurrent fits and is caused by abnormal bursts of chaotic electrical activity in the brain. Anyone can develop the condition at any time, although it is more usual to develop it before the age of 20 or after 60. The easiest way to visualise a fit is if you can imagine your brain as a computer. A surge in electricity will cause the computer to crash in much the same way as an excess of electrical activity will cause the brain to fit . . . I fall unconscious to the ground, often in mid-sentence and then twitch, chew my tongue and make screeching noises, which friends say sound like I am in excruciating pain. This can last up to 10 minutes, after which I wake up dazed and confused, invariably bruised and battered, muttering incoherent half-sentences. Within 15 minutes, however, I am fully conscious and able to continue the conversation where I left off . . .

Witnessing someone having a fit must be very disturbing; I have never actually seen one. In my mind's eye I have an image that has been conjured up by Dostoyevky's depiction of a fit in *The Idiot* and by a continuing narrative of all the quirky things I do and say when I regain consciousness or as I hit the floor.

I have built up a very personal relationship with the floor over the years. It's a strange sensation repeatedly waking up on the floor, your eyes level with chair legs, shoe soles and dirt. The average person walks into a bar, looks around and orders a drink. I walk into a bar, look at the floor and try to imagine how much it would hurt to fall on it. My stories from holidays abroad frequently involve a description of ambulances, pavements and the differences in medical care.

Biographical writing and 'ghosting'

It may be that you are attracted to the idea of writing about the life of someone else rather than your own. There is always a demand for well-written profiles of individuals whose experiences or expertise make them worthy of interest to a particular audience.

What's more, some writing that appears to be 'autobiographical' is in fact written by a journalist on behalf of the person whose life it documents. Such writing is known as 'ghost' writing.

In both cases, this writing task involves the following stages:

Choose a subject, medium and possible style model	**Don't** go for someone famous. Enough has already been written about them and it will be hard for you to do anything original. **Do** choose someone you know; this could be: • a relative who has had an interesting experience (fought in a war/lived abroad/set up a new business/worked in an interesting job/overcome an illness/gained an award or qualification) • a fellow student who is doing or has achieved something notable (represented the town/county/country, won a scholarship, gained an award, an unusual hobby/skill, played in a band) • someone you have worked for (their career, how they became a manager, other jobs they have had) • someone in your community (business person, sports person, doctor, religious leader, politician, councillor, head teacher). You could write an article for a local newspaper or magazine, or script a feature for your local radio station.
Do some homework	Do some research about your subject's achievements before you talk to him or her.
Interview your subject	Contact your subject and explain what you are doing – and gain permission to use him or her as a subject for your writing assignment. Think in advance about what you want to find out about your subject – have some questions prepared, but don't stick to them rigidly, and go with the flow of the conversation. Use a tape recorder to record your interview – but gain permission first. Alternatively, take detailed notes.
Re-work your raw material	Your finished piece – whether article, radio feature or contribution to a website – will be completely different from the interview. Look for an 'angle' on your subject with which you will 'hook' your audience in your opening few sentences, and adopt a suitable format and style from your style models. If you wish to write an article, why not take a couple of photographs of your subject? When ghost writing, the same steps apply – but write in the first person, as if you were the person concerned.

Commentary tip

When writing about your biographical piece, refer in detail to the raw material you gained in your interview and explain how you chose to re-write and re-arrange it – and why.

Quote both from your final text and your notes/tape recording to show this.

ACTIVITY 13

Reprinted below is the opening of an article which appeared in *You* magazine (the supplement of the *Mail on Sunday* newspaper). It focuses on the life and achievements of a person its readers are unlikely to have heard of before.

(a) Study the piece and identify the 'angle' or 'hook' which the journalist has used to make the subject sound interesting.

(b) Suggest a subject known to you and an 'angle' on his or her life which you could use as a way to shape a piece about him or her. It could be someone you work with or who lives near you, who has reached some kind of milestone in life; or it could be a fellow student whose achievements might interest the readership of a local newspaper or college magazine.

(c) Attempt a first draft of this piece.

THE DAY I BECAME MARILYN

UNA PEARL WAS A 20-YEAR-OLD FILM EXTRA FROM CROYDON WHEN SHE LANDED THE PART OF MARILYN MONROE'S BODY DOUBLE. HERE SHE TELLS *SARAH WISE* HOW IT FELT TO POSE AS THE ULTIMATE SCREEN GODDESS

As jobs go, it must be one of the strangest – standing for ten hours a day under blazing hot lamps, caked in heavy make-up and wearing a tight, unyielding dress, pretending to be Marilyn Monroe. But for 20-year-old film extra Pearl King, who had adopted the stage name Una Pearl, being Marilyn's stand-in for the 1957 film *The Prince and the Showgirl* 'was one of the happiest times of my life. I loved every minute of it, no matter how exhausted I felt – and we were all exhausted at the end of that shoot.'

It was certainly tiring work being a 1950s body double. In the days without the computer technology that allows directors to alter skin colour and body shape post-shooting, body doubles were used to dummy-run scenes, testing out hundreds of postures and positions for the lights and cameras.

Today, Una is a glamorous 60-something mother of two grown-up daughters, with a sweep of platinum hair and a peaches-and-cream complexion, living in contented obscurity in Epping Forest. She gave up acting in 1963, when she married her husband, John, a Lloyd's underwriter, and started a family; but several boxes in her attic contain well-preserved mementos of her time as a shadow of the stars. Una 'was' Brigitte Bardot for a parachute jump in the 1959 film *Babette Goes to War*; in Stanley Kubrik's *Lolita* (1962), she stood in for 15-year-old actress Sue Lyon (who thought Una had been sent on set to take her entire role), and she body-doubled perfect Englishwoman Deborah Kerr in the 1960 drawing-room farce *The Grass is Greener*, alongside romantic leads Cary Grant and Robert Mitchum.

Dramatic monologues

One form of writing which often produces interesting work is the **dramatic monologue**. In this, you create a character who tells a story directly, as if speaking aloud to a friend or confidante. These pieces can work particularly well on radio, as little visual action is usually involved, but they can be equally effective for the stage or TV. If you are also studying Drama or Performing Arts, you may have a ready-made outlet for your script.

Dramatic monologues have many uses – even museums may personalise the information they present by putting words into the mouths of actors representing historical characters, who guide visitors around exhibitions. They have sometimes featured in the writing assignments set for Module 5, Editorial Writing.

Dramatic monologues also allow you to apply many aspects of your AS English Language studies – and to discuss these in your commentary. For example, you can use your understanding of the nature of spoken language to make your character talk realistically; you can establish aspects of his or her character by including regional elements of language, and you could even draw on aspects of your work on language and gender by employing 'typically' gendered speech.

Many of the most interesting monologues are much more than mere stories; the narrator is likely to spend as much time giving us opinions and observations as mere narration, and thus he or she reveals aspects of character to us. We may also gradually realise that the character telling the story may not be 'seeing' things quite straight; perhaps he or she is a child, or has only limited understanding, or is subject to a particular prejudice or 'blind spot'.

ACTIVITY 14

Perhaps the most well-known examples of this genre produced in recent years are the two series of *Talking Heads* by Alan Bennett. It is likely that you will find a copy in your school/college library. Read and study at least one of the monologues, and as you do so, answer the following questions:

- What is the approximate balance (in percentage terms) between narrative and reflection or observation?
- Which **idiolectal** features of the narrator's language help establish personality or character?
- Are there any hints to the reader or listener that the narrator's judgment or understanding of things may not be 100 per cent reliable?

ACTIVITY 15

Before you can start writing your own monologue, you will need to decide a number of things about your central narrator character. It is best to choose the kind of person you understand well – perhaps someone in your own age group. Use this prompt sheet to help you – the final question should provide you with the initial spark for the story he or she is going to tell.

- What gender is your character?
- How old is he or she?
- If in education, what does your character study, and where?
- If in work, what is his or her job?
- Who is the most important person in your character's life?
- List three things or people your character likes and dislikes.
- Does your character speak with a regional accent or RP?
- Does he or she use a regional dialect or Standard English vocabulary and grammar?
- List five other distinctive characteristics of the way your character talks (aspects of his or her idiolect).
- In what way is your character's narrative going to be slightly distorted, unreliable or biased? Is he or she prejudiced? Naïve? Slightly 'disturbed'?
- Think of something that happened to your character today that he or she wants to talk about. Avoid deaths and disasters – something apparently trivial is fine to get you started.

Commentary tip

If you write a monologue, make links in your commentary with Module 2 work by writing about:

- how you have incorporated idiolectal features to create your character
- any accent/dialect or general speech features you have included to establish your character
- any aspect of language and gender that you have consciously applied to your monologue.

Writing to entertain is not limited to fiction, and it isn't necessary to have a particularly vivid imagination to turn the material of 'real life' into highly engaging text. The kinds of 'true life' feature articles that appear in many magazines, for example, may have an informative (or even instructive) dimension to them, but they are usually read recreationally, even when they deal with relatively serious subjects, as with the following example.

ACTIVITY 16

(a) As you study the following article, closely consider how it engages the interest and emotional sympathy of its readers. Although it is based on fact, there are several strongly narrative elements in the piece which we might also find in fictional stories. These are listed in the table below; find examples in the text.

Narrative elements	Examples
A central character with whom the readers of the magazine can identify and/or sympathise	In what ways is this true of the 1st person narrator of the story?
The representation of other characters	Who are they, and what is their role in the story (friend, supporter, adviser, etc.)?
The action springs from a significant event in the character's life	In what ways did the events of the story change life for Sarah?
Several dramatic incidents/episodes	How is language used to convey these?
Dialogue used to bring these alive	Note how selectively this is done.
Dramatic language to bring home the 'action' in the story	Suggest some examples.
An ending which resolves the issues of the narrative in a satisfying way	How does it do so?
A 'moral' or implied meaning/message	What 'meanings' emerge by the end of the piece?

(b) Collect two or three more examples of this kind of 'real life' story feature from popular magazines (e.g. *J17, Cosmopolitan, Bella, Best, New Woman, More!* and *Chat*) and survey them, applying the same set of questions.

(c) Perhaps you have had an experience which you can exploit for a piece such as this – though, of course, it could be for a very different audience. If so, sketch an outline of the article before attempting a first draft, and try to include some of the elements included in the table above.

(d) It is likely that this article was at least partly 'ghost' written (see page 205 above) by a journalist who had interviewed Sarah Phillips, the subject of the story. Someone you know may have had an experience that would make an interesting read – an unusual encounter or experience, a triumph or disaster, an achievement or a disappointment.

Interview your subject following the same procedure as for biographical writing (see page 203 above) and tailor your piece to the 'house style' of an appropriate magazine or other suitable medium.

Just a bit

Should I..? Yeah! Well, you're meant to let your hair down on holiday...

By Sarah Phillips, 19, from Herne Bay, Kent

'Now boarding the 7.05 flight to Ibiza,' boomed the voice over the loudspeaker. I smiled at my mates Jenny and Emmie. It was finally here – the holiday we'd been planning for months.

I was 17 and it was the first time I'd been abroad without Mum and Dad. I loved clubbing, so Ibiza seemed the perfect choice.

We were staying in a resort called Figueretes, which was pretty quiet. So on the third night, we decided to head for San Antonio – we'd heard the nightlife there was amazing.

Emmie had gone out with some other mates she'd met, but me and Jenny couldn't wait for our first big night out in Ibiza.

'Come on, Jen,' I sighed, slumped on the bed in our apartment as she put on a third coat of mascara. She always took ages to get ready. Me, I'm one of those girls who's ready in 10 minutes.

We couldn't have looked any different – her dressed up to the nines in a silver slinky number and strappy sandals, and me – my hair all scruffy and trainers on. But we were great mates. Jenny and Emmie were both older – Jenny 29 and Emmie 28. And they were quite protective with me.

We jumped on a bus to San Antonio and got there at about 8pm.

'Sex on the beach?' laughed Jen, as we pushed our way through the crowd to the first bar. The cocktail had become our favourite holiday tipple. and it was always a laugh to order it.

A few cocktails later, we headed for the dance floor. One of my favourite DJs, Dave Pearce, was playing, and I was desperate to get a photo with him.

'Just do it,' said Jenny.

So I did, walked right up and introduced myself. I couldn't believe I was there chatting to him.

'Are you coming to Eden tonight?' he asked.

But it'd cost an extra £50 and we didn't have enough money. None of us were that well off – we all worked on the tills in Safeway.

'No worries, girls, I'll get you on the guest list,' said Dave. Wow! I felt a bit like a celeb. Dave headed off, and me and Jen went to another bar. We got chatting to these blokes, Wayne* and Stewart*, from Birmingham and we really hit it off. But we weren't looking for anything romantic. I was seeing Dave* back home. And anyway, this was a girly holiday – we weren't interested in lads.

'I'm horny, horny horny horny...' Jenny started singing when our favourite holiday song came on.

We were all dancing, but Wayne took me to one side. 'Have you ever taken drugs?' he asked, and I nodded, a little embarrassed.

'Just the once – at a club in Kent.'

He asked me if I wanted to share an ecstasy pill. I knew it was risky, but the last time had been great – it'd given me loads of confidence – and anyway, I was on my hols. It was only half an E. Where was the harm?

As the night wore on, I couldn't even tell I'd taken anything.

'That wasn't very good,' I shouted to Wayne over the music, but he was too drunk to care.

I headed to the bar. 'Agua por favor!' I yelled. From now on, I'd stick to water.

We left the club about 2am – it was weird, last time I took ecstasy, it kept me up all night, but this time I was exhausted.

'Hungover?' said Jenny, coming in to my room in her PJs the next morning. She buried herself in my pillows.

'I feel like someone's beaten me over the head with a hammer.'

I felt awful, too, but I hadn't been drunk. I'd only drunk water when I was

All I wanted was to go home to my mum

SARAH'S NOT-SO-ECSTATIC TRUE STORY

# of fun

at Eden – I never drink alcohol when I'm out clubbing.

Must be the heat, I thought, as I clutched my stomach in pain. Either that or I'd swallowed some water when I'd been scuba diving the other day.

Whatever it was, it got worse. A few days later, I couldn't leave the apartment. I felt sick all the time and I had the runs. But that's normal when you're abroad, isn't it?

Emmie went home early – she broke her foot and then her little girl had an accident at home. The holiday was turning into a nightmare. My first time abroad and I was on the phone to my mum every day. But I still had another week out here.

'I want to come home, too,' I'd cry, but I couldn't really leave, I felt too bad about Jenny. At least she was having a good time.

Eventually, the two weeks were up, and we headed home. Emmie and her fella Paul picked us up from the airport. I walked through the barrier and Emmie looked at me in horror. I'd turned yellow.

'It looks like jaundice. You could have something wrong with your liver,' she said. Her mate had had liver problems, so she knew the signs.

I was back and forth to the hospital. The doctors thought I had hepatitis. They told me to stay off work for a couple of months – *it must be serious.*

I felt rough for a while, but gradually, my liver seemed to repair itself. I felt loads better.

'I think it's time you had a night out,' said my mate Claire. I'd been cooped up for long enough.

So, the next week we went to our favourite club – Amadeus in Kent. Had a few too many vodka and Cokes.

The next morning, I had a killer hangover. I couldn't shake it. A week later, I started to feel sick. I was going yellow again with jaundice.

Gradually I got worse. I was texting my boyfriend Dave one day and didn't know what I was writing. My sister Tracey tried to take my mobile off me, but I went mad. Mum phoned my dad and asked him to come round. She thought I was drugged up. Dad took me to the hospital. By then I was out of it and I was hysterical – locked myself in the toilet, screamed and ranted like a loony.

The doctors put me on a ventilator and a dialysis machine. It didn't work. I slipped into a coma and needed a liver transplant.

One of the doctors asked Dave if he knew if I'd ever taken drugs.

'She's taken ecstasy once or twice,' he said, and the doctors looked at me.

'Why didn't she tell us this before?'

Truth was, I'd worried it might have been the drugs that had made me ill. But I thought Mum would go mad if she found out, so I hadn't said anything.

I thought Mum would go mad if she found out, so I hadn't said anything

We found out later that the toxins from the E I'd taken on holiday had been poisoning my body. Of course, I was out of it, didn't know how ill I was. But Mum told me later that I'd nearly died.

'It's really not looking good. Her body is very weak,' the doctor had told Mum. 'She's probably only got another 72 hours.'

Mum stayed with me, holding my hand, hoping against hope for a miracle.

And she got one – the doctors found a liver. A transplant might just save my life.

When I came out of theatre, I was babbling. 'Where's my baby?' I asked. I don't have any kids. I was hallucinating, but Mum just laughed, tears of joy streaming down her face. I was alive. That's what mattered.

It took me another three months before I was completely better. I'd been through hell, put my family through it, too, all because I'd wanted a laugh.

People think that's what ecstasy is – just a bit of fun. But it kills people.

I even split up with Dave over it. He took a few Es after I came out of hospital. He lied to me about it because he knew I disapproved, but I caught him at it when we were out clubbing one night.

He chose drugs over me, and we split up. I won't be around people who do drugs now.

I met a lad in a club a few months ago, and realised he was off his face.

'You're on E, aren't you? You mad, or what? It nearly killed me.' Then I showed him the scar from my transplant. He looked like he was going to throw up. He couldn't get away fast enough. I hope it made him think twice before he took it again.

I don't even smoke fags or drink any more – I can't because of my liver, but I wouldn't anyway. I'm lucky to be alive. I got a second chance at life and I'm not going to do anything to mess it up.

*'Wayne', 'Stewart' and 'Dave' are not their real names.

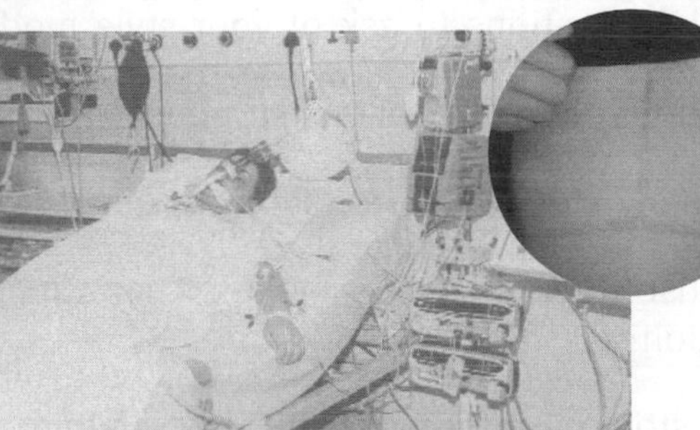

I hope what happened to me puts others off

27

Prose fiction

Writing good prose fiction is difficult – and unless you are a regular reader of fiction yourself it is often unwise to attempt this for your Original Writing coursework. Moreover, on an A Level course you will not have time to develop a narrative of anything like the length or complexity of a novel, and however popular it is as a school writing exercise, there is only a limited market for the short story.

But it may be that you have a particular interest in fiction of a certain type or **genre**, and that there is a particular medium in which short examples (up to 1500 words) of the genre do appear. Such genres might include:

- crime/detective fiction
- romantic fiction
- action/adventure
- science fiction/fantasy
- horror/thriller.

Many genres of fiction have shared characteristics which writers adopt with varying degrees of originality. For your chosen genre, you will need to read widely within the genre and carry out an investigation of the following:

- Story titles and characters names. (Would 'Mist in the Morning' be a more appropriate title for a crime thriller or a romantic story? What might we predict about a tale that has 'Lex Zoldark' as its central character?)
- Settings and locations. (For which genres of story would a crumbling mansion adjacent to a graveyard be a suitable setting?)
- Typical storylines. (Boy meets girl, they overcome problems and live happily ever after.)
- Common stylistic features (Many dynamic verbs are used in action/adventure stories, and adjectives/adverbs in descriptions for horror stories.)

As you investigate any genre, as with other kinds of Original Writing, you should spend time studying good examples, or style models. Whatever genre of fiction you study, the questions to ask of your style models will be similar:

- What does the writer establish about characters and setting?
- How many characters are involved, and of what kind?
- What use does the writer make of narration, dialogue, description and reflection?
- Is the story narrated using the first or third person – and whose point of view does the narrative primarily present?

- What is the 'crisis' of the narrative, and how is it resolved?
- How does the writer achieve an effective ending?

ACTIVITY 17

Here, we will look at the opening of a story, 'Stepping In', which appeared in *Bella* magazine's popular 'Tales with a Twist' series of family-orientated if somewhat formulaic short stories.

(a) Answer as many of the questions above as you can for the extract given.

(b) Now provide your own ending to the story in a style that is consistent with the first part of the tale. Remember to try to achieve some sort of 'twist' at the end.

Compare your study of the first part of the story with the commentary on page 231.

STEPPING IN

JAN COULDN'T GET EXCITED ABOUT CHRISTMAS – HAD THE MAGIC GONE FOREVER?

Jan glowered at the tree. 'I hate Christmas!' she said. Tim had brought the tree home, grumbling at its price, and it stood in the corner, bare and dismal, waiting for her to decorate it. Any time now it would start shedding its needles all over the carpet and making more work.

Her mother frowned. 'Don't say that. It's the season of goodwill.'

'Huh!' Jan poked about in the box of decorations. A tawdry looking lot they were, too. 'It'd be better scrapped.'

'You don't mean that,' Mum protested. 'You loved it, once.'

'Of course I did, once. Christmas is for kids. Santa Claus, Away In a Manger, Little Donkey . . . I go along with it because I don't want our children to miss out. But what's in it for adults? Mothers, especially. Hard labour and an empty purse.'

The presents – modest though they were – had cost the earth. Then there were the drinks you had to lay on for anybody who dropped in, the cards, the stamps, food for the regulation blow-out, and all the things you'd forgotten to budget for, like marzipan for the cake and chocolate liqueur.

Not to mention crackers. All silver stars on the outside and nothing inside but a paper hat and a silly plastic toy.

'You're tired,' Mum said.

You could say that again, Jan thought. Especially this year, what with just recovering from flu and the worry about Tim's job, besides the usual 1001 things that had to be done.

Mum was bringing round old Mrs Bates for Christmas dinner, and there'd be Tim's Uncle Frank with his endless 'Did I tell you about the time when . . .'

Commentary tip

In Module 2 you may have studied the ways that characters of different gender, class or region are represented in fiction. Perhaps in your story you have followed the pattern and deliberately worked with the stereotypes that you think the genre demands. More interestingly, you may have decided to defy these expectations. Either way, discuss these issues, and make the link to your Module 2 work.

Fiction for younger readers

It may be that you wish to try your hand at a piece of fiction for children. It is however, a lot more difficult than may at first appear to capture the interest and imagination of children; a good idea for characters and storyline needs to be matched by a controlled yet imaginative use of language.

What makes a successful piece of children's fiction? The only way to find out is to look at a variety of texts aimed at children of all ages – and to talk to children themselves!

ACTIVITY 18

Below is a list of some characteristics of successful children's fiction as suggested by a group of students. This is followed by two extracts from contrasting examples. *Shrek* is the source of the successful animated film, and *Percy the Small Engine* is an example from a previous generation of writing for children – part of the Rev. W. Awdry's popular series of which 'Thomas the Tank Engine' is the best-known character.

As far as you can judge from these short extracts, and using any additional examples you can find, suggest how far – if at all – each of the following characteristics applies:

- central character(s) with whom younger readers can identify – these may be children, animals, mythical creatures or even humanised inanimate objects
- a fast-moving series of adventures/episodes
- the story at some level reflects issues which do arise in children's lives
- a clear sense of 'good', 'bad, 'right' or 'wrong'
- an underlying 'moral' or message
- some playful uses of language
- language may be limited in complexity (e.g. in terms of syntax, abstraction and lexical range) but does stimulate and enrich the readers' linguistic experience
- the ending 'rewards' the central character in some way.

Compare your discussions of these extracts with the commentary on page 232.

TEXT A **SHREK**

His mother was ugly and his father was ugly, but Shrek was uglier than the two of them put together. By the time he toddled, Shrek could spit flame a full ninety-nine yards and vent smoke from either ear. With just a look he cowed the reptiles in the swamp. Any snake dumb enough to bite him instantly got convulsions and died.

One day Shrek's parents hissed things over and decided it was about time their little darling was out in the world doing his share of damage. So they kicked him goodbye and Shrek left the black hole in which he'd been hatched.

Shrek went slogging along the road, giving off his awful fumes. It delighted him to see the flowers bend aside and the trees lean away to let him go by.

In a shady copse he came across a witch. She was busy boiling bats in turpentine and turtle juice, and as she stirred she crooned . . .

'What a lovely stench!' Shrek cackled. The witch specialized in horrors, but one single look at Shrek make her woozy.

When she recovered her senses Shrek said, 'Tell my fortune, madam, and I'll let you have a few of my rare lice.'

'Splendid!' crowed the witch. 'Here's your fortune.

'Otchky-potchky, itchky-pitch,

Pay attention to this witch.

A donkey takes you to a knight –

Him you conquer in a fight.

Then you wed a princess who

Is even uglier than you.

Ha ha ha and cockadoodle,

The magic words are "Apple Strudel".'

'A princess!' Shrek cried. 'I'm on my way!'

Soon he came upon a peasant singing and scything. 'You there, yokel,' said Shrek. 'Why so blithe?'

The peasant mumbled this reply:

'I'm happy scything in the rye,

I never stop to wonder why.

I'll hone and scythe until I die.

But now I'm busy. So goodbye.'

'Yokel,' Shrek snapped. 'What have you in that pouch of yours.'

'Just some cold pheasant.'

'Pheasant, peasant? What a pleasant present!'

The last thing the peasant saw before he fainted was Shrek's glare warming up his dinner. Shrek ate and moved on.

Wherever Shrek went, every living creature fled. How it tickled him to be so repulsive!

TEXT B PERCY THE SMALL ENGINE

Percy is a little green tank-engine who works in the Yard at the Big Station. He is a funny little engine, and loves playing jokes. These jokes sometimes get him into trouble.

'Peep peep!' he whistled one morning. 'Hurry up Gordon! the train's ready.'

Gordon thought he was late and came puffing out.

'Ha ha!' laughed Percy, and showed him a train of dirty coal trucks.

Gordon didn't go back to the shed.

He stayed on a siding thinking how to pay Percy out.

'Stay in the shed today,' squeaked Percy to James. 'The Fat Controller will come and see you.'

James was a conceited engine. 'Ah!' he thought, 'the Fat Controller knows I'm a fine engine, ready for anything. He wants me to pull a Special Train.'

So James stayed where he was, and nothing his Driver and Fireman could do would make him move.

But the Fat Controller never came, and the other engines grumbled dreadfully.

They had to do James' work as well as their own.

At last an Inspector came. 'Show a wheel, James,' he said crossly. 'You can't stay here all day.'

'The Fat Controller told me to stay here,' answered James sulkily. 'He sent a message this morning.'

'He did not,' retorted the Inspector. 'How could he? He's away for a week.'

'Oh!' said James. 'Oh!' and he came quickly out of the shed. 'Where's Percy?' Percy had wisely disappeared!

When the Fat Controller came back, he did see James, and Percy too. Both engines wished he hadn't!

James and Gordon wanted to pay Percy out; but Percy kept out of their way. One morning, however, he was so excited that he forgot to be careful.

'I say you engines,' he bubbled, 'I'm to take some trucks to Thomas' Junction. The Fat Controller chose me specially. He must know I'm a Really Useful Engine.'

'More likely he wants you out of the way,' grunted James.

But Gordon gave James a wink . . . Like this.

'Ah yes,' said James, 'just so . . . You were saying Gordon . . .?'

Now is your chance to create a piece of fiction of your own. As you develop your ideas you may wish to think about the kinds of illustrations you would use. They are important in helping to contextualise unfamiliar language – but you do not need to produce these for yourself. Make sure you test your work on some 'guinea pig' readers of the age group you are aiming at, and ask them for their honest opinions.

Commentary tip

If you attempt a piece of children's fiction, there will be plenty of issues to discuss in your commentary:

- your choice of central character and storyline
- how you have controlled the syntactic complexity of your language
- how you have made the language interesting and challenging, as well as accessible
- how you provided sufficient contextual information to allow readers to guess the meaning of unfamiliar language.

Choosing your assignment

As you make your choice of writing assignment, you may find it helpful to submit your proposal to your supervising teacher; as with previous assignments, make sure you cover the following key points:

Proposal/Pre-commentary: Writing to entertain

Key point	Explanation
Content/subject matter	What/who are you going to write about?
Genre/medium	What kind of text are you going to write, and where might it appear? Be as specific as you can. Is this different from your other pieces?
Target audience	Which group(s) of people are you hoping to reach? Is this a distinctly different audience from your other pieces?
What style models do you intend to study?	Note the titles of similar texts, aimed at a similar audience, but *not* on the same topic.

Writing to persuade

The primary purpose of persuasion includes not only texts which set out to persuade us to do something – give money, buy a product, vote for a political party – but also any piece of writing that seeks to influence us, or change our opinions, or challenge our beliefs and assumptions. Some obvious examples include:

- advertising and marketing campaigns
- letters to newspapers, magazines, MPs, etc. on controversial topics
- newspaper or magazine articles putting forward a particular point of view or argument
- flyers and leaflets on a controversial subject
- reviews of films, CDs and other consumer products and services
- political pamphlets, speeches and election addresses
- other speeches and presentations.

Many forms of writing have a persuasive element, and you could argue that for some of the examples listed here (such as reviews) the informative function is equally important. As always, it is important to be alert to the ways in which these purposes overlap and help shape the distinctive nature of texts.

There are strong links between the study of writing to persuade, and the study of Language and Power for Module 2 (see pages 88–114 Module 2). It may be a good idea to study these two parts of the course in tandem. As part of your study of Language and Power, you will be examining the power of rhetoric and investigating what it is that makes language influential, impressive and powerful – the very things you need to do when producing a persuasive text of your own.

Commentary tip

Refer to the section in Language and Power on rhetoric and persuasive language (page 102 Module 2) – and identify some specific examples in your own writing of any of these techniques.

Appealing to heads or hearts

What makes a piece of language persuasive or influential? One way of starting to answer this question is to think of it in terms of three key elements – the **who**, the **what**, and the **how**. The framework below can be applied to persuasive texts:

Key element	Explanation	Some language features to consider
Who is addressing us?	What is our relationship with the author/source? How much should we trust/respect him or her?	At what points – if at all – does the author/speaker use 'I' or 'we' – and with what effect? How does the author establish or claim authority or expertise on the topic? What sort of relationship does the author establish with his or her readers/listeners?
What exactly is he or she telling us?	How strong is the case or argument being put forward? Does the logic stand up to analysis? Does it convince us *intellectually* about the truth of what is being said?	What is the main conclusion the text tends towards? What does it want us to think/believe/do as a result of reading/hearing the text? What are the main arguments? What facts or other pieces of evidence are given in support of these? How clearly does the logic lead to the conclusion? (Look for words such as 'so', 'therefore', 'because', 'however'.) Does the text deal with any possible objections or counter-arguments to the case it is making?

How does he or she convey ideas to us?	presentation of the message? Does it create an *emotional*, as well as an intellectual, response?	How does the text convey opinions and subjective judgements? (Look, for example, at the kinds of adjectives used to make evaluative comments.) How does the text make us care about the issue? At which points is the choice of language particularly emotive? Which rhetorical/persuasive techniques give the text its particular impact?

ACTIVITY 19

Apply the sets of questions in the table on page 219 to the examples below – and supplement these with additional texts of your own. For example, study some examples of film, music and other reviews in popular magazines and newspapers.

Compare your responses with the commentary on page 232.

TEXT A

SHELTER

Dear Friend

Forgive me if I sound angry. But hearing the stories I hear every day, and knowing how badly many homeless families are treated in Britain today, I find it hard to be cool and unemotional about it.

Ours is supposed to be a civilised society – and yet the conditions in which many homeless families are living are nothing short of scandalous. The latest figures show that in England alone, a total of 81,270 households are living in temporary accommodation – the highest number ever. Of these, 12,000 households, including thousands of children, are living in bed and breakfast accommodation – the worst and most insecure form of temporary housing. Often whole families are crammed together in a single room for several months at a time.

Every day Shelter hears from people living in overcrowded conditions where they are forced to share basic amenities with several other families. We hear about people being placed in houses with dangerous stairs, poor ventilation, defective gas fires, unsafe wiring, filthy kitchens and stinking toilets. We hear about children suffering from bronchitis, asthma and stomach aches because of their disgusting living conditions. We hear of parents sinking into depression as they struggle to cope.

We can't let this go on. It's degrading, inhuman and plain **wrong.** That is why I want to ask you to share our anger and concern – and to turn it into **practical action** by pledging £2 a month to help us win a better deal for Britain's homeless people.

If you are wondering how £2 can help, let me give you an example – among thousands I could choose – of how Shelter works to help people in housing need.

Louise is a mum with two young children, who was made homeless when her landlord sold the flat she rented. Her local council placed her in bed and breakfast accommodation, where for six long, dreadful months she had to endure the sheer hell of bringing up her children in one cramped room . . .

This is where Shelter's work is vital. We are Britain's leading charity working with homeless and badly housed people. Our housing aid centres and our free national 24-hour housing helpline, Shelterline, give advice, information and practical help to well over 100,000 people every year. **But as a charity we struggle to raise the money to keep these services going – and there is so much more we need to do.** That is why your £2 a month really is important to us. It will help us raise the regular income we need to be here for families like Louise's, 24 hours a day, 365 days a year.

. . . **Please help us to make it happen by using the form enclosed to pledge £2 a month,** or as much as you can spare. Thank you.

Yours sincerely

Christine Parrish

Director of Housing Services

TEXT B

YOUR £10 CAN HELP TO CHANGE THESE YOUNGSTERS' LIVES

Amelia Hill visits Fairbridge, a group that unlocks the potential of teenagers crushed by inner-city deprivation.

Fairbridge doesn't assist sufferers of a particular disease. It can't produce figures showing how many people it has helped to achieve a concrete goal. Instead, it targets teenagers suffering from inner-city deprivation.

Fairbridge works quietly and efficiently from 12 bases across the country to catch youngsters aged from 13 to 25 who have slipped through all society's safety nets.

These are people who have been crushed by life; victims of physical and emotional abuse, and long-term sufferers of drug and alcohol addiction. They are typically homeless, have little – if any – education and are angry, aggressive and abusive to those who reach out to them . . .

Fairbridge enabled 241 young people last year to develop the self-confidence to take part in team activities for probably the first time in their lives; learning to make and keep commitments, turn up on time and trust both themselves and others.

. . . 'We offer these young people a good deal,' said Tony Maybery, manager of the Southampton centre. 'They take part in activities they enjoy on an entirely voluntary basis. All they have to do is commit to explore their behaviour and attitudes.'

The group receives financial donations from a range of bodies, including AOL and Barclays, as well as support from a range of businesses such as Waitrose and members of the Guild of Food Writers, who regularly visit centres to help teach the youngsters how to cook.

Just over half its annual funding of £340,000 comes from statutory grants but Fairbridge is determined to make up financial shortfalls with trust money and public donations.

. . . 'By making a donation to Fairbridge, the public can give young people someone to believe in and that's when they start to believe in themselves,' said Allan.

'We're the last opportunity for many of these children to put their lives back together.'

The Observer

The structure of arguments

When constructing your persuasive text it is important to be clear about the points you wish to make, and the conclusion you want your readers to reach. Whether you can persuade someone to accept this conclusion who did not already do so will largely depend on the reasons you give in support, and how you lead your reader/listener logically from one reason to another until you reach your conclusion.

ACTIVITY 20

In this Activity you will examine an example of an 'argument' and the way in which different reasons are assembled to lead to the conclusion. The text is an extract from an editorial in *When Saturday Comes*, a weekly football magazine.

After reading the piece, below, answer the following questions:

- What is the conclusion of the text?
- List the principal reasons given in the text which lead to this conclusion.
- How does the writer acknowledge – and then counter – the reasons given for the proposal in the first place?
- What words/phrases are used – often at the beginnings of paragraphs – to build the argument from one point to the next?

IF THE CAP FITS

Both the Canterbury Bulldogs (one of the top rugby league clubs in Sydney) and the Australian Rules club Carlton (something like the equivalent of Arsenal in Melbourne) were plunged into crisis by the application of the salary cap, the very mechanism proposed as a solution to the problems of European football both by the ever-active imaginations of the G14 group and some Nationwide League chairmen.

Carlton were fined £330,000 and subjected to heavy penalties in the AFL's draft system, for making under-the-counter payments to several players in order to evade the salary cap rules . . . The Bulldogs were docked 38 points near the end of this season for similar breaches of the league cap, dumping them firmly at the bottom of the table and making a farce of the whole campaign . . .

The arguments over salary caps (and the draft systems that go with them in many American and Australian sport) tend to divide people along unusual ideological lines. On the one hand, the stated aim is to keep competitions balanced and not allow a few clubs to become far richer than the others for an indefinite length of time . . .

On the other hand, salary caps are generally resisted by players' unions, for obvious reasons, and by the restrictive practices zealots of the European Union, who see them as a blatant restraint of trade. While a more equal league and a reduction in the percentage of turnover spent by clubs on wages are both desirable goals, the current proposals for salary caps are likely to prove not only ineffective in achieving them, but also disingenuous in their motivation.

The first objection is that salary caps simply do not work . . . Examples from other countries and the experience of our maximum wage until its abolition suggest that clubs will always try to find a way around the caps. What's more, if they are caught, the consequences make a joke of the competition and are deeply unfair to fans who have invested time and money in following the league in good faith . . .

The second objection is that neither the G14 nor the Nationwide League chairmen (led by the most profligate of the First Division spenders) are in any position to demand a salary cap. On the most basic level, the idea that any cap should be based on a percentage of turnover (rather than an absolute sum) would serve not so much to iron out inequalities as to institutionalise them.

More iniquitous still is the idea that the G14 (now comprising 18 clubs) is entitled to dictate how other clubs should organise their finances. Their proposals on the salary cap . . . are in fact simply their latest ploy to gain legitimacy at the expense of the game's governing bodies.

As in many other areas of industry, this plea for a certain kind of regulation is essentially a smokescreen designed to cover up gross mismanagement. The proposals are likely to prove unworkable, unfair and illegal. But history suggests that is not likely to stop football charging enthusiastically towards an apparently neat solution to its problems.

Possible topics

The range of possible subjects for persuasive writing is enormous – and your topic doesn't have to be a matter of huge national or philosophical importance. There is already a great deal of material related to the more popular topics such as hunting, smoking, drugs, abortion and even euthanasia, so why not go for something a little different, possibly a little closer to home?

Activity 21

What follows is the beginning of a list of some possibilities, moving from very local topics right through to major philosophical questions. Use the various sections of the table as a framework to interview a partner and find out what he or she feels strongly about.

Domestic or personal issues	School or college-based issues	Neighbourhood issues	Town/regional issues	National issues	International political/ scientific issues
Should smacking of children be allowed? Do kids watch too much TV? Should children get more/less pocket money, or do more/less homework? Should people be encouraged to eat a healthier diet?	Dress code Recreational facilities – access and quality The value of Key Skills/ General Studies/other compulsory courses Access to IT facilities Homework/ coursework policy Student Charter issues	Community facilities for young people Litter, graffiti, vandalism Transport	Crime, drugs Unemploy-ment Transport, education, health services Sports team Charity campaigns	AS exams Student fees Drugs policy Religious/ single-faith schools Race/gender issues Censorship – sex and violence on TV The Euro Transport policy The NHS	Third World poverty Environment/ pollution GM foods War, terrorism The Middle East Cloning

As you make your choice of writing assignment, you should submit your proposal to your supervising teacher – covering the key points suggested below:

Proposal/Pre-commentary: Writing to persuade

Key point	Explanation
Content/subject matter	What are you going to persuade your readers/listeners to do, think or believe?
Target audience	Which group(s) of people are you hoping to reach? Is this a distinctly different audience from your other pieces?
Genre/medium	How are you going to reach them? What kind of text are you going to write, and where might it appear? Be as specific as you can. Is this different from your other pieces?
Your argument	What information are you going to include/need to collect? Outline in brief the structure of your argument. How will you appeal to heads and hearts?
What style models do you intend to study?	Note the titles of similar texts, aimed at a similar audience but *not* on the same topic.

Preparing your submission for assessment

Selecting your final pieces

On your AS course, you may have had the opportunity to attempt several potential coursework pieces in draft form; if so, you will now need to choose two pieces which you will develop to completion for your submission. As you do so, remember the requirements for the folder and the key words in the table on pages 175–6. You should also bear in mind the following guidelines:

- Choose two pieces which show a strong contrast of purpose, audience, genre and style. You are aiming to demonstrate your versatility as a writer.
- Choose pieces which reflect your own individual interests.
- Make sure that the pieces provide enough challenge; some types of writing – such as writing basic sets of instructions, or writing for very young children, may not allow you to demonstrate sufficiently high-level skills to achieve the higher mark bands.
- Find one or two examples of texts written for the same purpose/medium/genre as your chosen task, but on different topics. Study these style models closely – applying the same kinds of detailed questions to them as if they were texts for analysis on the Unit 1 paper.

A note on 'originality' and pastiche

After thoroughly researching the genre and style models of the kinds of writing you intend to produce, there is a danger that you could end up merely producing acceptable imitations of established kinds of text, or **pastiches**. Pastiches can easily topple over into **parodies**, where a writer deliberately exaggerates some of the distinctive features of a genre in order to mock them.

The principal challenge facing any writer is to work within the established expectation of a genre while doing something just a little different. If you disregard all the conventions and expectations of the genre, your work is unlikely to be published; on the other hand, you should be doing more than just slavishly copying a list of characteristic features and cloning existing texts.

For example, the film *The Blair Witch Project* used many of the rather clichéd expectations of the horror genre, while at the same time offering a different kind of experience for the viewers. Effective work for Original Writing will be of this kind – clearly rooted in a study of the appropriate genres and style models, but demonstrating your individuality in the way you work with these conventions. It can be a difficult balance to strike.

Drafting and re-drafting

It is likely that your final pieces will need to go through at least two or three drafts before you are completely happy with them. Make sure that you know the **internal deadlines** which your school or college sets for submission, and allow time for this process to take place. Each draft should represent your best attempt at the task; once you have completed a draft, you should seek feedback from the following groups of people:

- Yourself. It is important to become increasingly critical of your own work. Put your writing aside for a couple of days after you have finished a draft, and then return to it as objectively and critically as you can. It is a good idea to read your text aloud. This is particularly important for scripts and other texts intended to be heard, but it can also help you spot problems of expression with all kinds of writing.
- Your fellow Language students. Try a 'workshop' approach where you and your classmates offer helpful, critical comments on each other's work.
- Your teacher. He or she will act as your advisor or editor and offer constructive advice and criticism. Your teacher will *not* be able to correct errors or details, but will be able to offer quite substantial guidance on what you need to do to improve the piece.
- Your readers. You need to select a number of 'guinea pigs' who are typical of the kind of readers you are trying to reach with your pieces, and try out your writing on them. For their feedback to be useful, you might like to give them a short questionnaire which invites them to comment (anonymously) on some specific aspects of the piece – otherwise, they are likely to offer rather bland approval, out of friendship or kindness.
- A 'real' editor. For some kinds of writing it may be possible to submit a well-developed draft to an editor of the kind of medium you are aiming for – such as a student magazine, local newspaper, or a website – and invite comment. However, don't be too disappointed if you receive either no response, or only a flat rejection.

It is very important that you keep a copy or record of each draft of your piece. If you are working with a word processor, save each successive draft with a different file name; you will need to submit *each* draft in your folder and to discuss the changes you have made in your commentary.

Commentary tip

One alternative way of saving versions of your work is to make use of the 'track changes' function in a program such as Microsoft Word, which enables you to highlight changes you make to a draft. You can then discuss in detail your reasons for some of the more significant alterations you make.

Your teacher will also require you to keep any notes he or she gives you on the drafts, as well as any other feedback you receive from other sources.

Activity 22

As you revisit a draft of your work, ask questions such as the following. Make a note of your answers in your notebook and refer to these later when writing your commentaries.

- Is it well organised – is there a logical structure and is it easy to follow?
- In particular, does the opening sentence and paragraph do the job it needs to?
- How does it compare with the style models you have studied?
- What kind of relationship have you tried to achieve with your reader? Are your choices about whether to address readers directly using the second person, and whether to use the first person, all appropriate?
- What **register**(s) have you chosen to use, and are these suitable for your audience? Have you achieved the right level of formality/seriousness?
- Are your sentences well-constructed and accurately punctuated? Reading aloud will help you to judge.
- How accurate is your spelling? A high standard of technical accuracy is expected at A Level.

The commentary

When you are satisfied that you have completed the final drafts of your pieces, you should turn to writing the final version of your commentaries. If you have taken the advice offered earlier by writing ongoing commentaries on your work and keeping a working notebook, you will already have a lot of the raw material. Look back, too, at the 'Commentary tips' offered throughout this module.

Remember, the commentaries account for one-third of the total marks in this module. Here are some guidelines to help you to gain as many of these marks as possible:

Key point	Comments
Explain your **aim**	This is your chance to show that you have addressed complex and subtle language points. Don't spend too long giving a long narrative account of how you came to develop the idea, but do give a brief explanation of your aims, ideas and intentions. Briefly outline your aim, then discuss how the web of requirements of audience, purpose and genre made your task complex and demanding.

Key point	Comments
Reflect on the **choices** you have made and select the most significant ones to discuss	As a writer of texts you have made hundreds of choices within each language framework. These include: **Content (selection)**: what to include and what to leave out **Structure (discourse)**: how to begin, how to end, and how to get from one to the other **Form/lay-out (graphology)**: how to present your text on the page **Register (grammar/lexis)**: the level of formality/technicality to use **Tone and style (grammar, lexis, semantics, pragmatics)**: the degree of lightness/seriousness to adopt, how to address your readers/listeners, and how to use language to achieve your desired effect. In about 750 words per commentary, you cannot possibly explain every detail of these choices, but do pick out some of the most significant ones and include at least some detailed analysis of linguistic details from your text. Remember to quote relevant extracts from your work to illustrate your points.
Analyse the changes you have made	In the course of re-drafting your work it has probably changed significantly. Explain why you have made some of the revisions to your texts, and refer specifically to some changes in the drafts included in your folder.
Refer to **style models**	In explaining your choices of language and approach, refer specifically to any style models you have used.
Refer to **sources**	Make it clear exactly how you have used information from other sources, and demonstrate how you have changed and re-presented it by referring specifically to the sources you include in your folder.
Evaluate the results	Arrive at an objective judgment on your pieces. How successful are they? What do you think might still need to be revised if you had more time?
Keep to **word limits**	You'll probably need most of the 1500 words allowed for both commentaries to do justice to the task, but don't go beyond this; the best commentaries are brisk and selective, not leisurely and encyclopaedic!

Practicalities: assembling your file

When it comes to submitting your folder, your school/college will advise you about the practicalities of how to present your work. The file you submit should include the following key elements.

Key element	Comments
Contents page	Use a single sheet of A4 to list the contents of your file.
A short **'pre-commentary'** for each of the two pieces, simply stating the intended audience, purpose, genre and medium of each.	This can be a single sheet of A4 at the front of your folder. Do not include this in your word counts.
The **final version** of both pieces, free from all annotations and presented as professionally as possible.	It is good to make the pieces appear in the format in which they are intended to be published. However, no real credit is given for artwork and graphic design, so concentrate on the text rather than spending hours formatting and laying it out.
Bibliographies.	Include a bibliography if you have referred to other sources of information in preparing your submission. Give full details of author, title, publisher and date of publication, and website addresses.
An accurate **word count**.	Record this at the end of the piece. Ensure that the total length of the two pieces is between 1500 and 3000 words.
The **commentary** on each piece.	It is best to place each commentary immediately after the final version of each text, but before the previous drafts.
All **previous drafts** of both pieces – along with any comments/annotations made by teachers and readers.	Arrange these sequentially, from first draft onwards, and label them clearly for ease of reference.
Source materials.	You should include photocopies or printouts of any significant sources of information you have used. This is particularly important for informative texts, where you need to show that you have created a genuinely original piece of writing. Label your sources for ease of reference in your commentaries.
Style models.	Include examples of any style models you have studied when preparing your pieces. Again, label these for ease of reference.

Commentaries

Activity 4

1 In text **A,** note the word play on 'fill the gap', the amusing graphics, the attempts to enthuse readers with words like 'broaden horizons' and 'seize the freedom', and the direct address in the second person. The headline of text **B** links it to the wider 'A-Z of 2003' feature of which it is part, and its apparent 'shock' value – what, no more CDs? – invites readers to read on. Text **C** also goes for a shock effect with its 'prisoner' shot of the typical *Cosmo Girl* reader, which makes clear the meaning of the italicised headline word 'Real'. This, it seems to be saying, could happen to *you*! The opening paragraph is in the present tense and the second person, forcing its readers to undergo imaginatively the experience the article is discussing. The 'trail' for text **D** is provided by the anchor-man's link, and it functions, in effect, as the headline of the piece.

2 The gatefold-leaflet format of text **A** breaks the information into clearly defined sections, each with its own snappy headings. Paragraphing is also very clear, with some icons/symbols and emboldened questions drawing in the eye. Text **B** is a conventional magazine article, with regular paragraphing being the only graphological guide to the structure of the piece. Text **C**, however, uses panels, headings and 'pull quotes' to separate the article into reportage, case study, a set of numbered steps which will follow if someone is caught shoplifting, and a 'help & advice' section.

3 The two voices represent the 'studio' and the 'location' reporters, but in this piece of straight reporting no use is made of SFX or music. The report begins with an overview of the whole match, so there is no 'suspense' involved, but then follows the chronological sequence of first half – second half.

4 It's clear that the writer of text **A** assumes readers know what a 'gap year' means, and the register of the text includes several lexical items which most full-time students will recognise ('placement', 'sponsored events', etc). Some less common terms like the French word *vendange* are implicitly explained. Text **B** assumes in its readers a certain technological familiarity with the world of CDs and their 'skip facility', computing, music and an interest in the record industry generally – which is fair enough, given the medium in which it appears (the *NME*). Less technically, the opening paragraph of text **C** takes it for granted that its readers may be able to identify with the shoplifting scenario it describes and is careful to match the individual case studies to the target audience of the magazine in age and gender. The reporter in text **D** assumes basic interest in the rugby match he describes and a fair degree of familiarity with the terminology of the game, with its 'tries' and 'penalties'.

5 In text **A**, countries and cities are mentioned without explanation – so some basic geography is assumed. The references to students by first names does not imply we know them, but is designed to create an informal, friendly relationship. Text **B** includes unexplained references to technologically or music-related organisations like 'MSN' and 'WinMX', and to several musical artists, but *does* explain the initials 'RIAA' in full the first time it is mentioned. Text **C**'s reference to 'Winona' assumes that its readers will recognise the topical reference to the shoplifting case involving the Hollywood actress Winona Ryder. Text **D** assumes that most listeners may be familiar with the rugby players to whom it refers, though it does provide suitable labels (e.g. 'England and Lions pace man') for the benefit of more casual listeners.

6 No explanations are given by the reporter in text **D** of what 'tries' are or how many points they are worth – the assumption is that listeners are sufficiently informed on these basic aspects of the game.

7 In text **A** several examples of individual students' experiences are included to illustrate some of the general possibilities indicated. Text **B** includes a few facts and figures in straightforward numeric form – the '2.2 billion blank CDs' it mentions is included to convince its readers that there is a problem with music piracy. Text **C** is very much anecdote-led, with the 'true life' stories of two young girls occupying the bulk of the text, and even text **D** uses a human-interest angle to report the rugby game, choosing to focus on one well-known player even though he didn't make a decisive contribution to the game.

8 Standard English is used throughout text **A** but minor sentences like 'Planning a grand tour?', the use of contracted forms like 'they'll' and the slightly light-hearted flavour of some of the examples ('cleaning someone's car with a toothbrush!') don't allow the tone to become too serious. Text **B** is also remarkably formal and serious in tone, even though it includes numerous terms linked to modern music. However, it does slightly subvert 'standard' English practice by beginning sentences with 'Still' or 'So:', and includes some sentences that create the illusion of spontaneity and the spoken word ('Oh, and it's all our own fault'). The register of text **C** is notably different, being closer in places to the colloquial language it imagines its readers use ('scary stuff' . . . 'Mates won't cover for you') and directly quoting the subjects of its case studies extensively.

9 In text **A** some amusing graphics illustrate the main points in each section.

10 The second-person pronoun is used to address the reader throughout text **A** – this establishes an immediate and friendly relationship, and almost feels as if readers are being spoken to rather than written for. This is true to a lesser degree of text **B**, where the feel is still fairly personal, but not as insistently so. Text **C** goes further by forcing its readers to imagine themselves in the present tense carrying out an act of shoplifting. Text **D** remains entirely impersonal.

11 The only uses of first-person singular 'I' in any of the texts occur in passages quoted from specific people. The author of most short informative texts remains anonymous – and unimportant. The writer of text **B** uses the first-person plural, 'we'/'our', to suggest a unity of interest and identity between the writer and readers, but otherwise the texts avoid first-person usage.

12 There is clearly an element of persuasion going on in text **A**, as the Bureau which published the leaflet seems to wish to encourage young people to take a gap year of some kind. Text **B** is only persuasive in so far as it aims to convince its readers of the truth of its argument, but perhaps the pragmatic intention behind text **C** is to deter young people from shoplifting. Text **D** is largely informative but some colourful figurative language ('went off the boil', 'on the comeback trail') is fairly typical of sports reporting and hints at the need to entertain as well as inform listeners.

Activity 9

Text **A** is interesting because it addresses several different audiences – primarily victims but also bullies, parents and carers – all using the second-person pronoun 'you' throughout. It suggests that it has something to say to all of them, and the contents directs each group to its particular section. Celebrity endorsement in the introduction helps victims recognise that their situation is far from unique and can be very successfully overcome. The text uses headings which are phrased as first-person questions ('What can I do if I am being bullied?'), bullet points, and some emboldened and italic text for emphasis. The phrases/sentences in a series of bullets are usually syntactically similar, e.g. all begin with a verb, or contain imperatives. The instructions themselves are imperatives, but these are usually softened by phrases like 'try to . . .' and 'if you can help it'. Reassurance is offered by phrases like 'don't worry' and repeated comments that the recommended actions will make it 'harder' for the bully. The authorship of the text is of no interest or relevance, so the first person is avoided except in the heading already noted, where it is assuming the voice of the reader. Generally, the lexis is straightforward without being patronising – the text presumably has to speak to quite a wide range of students in terms of age and reading ability, so although the vocabulary is fairly simple ('upset', 'angry'), in some ways the language is quite mature ('don't become resigned to . . .').

Jamie Oliver's recipe (text **B**) is an interesting blend of first-person enthusiasm, expressed in short bursts like 'I love this salad', and 'One thing I do', and more straightforward imperatives – 'simply place the figs', 'weave around', etc. He doesn't follow the conventional lay-out for recipes; rather, his continuous prose seems designed to simulate his actual presence in the kitchen, as shown by the real time, future tense of 'At this point you'll think', and the colloquial 'it's pretty damn sexy'. His colourful and interestingly imprecise choice of verbs ('**throw in** some slices', '**rip** over some green or purple basil', '**drizzle** everything with the honey') helps convey something of the energetic personality most readers of the text will recognise from his TV series.

Activity 17

The very first sentence establishes quite a lot about the domestic, Christmas setting and the central character's mood (she 'glowered'). Other details in the paragraph (Tim's grumbling and the 'bare and dismal' nature of the tree) rapidly set the tone of the household as Christmas approaches. Characters are hastily sketched – the boring Uncle with his anecdotes, for instance, is a common enough stereotype. Although the story is told in the third person, it is largely the point of view of Jan we are presented with. She is likely to be the kind of character with whom many *Bella* readers can identify, and many of her thoughts and feelings are directly narrated. Dialogue is used selectively, with fragments of speech bringing to life the domestic episodes described in the story, but the descriptive detail is vital – note the kinds of adjectives used to describe the Christmas decorations ('bare', 'dismal', 'tawdry', 'silly').

Activity 18

It is impossible to reduce children's fiction to a formula, but these extracts do exemplify several features of the most popular titles. The central characters are all recognisable in different ways – Shrek as the unpopular 'loner', and Percy as the cheeky prankster who irritates the older children (represented here by the engines Gordon and James). *Shrek* follows one common narrative pattern by having the main character set out alone, presumably on a series of adventures which include encounters with a witch and a princess, who may represent the possibilities of evil and purity in the world; Percy's story ostensibly takes place in a railway yard but the scenario of practical jokes and pay-back (or 'pay-out' as the 1956 text puts it) may be a feature of many school playgrounds. When Percy gets his come-uppance (as he does later) a lesson about the consequences of 'naughty' or cheeky behaviour is duly learned. *Shrek* makes rather more playful and adventurous use of language; the writer does not shy away from words like 'vent' and 'cowed', 'copse' and 'blithe', though the immediate contexts in which they occur (including a picture on each page, not all reproduced here) provide plenty of clues. Note too the playful language in the rhymes and the rhyming of 'Pheasant, peasant? What a pleasant present!'.

Activity 19

The *Shelter* appeal is insistently personal, with the Director of Housing Services, Christine Parrish, identifying herself and her feelings of anger throughout. This works because of who she is – a significant figure within the organisation. The use of the first-person plural ('Ours is supposed to be a civilised society', 'We can't let this go on', etc.) binds her to her readers and appeals to our sense of collective responsibility for the crisis she describes. Finally she addresses readers in the second person ('If you are wondering . . .', 'your £2 a month') to make her appeal as direct as possible. The piece claims to be have arisen from anger rather than being 'cool and unemotional about it', though there is *some* appeal to our intellects in the form of some statistical information. The logic is straightforward – we aspire to be a 'civilised' society; but many people live in very poor conditions – therefore, something should be done. You can afford to give a little, and a little can go a long way, so you should make a monthly donation of £2.

However, the appeal is primarily to our emotional response, whether it be compassion or a sense of shared guilt. The use of an individual case study is more emotionally effective than simply sticking to facts and figures, and there are plenty of overtly rhetorical techniques (such as the triad 'It's degrading, inhuman and plain **wrong**'). The contrast between the 'civilised' values of our society and the conditions of the homeless is underlined by many lists including a string of emotive adjectives such as 'filthy', 'stinking', etc.

The *Observer* piece is less emotional, rhetorical and personal in style; the author takes a back seat and persuades us by providing evidence to support the conclusion that the Fairbridge organisation does good work and fulfils an important social need. It announces this conclusion early in the piece, and then backs it up with a mixture of general statements, facts, figures and quotes. It makes no direct appeal to readers for cash – the opportunity to donate appears elsewhere in the newspaper – but allows the case to speak for itself.

Glossary

accent The pronunciation characteristic of a particular region or social group *p66*

adjacency pair The basic unit of turn-taking in conversation *p59*

adjectives A word that gives more information about or describes a noun or pronoun *p46*

adverbs A word that gives more information about a verb, an adjective or another verb *p46*

agenda In conversation, the topic(s) covered by the discourse *p59*

alliteration Repetition of similar (usually initial) consonant sounds in successive words *p50*

colloquialism Literally, the language of speech; in practice, very informal use of language *p20*

compound sentence Sentences which consist of several clauses joined by *and, but, or* or *so p72*

conjunctions Words such as *and, but* and *because* which join elements of a sentence together *p46*

connotation The implied or associated meanings of a word or phrase (see also **denotation**) *p52*

context-bound/context-free The degree to which the meanings in a spoken or written text refer to elements of the contexts in which they are produced and received *p23*

covert prestige The unofficial prestige that non-standard varieties of accent or dialect may enjoy within a speech community *p168*

data Any sample of spoken or written language gathered for research and analysis *p3*

declarative The most common sentence type, a statement *p42*

deficit model View of language in which varieties which do not correspond to the dominant prestige variety are viewed as inferior or corrupt *p132*

deictic references Words such as *this, that, there,* which refer to people, places or things beyond the text in which they appear *p72*

denotation The literal, primary meaning of a word or phrase (see also **connotation**) *p52*

dialect The distinctive vocabulary and grammar of a geographical area within a language community *p64*

dialectology The study of dialectal variations *p11*

digraph A combination of two letters (such as – *sh*) which consistently represents a single **phoneme** *p48*

discourse structure The way in which spoken and language texts are organised and sequenced *p35*

double/multiple negative The use of two or more negative elements or markers in non-standard verb constructions *p74*

dramatic monologue Form of narrative in which a sole narrator 'talks' directly to the reader/audience in a continuous monologue *p205*

dysphemism A deliberately blunt expression of a delicate subject *p53*

ephemera Texts which are designed only to have a short-term use and not to be permanent *p24*

euphemism A polite or understated reference to subject of some delicacy *p53*

eye-dialect Term used to describe the non-standard spelling and punctuation used by some writers to give the impression of a regional variety of speech *p134*

figurative language Language which uses metaphors, simile and other non-literal expressions *p53*

forensic linguistic The application of linguistic study to problems of authorship of texts, sometimes in a criminal context *p64*

generic form Form of a word which refers to a whole class/type *p116*

genre A recognisable type of text/discourse with characteristic elements or ingredients *p69*

grammar The system which enables words to be combined meaningfully into different kinds of texts. Usually includes **mophology** and **syntax** *p40*

graphology Those features which contribute to the visual appearance of a text on the page *p69*

hedges Words/phrases used to indicate a degree of uncertainty or tentativeness *p121*

idiolect The distinctive features of a person's language which mark them as an individual *p43*

Imperative The command form of a verb or sentence *p42*

influential power The power to persuade and influence *p90*

instrumental power Power used to apply and exert power and authority *p90*

interrogative The question form of a sentence *p42*

jargon Usually the specialised, technical language associated with a specific field of activity *p64*

language repertoire The range of language styles which an individual speaker uses *p82*

lexis The collective term for the word stock, or vocabulary, of a language or text *p45*

linguistic relativism The view that every language embodies a unique way of thinking about the world, associated with the linguists Sapir and Whorf *p117*

marked/unmarked forms Marked forms of words indicate explicitly the gender, tense or person involved; unmarked forms do not *p116*

maxims Guiding principles associated with H P Grice's analysis of conversational discourse *p93*

metalanguage The language used to discuss language itself *p5*

minimal responses In conversation, short utterances made in response to a speaker (such as *yes, mm, I see*) *p121*

mode Usually, whether a text is spoken or written *p14*

morpheme The smallest units of meaning *p43*

morphology The study of the ways in which the forms of words vary according to grammatical meaning *p43*

noun Class of words which refer to people, places, & objects (**proper** and **concrete**), feelings and ideas (**abstract**) *p44*

onomatopoeia The phonetic imitation in language of actual sounds (e.g. buzz, pop) *p50*

oratory The craft of public speaking *p102*

overt prestige The obvious and official high status and authority of such forms as Standard English and Received Pronunciation *p126*

paralinguistic features Gestures and accompanying facial expressions which contribute to the communication of meanings in speech *p72*

parallelism The successive repetition of similar phrase or sentence structures *p163*

parody A text which imitates and exaggerates distinctive features of another text for humorous effect *p224*

pastiche A text which successfully imitates the distinctive features of another text *p224*

phatic talk In conversation, (small) talk whose primary function is to develop/reinforce social relationships *p92*

phonemes The basic sounds (vowels and consonants) on which a language is based *p48*

phonology The study of the sound system of a language *p48*

present perfect tense Verb tense indicating an action completed in the past that is relevant now such as *I have walked here, I have not told her,* etc. *p76*

pragmatics The study of the meanings which are implied and understood in the way we use language *p54*

prepositions Class of words which define positions and relationships (*to, below, under, into,* etc) *p46*

prescriptivism Approach to language which attempts to impose (or prescribe) 'rules' of 'correct' usage *p132*

progressive tenses Those verb tenses formed with the morpheme *–ing p76*

pronouns Class of words which are used to substitute for and refer to nouns (*she, it, us,* etc) *p46*

prosodic features Those aspects of the use of the voice (intonation, stress, tempo, pitch) which contribute to meanings communicated in speech *p23*

question tag Short question forms which occur at the ends of phrases *p121*

Received Pronunciation (RP) The accent of educated professional speech *p26*

register Either the level or formality or degree of topic-specific language in a text *p69*

rhetoric Term used to describe a range of techniques associated with powerful and persuasive language *p102*

schwa The most common short vowel sound in English (='uh') *p49*

semantic field A group of words with related or similar meanings *p51*

semantics The study of meanings *p51*

sentence boundaries The points in a text where sentences begin or end *p73*

slang Informal language *p20*

Standard English The accepted vocabulary and grammar of educated, 'correct' English *p20*

stress The emphasis placed on a particular word or syllable *p51*

style model An example of a type of text which serves as a model for original writing *p176*

sub-text The implied or intentional meanings in a text *p60*

syntax The aspect of grammar concerned with the construction of sentences and word-order *p41*

taboo Language which is considered offensive (includes 'swear words') *p20*

transcript A written record of spoken language *p9*

verbs Class of words which describe actions, feelings and states *p45*

vulgarism Language which falls short of **taboo** but which is regarded as coarse or impolite *p20*